GARDEN ORNAMENTS
by
KENNETH LYNCH
WILTON, CONNECTICUT 06897-0488

This book is one of
THE ARCHITECTURAL HANDBOOK SERIES
published by
THE CANTERBURY PUBLISHING CO.
WILTON, CONNECTICUT 06897-0488

TELEPHONE: KENNETH LYNCH & SONS   (203) 762-8363

READER SERVICE BUREAU

NOTICE TO READERS ! SPECIAL HELP FOR ARCHITECTS
ETC. IS AVAILABLE TO YOU FREE TO ANSWER
QUESTIONS CONCERNING COST, INSTALLATION
PROBLEMS, SPECIFICATION WRITING, MATERIAL
AVAILABILITY, PAST PERFORMANCE — ETC.
CALL
KENNETH LYNCH & SONS, WILTON, CONN
AND HAVE YOUR BOOK AT HAND — ASK FOR
READER SERVICE ON THIS SUBJECT—THIS IS FREE.
NOTICE: *see addendum which should be enclosed.*

Please acknowledge receipt of this book with date, name and address,

ALL CORRESPONDENCE TO: BOX 488, WILTON, CONNECTICUT 06897-0488.
(203) 762-8363   FAX (203) 762-2999

THIS IS ONE OF OUR MANY BUILDINGS   Please come to see us and The Craft Center Museum Gardens

The above picture is the original building of the Craft Center at Wilton, Connecticut. You are invited to come and visit us.

Many people have asked about the Lynch family and the work they have done in the past.

Tales are told amongst ourselves about the migration of this family from Connemara, Ireland, a wild, windswept, almost barren spot of land where they say there are "two stones for every dirt," and one could hardly blame them for migrating. Many of the Lynches lived in Galway which seems to be sort of a center for people of that name.

Just when the first Lynch came to America is not known accurately for the stories vary by nearly a hundred years. However, we know that Thomas Lynch was a signer of the Declaration of Independence and from the founding of this great country of ours, Lynches have always been heard about.

Our particular branch of the Lynch family was very hard working, very poor but certainly very talented in the working of metals.

With the coming of the twentieth century, many of the young men in the Lynch family turned to the professions and the clergy rather than taking up the traditional practice of shoeing horses, forging iron and casting bronze. Many of the things which we make today in these shops at Wilton are part of a tradition of working with materials which may seem foreign to the smith.

For instance, we have a very good woodwork shop for certain types of wood work, particularly our park benches and our small prefabricated buildings. This is the direct outgrowth of a wagon shop.

Our work in cast stone began informally about **eighty-three years ago when an architect** asked us to cast some stone just the way we would cast bronze, that is, cast it right into French sand, and we proceeded to do this and were impressed with the results and over the years developed a stone department so that today we have a very substantial cast stone business.

It took quite a few years for us to decide to embrace plastics. However, although fiberglass is the king of plastics and we feel that our Armorstone© is the thing that made it the king of plastics, it took many years for us to decide to include this and we are so confident of its value that we let it stand in line along with the justly famous materials such as bronze, lead and wrought iron, etc.

We invite you to come to Wilton and see the museum here which has the best exhibit in hand metalworking tools in the world, and you will find that this is indeed a *"Profitable Hour from New York."*

KENNETH LYNCH & SONS, Inc.
Box 488, Wilton, Conn. 06897
A profitable hour from New York City

INDEX

ALL CORRESPONDENCE TO BOX 488, WILTON, CONNECTICUT 06897.

STONE FIGURES - SEASONS

No. 1156. Stone Season, "SPRING," 72″ high not including pedestal.

No. 1158. Stone Season, "AUTUMN," 72″ high not including pedestal.

No. 1157. Stone Season, "SUMMER," 72″ high not including pedestal.

No. 1159. Stone Season, "WINTER," 72″ high not including pedestal.

N.B.: THE ABOVE PEDESTALS ARE NO. 1092
AND ARE 20″ HIGH BY 19″ SQUARE AT TOP AND 25″ SQUARE AT BOTTOM.

©1974
Kenneth Lynch & Sons
Wilton, Conn. 06897

STONE FIGURES · SEASONS

No. 1071. Stone Season,
"SPRING," 64″ high not
including pedestal.

No. 1072. Stone Season,
"SUMMER," 64″ high
not including pedestal.

No. 1073. Stone Season,
"AUTUMN," 64″ high
not including pedestal.

No. 1074. Stone Season,
"WINTER," 64″ high not
including pedestal.

N.B.: THE ABOVE PEDESTALS ARE NO. 1092
AND ARE 20″ HIGH BY 19″ SQUARE AT TOP AND 25″ SQUARE AT BOTTOM.

No. 2395. Stone Season. SPRING 60'' high. Not including pedestal.

No. 2396. Stone Season. SUMMER 60'' high. Not including pedestal.

No. 2397. Stone Season. FALL 60'' high. Not including pedestal.

No. 2398. Stone Season. WINTER 60'' high. Not including pedestal.

N.B.: The above pedestals are no. 2430 and are 20'' high x 16'' sq. at top and 21'' sq. at bottom.

© 1974
Kenneth Lynch & Sons
Wilton, Conn. 06897

No. 993. Stone Season,
"SPRING," 52" high.

No. 994. Stone Season,
"SUMMER," 52" high.

No. 995. Stone Season,
"AUTUMN," 52" high.

No. 996. Stone Season,
"WINTER," 52" high.

© 1974
Kenneth Lynch & Sons
Wilton, Conn. 06897

STONE FIGURES · SEASONS

No. 1290, No. 1291, No. 1289, No. 1288. Our models for these figures were made in Terra Cotta (Circa 1880). The design is, of course, older. They are from an important museum collection of that period. They lack the sharp detail of both earlier and later work. However, this style has many admirers.

No. 1288 "SPRING,"

No. 1289 "SUMMER,"

No. 1290 "AUTUMN,"

No. 1291 "WINTER."

Set of Stone Seasons, 49" high.

Bases are 13½" in diameter.

© 1974.
Kenneth Lynch & Sons
Wilton, Conn. 06897

THE FOUR SEASONS
CANTERBURY BRONZE OR ETERNITY LEAD

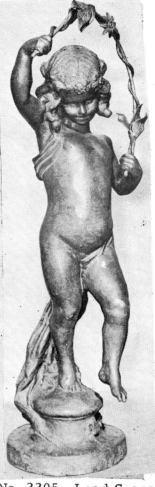

No. 2204. Lead Season, "SPRING," 43" high. English origin.
Bronze or Lead

No. 2205. Lead Season, "SUMMER," 45" high. English origin.
Bronze or Lead

No. 2207. Lead Season, "WINTER," 43" high. English origin.
Bronze or Lead

No. 2206. Lead Season, "AUTUMN," 43" high. English origin.
Bronze or Lead

A group of Seasons prepared for shipment.

© 1974
Kenneth Lynch & Sons
Wilton, Conn. 06897

7

No. 1107 "WINTER"   **No. 1104 "SPRING"**   **No. 1106 "AUTUMN"**   **No. 1105 "SUMMER"**

Set of Stone Seated Seasons, 29½" high. Pedestal is 15¾" high x 31" wide.

No. 1338. "AUTUMN"   **No. 1339 "SUMMER"**   **No. 1340 "WINTER"**   **No. 1341 "SPRING"**

Stone Seasons, set of four, in classical manner, 32" high, base 16" square. Pedestals are No. 1080 and are 20" high x 20 wide x 13" deep.

©1974
Kenneth Lynch & Sons
Wilton, Conn. 06897

Set of Four Seasons, stone, 20″ high.
Reading from left to right they are Nos. 1265, 1264, 1263, 1262.

Set of Four Seasons, Stone, 30″ high.
No. 1023 "SPRING," No. 1024 "SUMMER," No. 1025 "AUTUMN,"
No. 1026 "WINTER."

THE FOUR SEASONS
CANTERBURY BRONZE OR ETERNITY LEAD

Spring - No. 2014   Summer - No. 2015   Autumn - No. 2016   Winter - No. 2017

Set of Bronze or Lead **seasons- height-16 1/2" to 18"- English Models.**

Spring — No. 2200   Autumn — No. 2202   Winter — 2203   Summer — No. 2201

Set of Seasons — Heighth 19'' — Bronze or Lead

©1974
Kenneth Lynch & Sons
Wilton, Conn. 06897

THE FOUR SEASONS

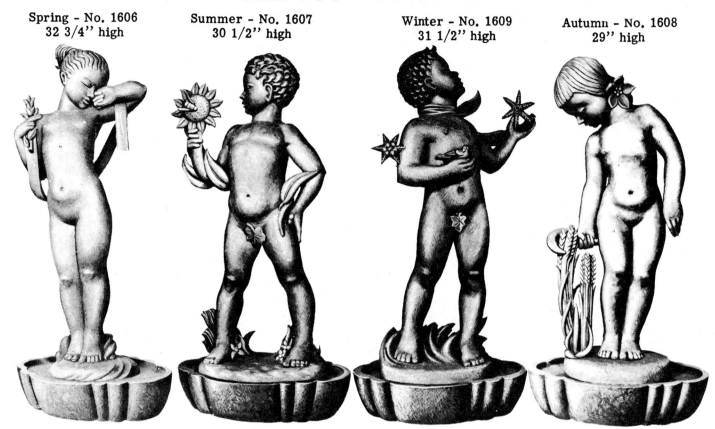

Spring — No. 1606
32 3/4'' high

Summer — No. 1607
30 1/2'' high

Winter — No. 1609
31 1/2'' high

Autumn — No. 1608
29'' high

These are by Gifford M. Proctor, F.A.A.R., N.S.S. This set of seasons executed by a great master, exclusively for us.
SPRING — a lovely little girl with a flower in her hand just awakening with the blooms.
SUMMER — a wonderful strong young man with a sun flower in his hand and a bee on the sun flower.
AUTUMN — a charming little girl with a scythe and some wheat.
WINTER — is a bright fellow with a scarf around his neck — snowflakes in his hand and on his shoulder — and a bird nestling against his body.

The bases can be piped for water jets. Sizes shown include the bases which are 15'' wide, 10'' deep, and 4½'' high.
Bronze or Lead.

Summer — No. 2464 **Autumn — No. 2465** **Winter — No. 2466** **Spring — No. 2467**

© 1974
Kenneth Lynch & Sons
Wilton, Conn. 06897

Set of Seasons in Bronze or Lead. **fine old English models — 25'' tall.**

11

STONE FIGURES - SEASONS

STONE

Set of Four Seasons, Peasant Children, 42″ high. No. 1224 "SPRING,"
No. 1225 "SUMMER," No. 1226 "AUTUMN," No. 1227 "WINTER."

Set of Four Seated Seasons, stone, 24″ high.
Reading from left to right they are Nos. 1269, 1266, 1268, 1267.
NOTE: Pedestals are 21″ high and are NO. 507-A and can be seen in
the Pedestal Section of this catalog.

© 1974.
Kenneth Lynch & Sons
Wilton, Conn. 06897

No. 2393. Architect. 50'' high. Base 13¼'' square. 300 lbs.

No. 2394. The Painter. 50'' high. Base 13¼'' square. 300 lbs.

No. 2384. The Musician. 50'' high. Base 13¼'' square. 300 lbs.

© 1974
Kenneth Lynch & Sons
Wilton, Conn. 06897

No. 2385. The Sculptor. 50'' high. Base 13¼'' square. 300 lbs.

CLASSICAL FIGURES
STONE

No. 2389. The Hunter (Large) 60'' high. Base 16'' square. 500 lbs.

No. 2391. The Hunter (Ephebo) 52'' high. Base 15'' square. 300 lbs.

No. 675. "EFEBO AND DOG," stone, 52'' high. No. 676. "DIANA," stone, 52'' high.

No. 2390. Diana (Small Huntress) 52'' high. Base 15'' square. 300 lbs.

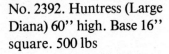

No. 2392. Huntress (Large Diana) 60'' high. Base 16'' square. 500 lbs

N.B. The above pedestals are:

No. 2430 Large — 20'' high — 16'' square top — 21'' square bottom. For Numbers 2389 & 2392.
No. 2430 Small — 20'' high — 13½'' sqare top — 14½'' square bottom. For Numbers 2390 & 2391.

No. 1032. Stone
"SOUND", 59" high.
Base 18½" x 14½".

No. 1033. Stone "TASTE",
59" high. Base 18½" x
14½".

No. 1057. Stone
"SMELL", 59" high. Base
18½" x 14½".

No. 1058. Stone "SIGHT",
59" high. Base 18½" x
14½".

Set of Five Senses, 59" high.

No. 1056. Stone
"TOUCH". 59" high.
Base 18½" x 14½".

© 1974.
Kenneth Lynch & Sons
Wilton, Conn. 06897

STONE FIGURES
Set of Four Elements.

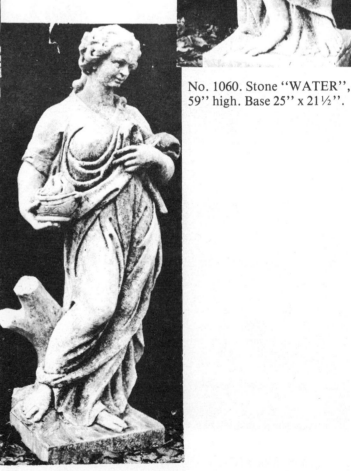

No. 1061. Stone "EARTH", 59" high. Base 25" x 21½".

No. 1060. Stone "WATER", 59" high. Base 25" x 21½".

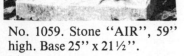

No. 1059. Stone "AIR", 59" high. Base 25" x 21½".

No. 1062. Stone "FIRE", 59" high. Base 25" x 21½".

No. 4798. Stone figure of Justice 66″ high on a 16″ square base. The scales are bronze.

No. 4660. Statue of Justice. 6 feet 3″ high. Furnished in bronze or lead with bronze staff and scales. This is an adaptation of Figure No. 2859 and is most beautifully modeled with the folds of the garment being in excellent detail.

© 1974.
Kenneth Lynch & Sons
Wilton, Conn. 06897

No. 2859. Lead figure, 6' 3'' high. Late 19th century. One of several copies. This copy was produced by the Bromsgrove Guild. These people were very good lead workers, producing lead on into the early 20th century, ceasing their lead operation somewhere in the early 1930's.

Now Available in Bronze or Lead.

No. 4991. Stone Costumed Figure with Musical Instrument. Unusually bold carving makes this figure an excellent resting place for bits of vegetation which will support moss and assist the patina in years to come.

This figure is 50" high. The base is 4½" thick and the dimensions are 12" x 15".

Stone Only.

Set of Four Elements, Stone, 31″ high.
From left to right they are: No. 1270 "AIR", No. 1271 "FIRE",
No. 1272 "EARTH", No. 1273 "WATER".

Set of Five Senses, Stone, 40″ high.
From left to right they are: No. 1117 "TOUCH", No. 1114-A
"SMELL", No. 1116 "TASTE", No. 1114 "SIGHT", No. 1115
"HEARING".

© 1974.
Kenneth Lynch & Sons
Wilton, Conn. 06897

ELEMENT FIGURES
CANTERBURY BRONZE OR ETERNITY LEAD

No. 1602 - FIRE

No. 1604 - WATER

No. 1603 - EARTH

Now Available in Bronze or Lead.

No. 1605 - AIR

These beautiful elements symbolize fire, air, earth and water are the work of that Master Sculptor Mr. Gifford M. Proctor. They are approximately 30'' high and their bases are so constructed that they can be piped with jets of water. They should be on stone pedestals about 14'' to 18'' tall or mounted on special bases within a pool.

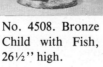

No. 4507. Bronze Child with Bagpipe, 12½'' high.

No. 4510. Bronze "FISHER BOY," 20'' high.

Now Available in Bronze or Lead.

No. 4508. Bronze Child with Fish, 26½'' high.

No. 4512. Fountain figure, bronze or lead, 25'' high. NOTE: This figure includes a bronze frog which squirts water at a child.

No. 4511. Bronze or lead figure of Child with Duck, 29'' high.

© 1974.
Kenneth Lynch & Sons
Wilton, Conn. 06897

No. 1118. Stone "PAINTER," 40" high; pedestal 20" high, 18" square.

No. 1119. Stone "MUSICIAN," 40" high; pedestal 20" high, 18" square.

No. 1121. Stone "C R A F T S - M A N," 40" high.

No. 1120. Stone "D E S I G N - ER," 40" high.

Pedestals shown are No. 960.

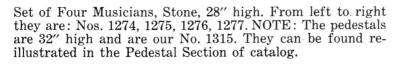

Set of Four Musicians, Stone, 28" high. From left to right they are: Nos. 1274, 1275, 1276, 1277. NOTE: The pedestals are 32" high and are our No. 1315. They can be found re-illustrated in the Pedestal Section of catalog.

No. 1036. Stone figure with instrument, 35½" high, 11" square base. Can be piped.

No. 1037. Stone figure with pipes, 35½" high, 11" square base. Can be piped.

WHEN THE GODS WERE CHILDREN
CANTERBURY BRONZE OR ETERNITY LEAD

No. 1634. "Ceres" (Demeter)
29" high including base.
Available in Bronze or Lead.

No. 1635. "Venus".
32 1/2" high including base.
Available in Bronze or Lead.

No. 1636. "Apollo"
31 1/2" high including base.
Available in Bronze or Lead.

No. 1637. "Hercules."
31" high including base.
Available in Bronze or Lead.

"VENUS". A child of Jupiter and Diana. Goddess of love and beauty. "Everywhere at the touch of her feet the herbage quivered into flower." Goddess of gardens and flowers, the rose, myrtle and linden.

"CERES". A child of Saturn and Rhea. A divinity of earth, sister of Jupiter, Juno, Pluto, Vesta and Neptune. Goddess of agriculture and civilization. Goddess of fruitful soil.

"APOLLO". A child of Jupiter and Letona, and a twin of Diana. God of manly youth and beauty, poetry and music. He was also the God of healing. He was the ideal of fairness, a pure and just God requiring clean hands and a pure heart of those who worshipped him.

"HERCULES". A hero, the son of Jupiter and Alcmene. Celebrated for his strength. As a child he strangled a serpent sent by Hera to devour him. He and Achilles were educated by Cheiron, a learned centaur.

© 1974
Kenneth Lynch & Sons
Wilton, Conn. 06897

CANTERBURY BRONZE OR ETERNITY LEAD

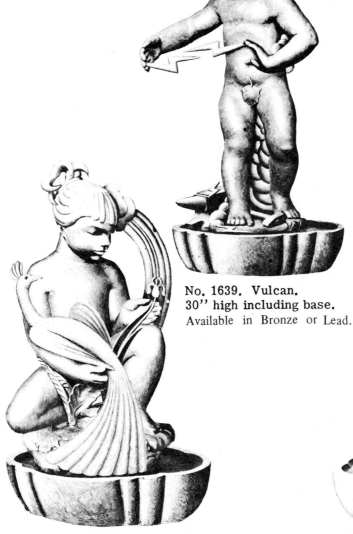

No. 1639. Vulcan.
30'' high including base.
Available in Bronze or Lead.

No. 1641. Neptune.
31'' high including base.

Available in Bronze or Lead.

No. 1638. Iris.
26'' high including base.
Available in Bronze or Lead.

No. 1640. Diana.
28 1/2'' high including base.
Available in Bronze or Lead.

"IRIS". Child of Thaumas and the ocean nymph Electra. Goddess
of the rainbow, messenger of Jupiter and Hera. The peacock was
her favorite bird. The base can be used as a reflection pool.

"VULCAN". Child of Jupiter and Juno. God of fire, God of metalworking. Consort of Venus. Forger of thunderbolts for Jupiter.

"DIANA". Child of Jupiter and Latona. Goddess of the chase and
the chaste. Twin sister of Apollo, Goddess of the woods.

"NEPTUNE". Trident spear is of bronze. Child of Saturn and
Ops. One of a large family of children. Brother of Ceres,
Jupiter, Juno, Pluto, and Vesta. God of the sea and water gen-
erally. Attributes include dolphin, horse, and trident.

©1974
Kenneth Lynch & Sons
Wilton, Conn. 06897

GARDEN FIGURES

No. 5556. Stone Piper, 30" high.

No. 5557. Stone Symbol Player, 30" high.

No. 5558. Stone Tambourine Player, 30" high.

No. 5559. Stone Horn Blower, 30" high.

No. 5521. Stone Flute Player, 30" high.

No. 5522. Stone Piper, 30" high.

© 1974
Kenneth Lynch & Sons
Wilton, Conn. 06897

No. 1154. Stone figure with fruit. 60″ high; the pedestal is 20″ high, 21″ square.

No. 1155. Figure with flowers, 60″ high, base 16″ square; pedestal is 20″ high, 21″ square.

No. 834. Grecian Caryatid. 91″ high, 30″ wide, 14″ deep.

No. 834-A. Grecian Caryatid (small). 43″ high, 15″ wide, 6″ deep.

Cast Stone.

No. 1313 and No. 1314. Stone, seated garden children. English origin, 12″ high.

No. 146. Cast stone garden seat, 16″ high.

These two figures are so artistically beautiful that no photograph could do them justice. They are highly recommended.

These figures should be used on pedestal No. 1317 which is 24" high x 18" x 18".

No. 1126. Stone, 48" high, 14" square base.

No. 1125. Stone, 48" high, 14" square base.

No. 4. Cast stone 31" high, 9" x 9" base.

No. 5. Cast stone, 31½" high, 8½" x 8½" base.

No. 11. Cast stone, 20" high, 7" by 7" base.

No. 10. Cast stone, 20" high, 7" by 7" base.

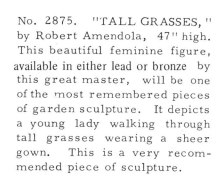

No. 2875. "TALL GRASSES," by Robert Amendola, 47" high. This beautiful feminine figure, available in either lead or bronze by this great master, will be one of the most remembered pieces of garden sculpture. It depicts a young lady walking through tall grasses wearing a sheer gown. This is a very recommended piece of sculpture.

No. 2875. "TALL GRASSES" in a southern garden.

GROWING THINGS

CANTERBURY BRONZE OR ETERNITY LEAD

No. 2911. Lead or bronze of this figure offered on a limited edition basis. This is the larger and slightly more mature model of "GROWING THINGS." It is 52" high; the pitcher can be piped. This is a breathtakingly beautiful piece of sculpture.

No. 1610 and No. 2911. "GROWING THINGS".
About forty years ago in the 1920's, Mr. Kenneth Lynch, Sr., who had at his disposal all kinds of sculpture, was trying to find the ideal garden piece. In an effort to find something which fitted this picture and after countless discussions with sculptors, he was able to finally convey the idea to Mr. Robert Amendola, F.A.A.R. Mr. Amendola agreed to try to develop what Mr. Lynch had in mind from Mr. Lynch's many pencil sketches. As a result, the wonderful figure called "GROWING THINGS", was done in the 33" height, shown on opposite page.

This received very wonderful acceptance from people all over the world. After further discussions in the following 15 years, Mr. Amendola and Mr. Lynch finally produced another figure, which they still call "GROWING THINGS NO. II" for it is still a development of the same girl (No. 2911).

Recently in an interview with Mr. Lynch he was asked to tell all the things this figure represented to him and the following words were recited: "Simplicity, uncomplicated, virtuous, innocent, unworldly, unspoiled, honest, sweet, trusting, loveable, beautiful, desirable, young, feminine, daughter-like, natural, delicate." Mr. Lynch went on further to say that all of this had to be related to flowers and gardens, and this seems to sum up what he sees in this figure.

Mr. Amendola worked very hard to capture the spirit of this piece in the larger size. It is now 53" tall and is indeed a most beautiful piece of sculpture. It is piped for water, and it will be a limited edition of 100 copies which, of course, will make it a valuable collector's item in no time.

© 1974.
Kenneth Lynch & Sons
Wilton, Conn. 06897

GROWING THINGS

CANTERBURY BRONZE OR ETERNITY LEAD

Growing Things," by Robert Amendola, F.A.A.R.
Figure of unusual grace and serenity. Mr. Amendola was at his very best when he did this beautiful piece of work for us.

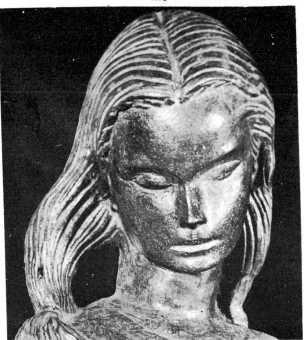

No. 1610. Lead figure, symbolic of Growing Things, 33" high, piped for water from pitcher. It looks very well on pedestal as shown in arrangement #1610-A.

The head of this figure is so beautiful we have had many requests to sell it separately as a decorative item. You may purchase it as 1610B. It is approximately 6" x 6". It is available in bronze and lead and should be mounted on a six inch square of marble.

© 1974.
Kenneth Lynch & Sons
Wilton, Conn. 06897

No. 1610-A. "Growing Things"© by Robt. Amendola. Lead only. Piped. 41 1/4" tall. 14" Diameter. Pool made from border #1503, 48" in diameter. (The figure is available in both bronze and lead).

SCULPTURE
CANTERBURY BRONZE OR ETERNITY LEAD

Girl with Shawl.

No. 2961. Figure 60" tall to top of shawl. The deep clefts in the lines of the garment make this a most beautiful piece of work.

Note details of back of figure. This is one of the finest castings that has ever been our privilege to make. The original model was European but was lost in the great War of 1914. Through the kindness and scourtesy of Gerry-Lewis Amendola and working from what photographic records we had, she produced this exquisite model, which is a joy to everyone who has ever seen it. This is available in either bronze or lead and will certainly be ranked as one of the world's great garden masterpieces.

© 1974.
Kenneth Lynch & Sons
Wilton, Conn. 06897

CANTERBURY BRONZE OR ETERNITY LEAD

No. 2961. Detail of back of figure.
Note great care given to lines of garment, buttons, etc.

No. 2961. Close up detail back of garment.

OTTER GIRL
BRONZE, LEAD OR STONE

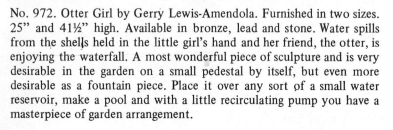

No. 972. Otter Girl by Gerry Lewis-Amendola. Furnished in two sizes. 25" and 41½" high. Available in bronze, lead and stone. Water spills from the shells held in the little girl's hand and her friend, the otter, is enjoying the waterfall. A most wonderful piece of sculpture and is very desirable in the garden on a small pedestal by itself, but even more desirable as a fountain piece. Place it over any sort of a small water reservoir, make a pool and with a little recirculating pump you have a masterpiece of garden arrangement.

© 1974.
Kenneth Lynch & Sons
Wilton, Conn. 06897

THE GARDEN GIRL

No. 4871. Lead figure and base using figure 4894 which is 55″ high. Base 16″ x 18″ and 4″ thick. The buckets can be piped for water to flow. The pool is lead and should be 48″ wide by 20″ projection. The bird is No. 2258.

No. 4881. Lead figure No. 4894 55″ high. The pool No. 1001 60″ wide with 30″ projection. Any base can be used to suit situation.

No. 4873. Lead figure 55″ high Bird bath No. 1231.

No. 4869. Composition using figure 4894 55″ high with Owl No. 4661 and pedestal No. 241.

© 1974.
Kenneth Lynch & Sons
Wilton, Conn. 06897

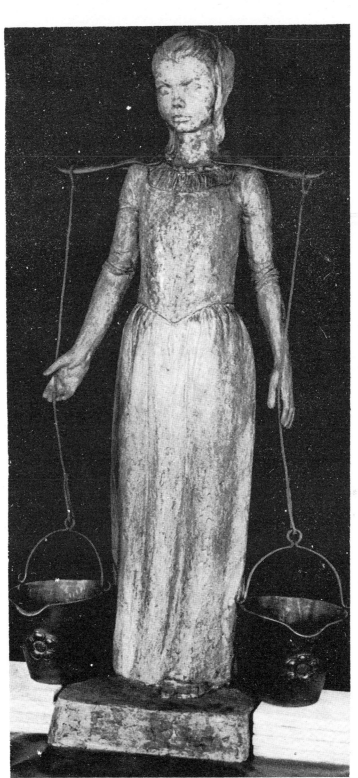

No. 4894. The Garden Girl. By Geraldine Lewis Amendola. Available in lead or bronze. It is 55″ high.
See opposite page for various suggestions for its use.
Of course, it can stand individually in the garden just as it is.
The detail on this figure is excellent right down to the stitches on the garment.
This classic piece of sculpture could only have been produced by an insired artist.
This is a signed numbered piece of original art.

No. 4879. Illustration of figure No. 4894 55″ high made of lead. Buckets can be piped.

No. 4875. Pool composition using lead figure No. 4894 55½″ high using a 1503 lead border 4′ in diameter.

No. 4870. Lead figure No. 4894 as shown with Dog in Basket. The figure is 55″ high with the base. The Dog is No. 272 and it is 24″ high. It is made of cast stone with lead colored basket handles.

No. 4872. Lead figure No. 4894 55″ high using a shell and base composition with No. 19 pool. Space required at least 6′ side to side and 4′ front to back.

No. 1976
The Little Puritan - cast stone.
Height of figure 41'' - plus 11'' below
grade. Note: Can be made less this 11''. It
is 12'' in diameter.
See detail.

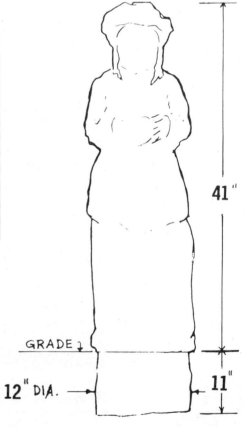

41"

GRADE

12" DIA.

11"

© 1974
Kenneth Lynch & Sons
Wilton, Conn. 06897

No. 4930. Girl with Apron. This delightful piece of sculpture used both as a bird bath, a planter, or a holder is a joy to behold. Gerrie Lewis-Amendola created this piece in 1973. It is sold in limited edition only and is available generally in Fairfield stone. On special order it can be made available in bronze.

It is 46″ tall.   NOTE: Pedestals are not included in the above sizes.

SCULPTURE

CANTERBURY BRONZE OR ETERNITY LEAD

No. 6089. The original model of a new piece of sculpture by this famous artist. It is designed to be made in bronze, lead or stone. It is 40'' high.

The artist was obviously inspired by a young girl with a little boy in her charge. This piece of work will be made in limited edition and signed by the author. The introduction of something to give it the proper elevation is, of course, important.

© 1974
Kenneth Lynch & Sons
Wilton, Conn. 06897

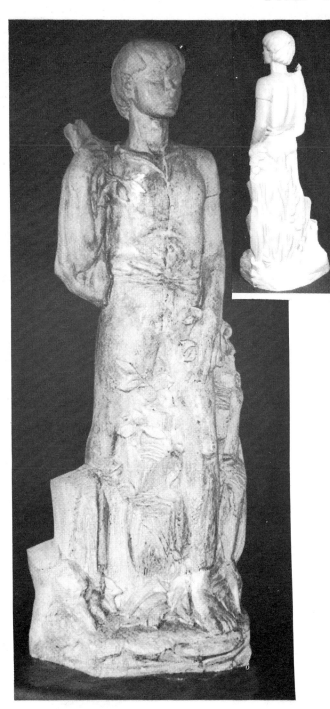

No. 5561. Stone figure of a youth intended to portray Young America of the period about 1790. The device he is holding with his right hand could either be arranged to be a bag of seed if he were a farmer or a jacket if he were a sailor. In his left hand he could either be as you see him or he could be holding an axe or a coil of rope or some other device that would indicate his occupation. This is an original work of art by Professor Robert Amendola. It is 56" high overall and the base is 17" x 19". Made in limited edition only.

No. 5561A. This is another version of the Youngling by Professor Robert Amendola. It is furnished in stone only and in this version there is a sapling as part of the figure. This figure likewise can be associated with other implements and devices. It is 56" high overall on a base 17" x 19".

©1974
Kenneth Lynch & Sons
Wilton, Conn. 06897

This English figure sometimes called the Supplicant or Platter Boy is available in bronze or lead and has been used as a game keeper with a fox, Bowman with hunting bow or a Warden with a fish.

No. 674. "PLATTER BOY," holding platter of roses. 50" high. This is a most magnificent piece in very fine detail. Without the platter, this piece is also known as "THE SUPPLICANT."

No. 674-H. Server or Page with purse and beautifully engraved tunic. In this pose he is frequently known as "THE SUPPLICANT." This is a valuable reproduction of a famous English piece, and we show him in other situations on this page.

No. 674-E. Server with Dog, 51" high.

No. 674-D. Server with Sundial, 51" high.

No. 674-C. Server with Shell, 51" high. Can be piped.

STONE FIGURES

No. 4955. Stone Figure of Gentleman in Period Costume, 61" high. The base is 14½" wide x 17½" front to back.

No. 4954. Stone Garden Figure of Peasant Girl, 60" high. The base is 16" wide x 18" front to back.

No. 4957. Stone Garden Figure of Peasant Lady, 59" high. The base is 15½" wide x 17" front to back.

No. 4956. Stone Figure of Peasant Girl, 50½" high. The base is 12½" wide x 17" front to back.

©1974
Kenneth Lynch & Sons
Wilton, Conn. 06897

GARDEN STATUARY

No. 1030. Stone "HUNTRESS". Note: This is a companion piece to the "HUNTER". 59″ high, base 19″ x 15″.

No. 1031. Stone "HUNTER". This is a most attractive piece of stoneware. 59″ high, base 19″ x 15″.

English Pixies, whistling, etc.

No. 214. Stone, 21½″ high.

No. 215. Stone, 17″ long.

No. 62. Stone, 22″ high on a 9½″ x 8″ base.

No. 213. Stone, 22″ high.

No. 212. Stone, 21″ high.

© 1974.
Kenneth Lynch & Sons
Wilton, Conn. 06897

No. 2428. Lead figure, Gany-maid, 66'' tall. Also available in bronze.

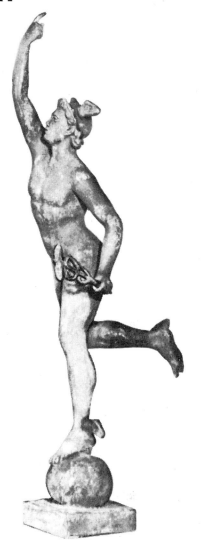

No. 2219. Mercury, lead figure, 48'' tall. The original of this figure came from Dr. Lister's garden in England.

Also available in bronze.

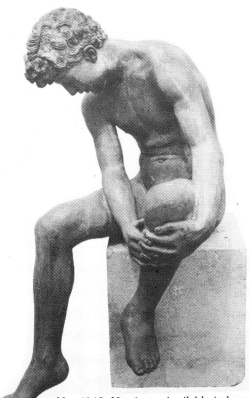

No. 4948. Narcissus. Available in bronze or lead. It is 42½'' high, 28'' front to back and 22'' from side to side. The base should be 19'' high.

No. 2450. Boy on Lead Base Holding Frog, piped for fountain, 9'' high, 10'' base, cast lead. Note: Also available in bronze.

No. 555. Hebe. 40'' tall, furnished in cast lead or cast stone. Note also available in bronze.

'No. 1070. STONE "HEBE" 66'' high on 16'' sq. base.

No. 2388. STONE "HEBE". 66'' high on 16'' sq. base.

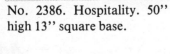

No. 2386. Hospitality. 50'' high 13'' square base.

© 1974
Kenneth Lynch & Sons
Wilton,.Conn. 06897

No. 1152. Stone "ABUN-DANCE". 68″ high, base 20″ square.

No. 677. Vintage, 60″ high, stone.

No. 678. Hospitality, 60″ high, stone.

No. 1153. Stone "MUSIC," 68″ high, base 20″ square.

THE YOUTHFUL NUDE

CANTERBURY BRONZE OR ETERNITY LEAD

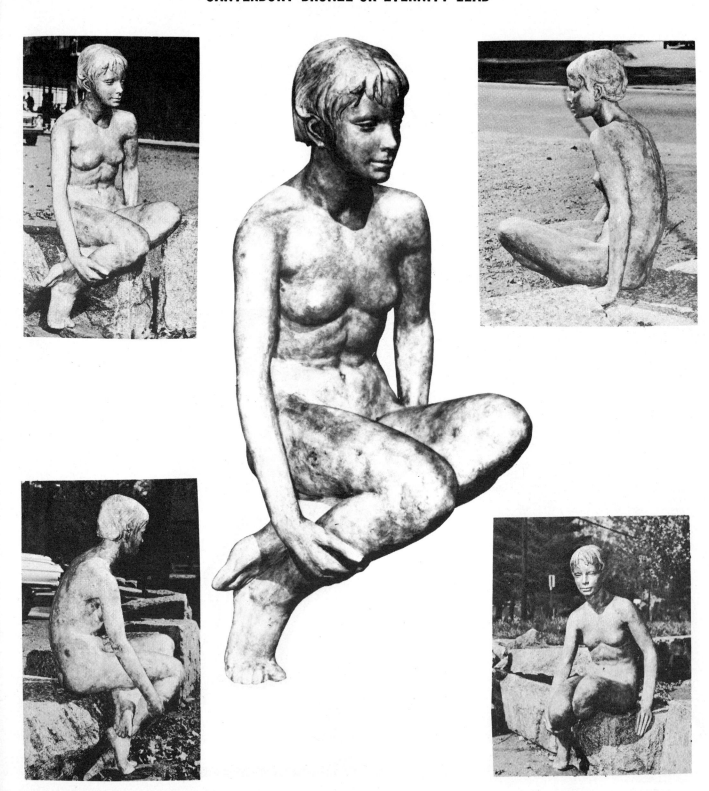

No. 2910. "Youthful Nude" available in bronze or lead. Designed to sit on rock and rock is included. It is life size. From bottom of stone to top of head it is 48". Width is 24". From toe to top of head 44". Geraldine Lewis Amendola sculpturess. Limited edition.

© 1974.
Kenneth Lynch & Sons
Wilton, Conn. 06897

CANTERBURY BRONZE OR ETERNITY LEAD

No. 4839. Detail of head on Chartes Angel.

Special lead casting of Antique French Angel. From privately owned model. Original in Frick Museum, N.Y.C.

No. 4839. Chartes Angel.   This figure is from the original models, one of which is in the Louvre and the other in the Frick Museum in New City. It is 47" high and it is a very wonderful piece of work. It is furnished in bronze or lead.

© 1974.
Kenneth Lynch & Sons
Wilton, Conn. 06897

No. 2214. Venus, 41″ high, furnished in cast lead or cast stone, antique finish.

Also available in bronze.

No. 518. Cast stone, 60″ high, excluding block.

No. 315. Cast stone Danish mermaid, similar to the one in harbor of Copenhagen, 42″ high, base 15″ x 24″.

No. 2460-A. Boy with Frog, lead or stone. Frog projects water away from the figure. 20″ and 36″ high.

Note: Also available in bronze.

No. 2460. Boy with Frog, lead or stone. Frog projects water toward figure. 20″ and 36″ high. Note: Also available in bronze.

No. 368. Child with Shell, lead or stone, piped. 20″ high and 36″ high.

Note: Also available in bronze.

© 1974
Kenneth Lynch & Sons
Wilton, Conn. 06897

No. 4552. Bronze Torso by G. Lewis, 13" high. Base is green and black marble, 6" cube.

No. 5424. Mermaid seated on rock. It is 52" high and the base is 30" x 19". It is a new model by G. L. Amendola. In our opinion this is the very best of the mermaid statues. This figure is available in Bronze, Lead and Stone.

No. 430. Fragment. Cast stone. 33" high, antique finish. Furnished with mounting wire. Stony texture only. Ideal on wall softly lighted at night.

 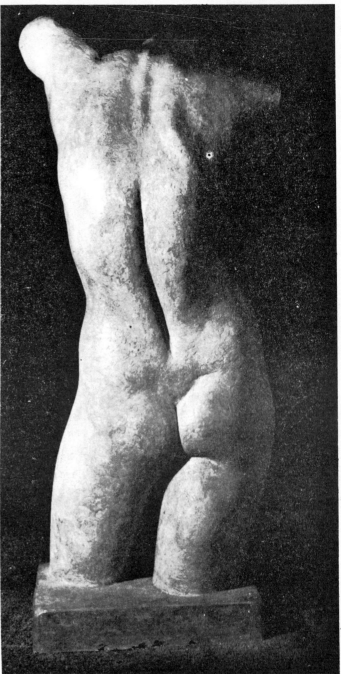

Illustration No. 4961. Torso by Gerrie Lewis-Amendola. It is 44" high overall. Base is 16" x 15". It is offered in bronze, lead and stone. This is unquestionably the best Torso we have ever seen. May we call your attention to a smaller version of this in bronze and lead (not stone). It is No. 4552 and 13" high

Torso No. 4961 by Gerrie Lewis-Amendola. Rear view. The care with which this sculpture is done is highly dramatic and impressive. This sculpture is viewable and enjoyable from all angles. Available in bronze, lead and stone. See smaller version No. 4552

©1974
Kenneth Lynch & Sons
Wilton, Conn. 06897

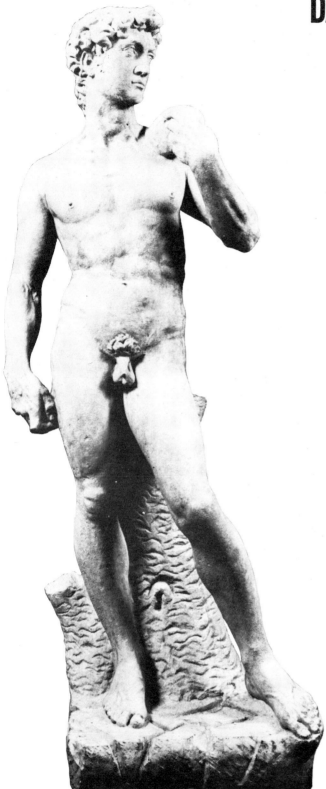

No. 5568. Stone figure of David. 59½" high. The base is 15½" x 17½". This piece was done by a member of the Academy at Florence, Italy. Like many of these pieces inspired by the original David, the author introduces his own interpretation

No. 4953. David in stone. 6'10" high. All reinforced with stainless steel armature. This David is an exactly half size model of the Great David done by Michaelangelo. This master sculptor had a desire to do the perfect figure of the young male and as a result made this heroic size carving and model. This masterpiece has been a constant source of inspiration for many sculptors. We were fortunate in having a fine Academy Master available to carve this almost exactly to half size. It is shippable and can be handled successfully. The base is 23" x 24" and it is on a base which elevates it at least 16".

©1974
Kenneth Lynch & Sons
Wilton, Conn. 06897

No. 961. Stone fountain figure, 33″ high, piped.

No. 962. Stone figure of bather, 33″ high.

No. 992. Stone fountain figure, 38½″ high, piped.

No. 1040. Stone Bathing Figure, 63″ high, base 18½″ x 15″.

No. 1123. Stone period figure, 36″ high, 12″ square base.

No. 1124. Stone period figure, 36″ high, 12″ square base.

No. 554. Winged Victory of Samothrace (Nike). Three sizes: 14″, 22″, & 48″ high, cast stone, antique finish.

© 1974
Kenneth Lynch & Sons
Wilton, Conn. 06897

No. 2341. Neptune (Extra Large) 82'' high. Base 24'' wide, 24'' front to back. 1,300 lbs.

No. 2340. ''Venus on the Sea''. 60'' high. Base 16'' square. 500 lbs.

No. 2342. Neptune (Small without trident). 60'' high. Base 16½'' square.

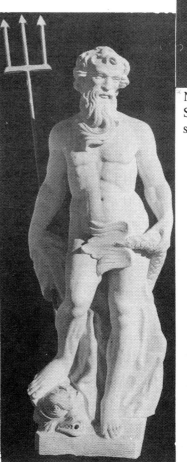

No. 2343. Neptune (Small) 60'' high. Base 16½''square. 500 lbs.

No. 2340. ''Venus on the Sea'' Rear view.

© 1974
Kenneth Lynch & Sons
Wilton, Conn. 06897

No. 1732. Stone figure "Julia Pouring."
60" high x 16" square base.

No. 2387. Stone Figure "Smell." 60"
high x 16" square base.

No. 2372. Stone figure "The Gleaner."
47" high. Base size 27" x 20".

© 1974.
Kenneth Lynch & Sons
Wilton, Conn. 06897

No. 1068. Stone, 48" high with 12" square base. This beautiful, helmeted figure was carved on private commission by an associate sculptor of Carl Milles for Kenneth Lynch.

No. 1034. Stone classical feminine figure offering fruit on a shell. 63" high, shell is 30" wide, base is 15" x 18½". This is a very fine piece of sculpture. Can be piped.

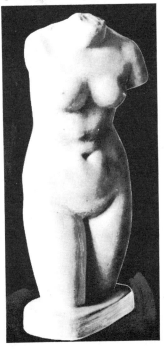

No. 553. Michael-angelo's David, height 30", cast stone, antique finish.

No. 889. Stone Child with Shell, excellent fountain piece, piped, 36" high.

No. 314. Cast stone, 57" high on a 10" x 17" base.

No. 271. Cast stone, 29" high on base 12" x 8".

No. 1721. Stone figure. Right and Left. 27'' high, base 9½'' diameter.

No. 1707. Stone figures. 18'' high, base 6½'' x 8½''.

No. 1722A Stone Cherub with Cymbals. 27'' high x 10½'' square base.

No. 1722. Stone Cherub with Tambourine. 27'' high x 10½'' square base.

© 1974.
Kenneth Lynch & Sons
Wilton, Conn. 06897

STONE SCULPTURE

No. 2344. Gibson Girl. 24'' high. 6'' x 6'' base. 17'' shoulder width. 75 lbs. Stone

No. 2381. Cherub For Lamp. Facing left. 40'' high. Base 15'' round. 225 lbs. Stone. Can be piped or wired for lights.

No. 2382. Cherub For Lamp. Facing right. 40'' high. Base 13'' round. 225 lbs. Stone. Can be piped or wired for lights.

No. 2399. Pedestal — 20'' high. 21'' wide. 28'' front to back. Top 18'' wide. Front to back 25''. 300 lbs.

No. 2383. Boy on Dolphin. 32'' high. Base 16'' wide. 23¼'' front to back. 250 lbs. Stone.

No. 1736. Stone Figure with Book.
36" high.

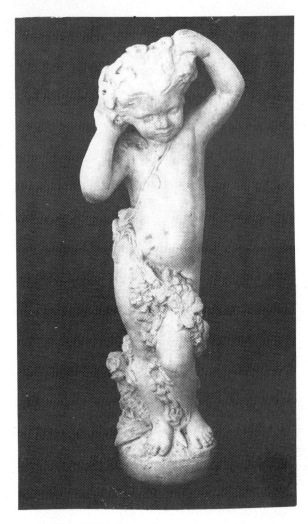

No. 1723. Stone figure "Innocence."
40½" high. Base is 9" diameter.

No. 2844. Lead figure with
birds, 20" high. Appealing
primitive feeling.

Note: Also available in bronze.

No. 845. Grecian Youth. 65" high, 26" wide, 19" deep.

No. 844. Grecian Maiden. 63½" high, 24" wide, 14" deep.

NOTE: Pedestals are not included in the above sizes

No. 1209. Stone, Roman bust, 31 1/2" high x 20" wide.

No. 465. Venus, cast stone. 19½" high, 5½" dia. base.

No. 103. Boy with Wheat, piped, cast stone. 35" high. 10" by 10" base.

No. 1208. Stone, Roman bust, 31 1/2" high x 20" wide.

No. 2864. Garden Figure, 33 1/2" high, Eternity lead. Exactly the correct period for certain things. Origin: England.

No. 2863. "SHEPHERD," 52" high on 15" square base. Note: This lead figure is also furnished with a shepherd's crook and similar arrangements. Original model courtesy of Mr. Carrol Cavanaugh of Norwalk, Connecticut.

No. 2862. "SHEPHERDESS," 51" high on 15" square base. This lead reproduction courtesy of the Carrol Cavanaugh collection.

No. 2882. Lead figure, piped, "FROGGY GOES A-WOOING", 20" high x 10 1/2" square base.

No. 2210. Cupid with sundial, lead figure, 30½" high.

No. 2876. Lead figure of child kneeling, probably looking into water, 10" high.

© 1974
Kenneth Lynch & Sons
Wilton, Conn. 06897

STONE FIGURES

No. 269. Cast stone, 41" high, 12½" base.

No. 1017. Stone fountain figures, piped, 34" high, 21" long, 14" deep.

No. 125. Cast stone, 22" high on a 9" by 10" base.

No. 65. Famous Verrocchio, cast stone, 31" high, base 12" by 12".

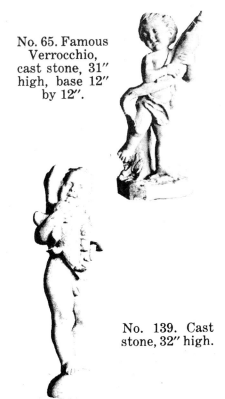

No. 139. Cast stone, 32" high.

No. 198. Cast stone, 30" high, 18" wide, 16" long.

No. 234. Cast stone, 10" high.

No. 233. Cast stone, 10" high.

No. 1067. Stone, Child with birds, 32″ high; base 15″ high x 14″ diameter.

309. Cast stone, 40″ high on a 10″ x 10″ base.

No. 308. Cast stone, 38″ high piped. Boy with frog and pipes.

No. 898. Cast Stone Sundial Figure, bronze gnomon, 36″ high.

No. 318. Cast stone, 29″ high.

No. 78. Pan with pipe, cast stone 26″ high on a 12″ x 12″ base.

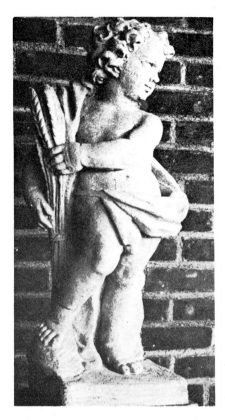

No. 27. Cast stone, 28″ high, 10″ x 9″ base.

No. 23. Cast stone, Child with Shell, 13″ high, base 5″ by 6″.

No. 318. Cast stone, 29″ high.

No. 312. Stone, 40″ high, 14″ base dia.

No. 4820. Lead figure now painted white (Circa 1870-1880). Sculptor unknown. From Hawley Estate designed by Stamford White. Base is 22″ in diameter. Unique — one only. 6'-2" high.

No. 2103. Dancing Girl on base with two frogs which squirt water. 22" high, & 38" high. Bronze and Lead.

No. 2103-A. Dancing Boy on base with two frogs which squirt water, 22" high Bronze and Lead.

No. 2452. "Love The Peddler", 30" tall.

Now Available in Bronze or Lead.

No. 2451-A. "Love The Peddler" with heart and bell.

Now Available in Bronze or Lead.

No. 2451. shell is piped for water. 30" tall.

Now Available in Bronze or Lead.

© 1974
Kenneth Lynch & Sons
Wilton, Conn. 06897

No. 2445.
Lead Dancing
Girl, 23" high.

No. 2444.
Lead Dancing
Boy, 23" high.

No. 896. Lead figure, Dancing Girl with lead shell with lead bird, 38" high. Piped in copper with two water jets at hinge of shell.

No. 903. Lead Dancing Girl Fountain, 23" diameter x 35" high.   Should be used in a pool.

No. 2239. Lead Dancing Girl, (2445) with 21" dia. lead shell and lead base 32" high.

No. 905. Lead Tri-form fountain on antiqued cast stone lattice urn which acts as water resevoir and contains recirculating pump-- shown with Dancing Boy figure, No. 2444. Heighth is 43", and the fountain diameter is 32". Other figures can be substituted.

©1974
Kenneth Lynch & Sons
Wilton, Conn. 06897

No. 2212 (left side) No. 2211 (right side). Pair of seated cupids, 31" high overall. Available in lead or bronze. The original antiques were made in lead. However, we have seen these exact cupids in bronze. They are made so that they can be seated either on a stone ball or on a wall coping or a pedestal of any kind. Furnished complete with proper anchorage.

No. 2212 and No. 2211. This illustration shows a pair of these famous cupids on stone balls and on stone pedestals. With this arrangement the overall height is 63". Other pedestal heights could be used. These cupids are available in either lead or bronze. They are antique reproduction pieces typical of the period.

  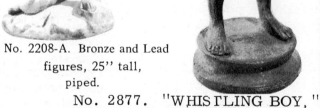

No. 2208. Bronze and Lead figures with shell, English origin, 25" high, 15" dia. shell.

No. 2208-A. Bronze and Lead figures, 25" tall, piped.

No. 2865. Lead garden pool figure, 24" high. Sculptor unknown, but very attractive piece.

No. 2877. "WHISTLING BOY," antique reproduction, 19th century. 14" high.

Now available in Bronze and Lead.

No. 804. Listening Angel Fragment. $11\frac{1}{2}$'' high, $8\frac{1}{2}$'' wide, 5'' deep. Stone.

No. 803. Listening Angel. 31'' high, 12'' wide, 12'' deep. Stone.

No. 699. Trumpeting Angel. This is a most excellent and most appealing piece of sculpture. It is cast stone and stands $20\frac{1}{2}$'' high. The Pedestal is No. 767. It is 34'' high and the bottom is 14'' x 14''.

No. 805. Angel Bracket - With Lute. 17'' high, 8'' wide, 5'' deep. Stone.

No. 805-A. Angel Bracket - With Trumpet. 17'' high, 8'' wide, 5'' deep. Stone.

©1974
Kenneth Lynch & Sons
Wilton, Conn. 06897

ETERNITY LEAD

**NOW AVAILABLE IN
BRONZE OR LEAD**

No. 1679.

No. 1679. Lead seated figure of child. 20" high, should be placed on a stone base about 12" high.

No. 2448. Lead figure, girl riding turtle, 14" high.

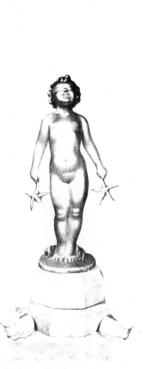

No. 2283. Lead figure, Child with Ducks on pedestal #24. Lead figure is 32" high.

No. 2022. Lead figure, 25" high, can be piped.

No. 2284. Lead figure, Child with starfish, 32" high on #24 pedestal. Many variations of this figure can be used. Frogs may be substituted for the starfish, etc.

No. 2038. Lead figure of Child, draped with scalloped tunic. Reproduction late 17th century. Can be piped.

©1974
Kenneth Lynch & Sons
Wilton, Conn. 06897

GARDEN PIECES
NOW AVAILABLE IN BRONZE OR LEAD

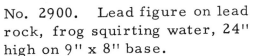

No. 2900. Lead figure on lead rock, frog squirting water, 24" high on 9" x 8" base.

Note: Also Available in Bronze.

No. 2453. Piping Boy, 32" high, pipes are lined with copper tubing for connecting to water. Lead or bronze.

No. 2884. Lead figure, piped for water. "JUDY WITH FLUTE," 42 1/2" high. This is a really great and beautiful piece of sculpture. Water comes from the stops on the flute. Geraldine Lewis, sculptress.

No. 906

No. 2453. Another application of Piping Boy, 32" high, lead.

No. 906. Lead Piping Boy on Shell, 40" high. Self-contained unit, water recirculates from the shell with its own built-in electric pump. NOTE: WE ALSO FURNISH THIS FIGURE WITH A SIMILAR PUMP ARRANGEMENT ON SHELL NO. 2007 WHICH GIVES YOU A GREATER WIDTH. ABOVE ONLY 21½" WIDE. NO. 2007 36", 40", or 48" wide.

©1974
Kenneth Lynch & Sons
Wilton, Conn. 06897

No. 2407. Cupid
birdbath, 30½'' tall.
Now Available in Bronze or
Lead.

No. 2446.
figure, Cupid with
stone and bronze
sundial.
Now Available in Bronze or
Lead.

No. 2408.
Cupid basket boy,
31'' high.
Now Available in Bronze or
Lead.

No. 2406.
Cupid shell
birdbath.
Now Available in Bronze or
Lead.

No. 2215. Dolphin
Base, 24'' high on 12''
tri-form stone base.

No. 2400.
Cupid with
sundial and bird-
bath or feeder.
30½'' tall.
Now Available in Bronze or
Lead.

No. 1664. Lead Boy
with tray and jet, can
be furnished without
jets. Overall height
including jet 41''

No. 2043. Child with
Fish, lead, 42'' high on
#2215 dolphin base.
76'' high overall.
Now Available in Bronze or
Lead.

© 1974
Kenneth Lynch & Sons
Wilton, Conn. 06897

CANTERBURY BRONZE OR ETERNITY LEAD

No. 2447. Bashful Girl Shell and Frogs, fountain or bird bath, piped, 26'' high, 15'' dia. shell. **Lead.**

No. 2644. Lead Garden Figure, 24'' high, piped for water. From Truesdale Collection. Very fine for a small fountain.

Note: Also available in bronze.

No. 2455. Bashful Girl, 22'' high, cast lead, 7'' by 7'' base. **Also cast stone.**

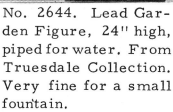

No. 1664. Lead Boy with tray and jet, can be furnished without jets. Overall height including jet 41''

No. 2443. Birdbath, piped frog with girl on shell, 18'' high, 15'' dia.

Now Available in Bronze or Lead.

No. 4658. Lead Bowl on Swan Pedestal, 25 1/2'' diameter x 26'' high to bowl. NOTE: Any figure may be used with this bowl, or may be used alone as a bird bath.

No. 1664. Lead boy and tray, 41'' high by 14½'' in dia. standing on our dolphin base 24'' high by 26'' dia. Note above photograph of this same base with special triform stone pedestal 12'' high, making the entire arrangement 67'' high.

GARDEN PIECES

No. 2021. Lead figure, 25'' high, can be piped.
Note: Also available in bronze.

No. 2442. Illustration of Jug Boy. 20½'' high, lead or stone.

Also available in bronze.

No. 2442. Lead figure; authentic, accurate reproduction of this famous Boy with Jug. The figure is 20½'' high, is piped for water, and in an arrangement such as shown in this illustration can be used with recirculating pump, etc. Note: Also available in bronze.

No. 2276. Lead figure, 16'' high, 15'' long on a base 5'' wide by 15'' long, can be piped.

Note: Also available in bronze.

No. 2132. Boy with Dolphin, 18'' high.
Bronze, Lead, Stone

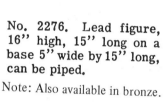

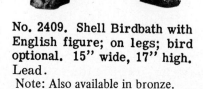

No. 2411. English lead garden figure, seated on lead rock, 15'' high. Note: Also available in bronze.

No. 2409. Shell Birdbath with English figure; on legs; bird optional. 15'' wide, 17'' high. Lead.
Note: Also available in bronze.

No. 2412. English lead garden figure on ball base, 15'' high.
Note: Also available in bronze.

© 1974
Kenneth Lynch & Sons
Wilton, Conn. 06897

No. 4929. Stone figure of child contemplating. This piece is available in two sizes. The larger is 34" long by 17" wide by 22½" high overall. The smaller is 15" long by 6½" wide by 10½" high overall. In the proper setting in a garden or at a pool edge, this is a most attractive piece of sculpture.

BY GERRIE LEWIS — AMENDOLA

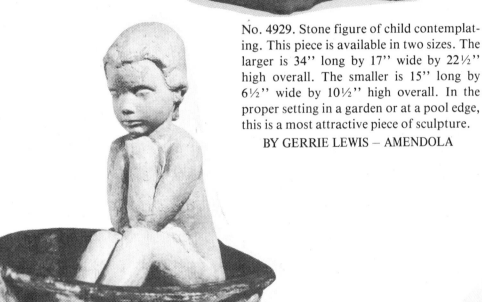

No. 4975. Seated child figure in walnut shell. This is the same figure as No. 4976 shown to the left. The shell is approximately 18" in diameter and it is reminiscent of the story of Thumbalina. Furnished in stone only.

BY GERRIE LEWIS — AMENDOLA

No. 4976. Seated child, 16½" high, 15" front to back. Furnished in stone only. An original work of art.

BY GERRIE LEWIS — AMENDOLA

© 1974
Kenneth Lynch & Sons
Wilton, Conn. 06897

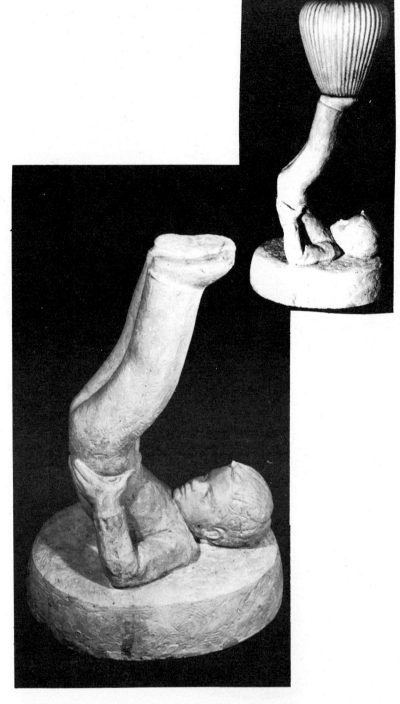

No. 4928. Child with baby. The larger size measures: 32½'' high overall, base 23 by 21''. The smaller size is 17½'' high overall, base 13'' by 10''. This is an original work of art. Furnished in cast stone only. It is a very fine piece of work by Gerrie Lewis Amendola.

No. 5565. "The Show-Off" by Gerri Lewis-Amendola. This delightful piece of sculpture shows a child showing-off what he can do with his feet in the air balanced on his back. There seems that there was just such a boy who continuously entertained his neighbors with his upside down pose balancing balls, planters, etc. We photographed him many times and finally decided it would make an excellent piece of sculpture. The figure itself is 25'' high overall and the base is oval, 17'' x 13''. Almost anything could be supported by this boy and we show some suggestions. He is available in bronze, lead or stone.

©1974
Kenneth Lynch & Sons
Wilton, Conn. 06897

No. 1324. "PAN WITH PIPES", 33" high on a base 12" x 13". Very stable. Base is designed to hide a recirculating pump. Lead or stone. Note: Also available in bronze.

No. 2061. Lead figure, girl with shawl, 36" tall. Also available in bronze.

No. 2023. figure. 30" tall

Now Available in Bronze or Lead.

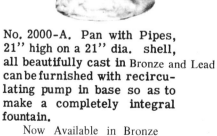

No. 2000-A. Pan with Pipes, 21" high on a 21" dia. shell, all beautifully cast in Bronze and Lead can be furnished with recirculating pump in base so as to make a completely integral fountain.

Now Available in Bronze

No. 2000. Pan with Pipes on shell, 17½" high, 15" in dia. Bronze and Lead can be furnished with pump in base circulating water from Pan's pipes. Note: Also available in bronze.

No. 2000-B. Lead Pan on lead rock. 13" & 17" high.

Note: Also available in bronze.

© 1974.
Kenneth Lynch & Sons
Wilton, Conn. 06897

SCULPTURE

CANTERBURY BRONZE OR ETERNITY LEAD

No. 642. Lead garden figure, 30" long x 42" high. NOTE: This is also furnished with stone snail and lead boy.

No. 1356. Lead Boys balancing or dancing around rim of fountain. Boys are 28" high. Larger pool could be used, of different design, etc. Your inquiry is invited.

No. 4686. Lead Balancing Boy, 40" high. The ball is stone. Looks well with four jets of water around it in pool.

No. 4689. Flute Player with Dolphin, 48" high x 40" long. The dolphin and base are of stone, and the flutist is lead with bronze flute. All piped.

No. 4687. Lead Circus Rider on stone Clydesdale, 42" long x 60" high.

No. 4688. Lead Balancing Boy, 28" high.

GARDEN STATUARY

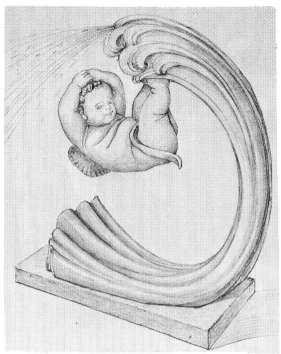

No. 1234. Baroque wave-like pedestal which can be used to support anything you feel would go well with it. It is 30" tall and can be piped. The figure on the pedestal is shown in another part of the catalog. It is No. 124 and is 21" high. Stone.

No. 1201. Stone Cherub riding wave. Piped up to 1" for filling pool or fountain effect. 2' high.

No. 75. 38" high stone, on a base 14¼" x 14¼", can carry large pipe.

No. 287. Stone, 37" high, piped, 10" x 10" base.

No. 1050. Stone, Boy, riding Sea Horse, 33½" high x 13½" square base. Can be piped.

No. 561. Boy on Seahorse. Cast lead or cast stone seahorse. In all cases, boy is made of lead. 31" high, can be piped. Note: Also Available in Bronze.

BELGIAN BOY

No. 248. Belgian Boy,
25" high on a 6 1/2" x
6 1/2" base, piped.
Lead or Stone. Now Available in Bronze

Photograph of Mr. Lynch with Belgian Boy in the background. This picture was taken in 1969.

Photograph of the actual Belgian Boy in detail.

The above figure No. 248 is a reproduction of the famous Belgian Boy which is one block from the Grand Plaza in the heart of Old Brussels, Belgium. The story is that this little child was lost for three days and he was the son of the Mayor of the town. The entire town stopped everything to search for the child and they could not find him. However, at the end of the third day the little boy was found standing on this exact corner with no clothes on doing what he is doing in this illustration, and the people were so over-joyed that they employed Belgium's best sculptor to model the child exactly as you see it, and they made this now famous fountain. The people love this little statue and its story very much and at various times of the year the statue is dressed as a military figure, as a political figure; anyone who is in the news might find his clothing in small size on the little boy. This is piped for water with copper tubing.

© 1974
Kenneth Lynch & Sons
Wilton, Conn. 06897

No. 25. Stone "FISHER BOY," 34" high. 19th century.

No. 902. Fisher boy & girl under umbrella. Piped in copper with brass spray head 50" high. Base 18" x 30". Base has concealed access door for recirculating pump. Cast stone.

No. 26. Stone "FISHER GIRL." Excellent 19th century piece, 31½" high.

No. 900. Fisher girl under umbrella. Antiqued cast stone, piped with all copper, verde antique patine, with adjustable brass spray head 42" high.

No. 156. Cast stone, 18" high.

No. 901. Fisher boy under umbrella. piped with all copper, verde antique patine, with adjustable brass spray head 44" high.

©1974
Kenneth Lynch & Sons
Wilton, Conn. 06897

No. 45. Stone garden sculpture. A most beautiful nostalgic piece of American 19th Century art. Size 44" high. Base is 22" diameter.

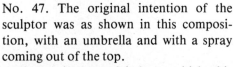

No. 47. The original intention of the sculptor was as shown in this composition, with an umbrella and with a spray coming out of the top.

The antique model from which this stone piece was made was in cast iron. Figure size 44" high. 22" diameter base.

The umbrella is 31" diameter. Adds to the height of the figures 11" inches making a total (+44") 55" in height.

No. 46. Stone garden figures piped for water feature. It can squirt vertically or at an angle towards front. Size 44" high. Base is 22" diameter.

© 1974.
Kenneth Lynch & Sons
Wilton, Conn. 06897

Note: Also available in bronze.

No. 2841. Lead Armorini from the collection of Mr. Carrol Cavanaugh. The winged child has a bow and there are two birds at his feet. This is a fine antique. Reproduction available. 32'' High 27'' Long. Base is 17'' Diameter.

Now Available in Bronze

No. 4977. Stone Mushroom with Leprechaun piped for water. While the mushroom should be used in stone, the Leprechaun could also be made in bronze or lead on special order. The mushroom is 13" high and 11½" in diameter. The figure is 15½" high overall and the base is 9½" x 5½". From the back of the head to the tail it measures 13". The pipes provide a delightful musical trickle of water.

No. 970. Stone "BOY WITH RABBIT," 25'' high on a 17'' x 11'' base. Claire Low, f.c.

No. 2005. Lead figure, 13 1/4'' high. Original from Cong, Ireland.

Now Available in Bronze

No. 2885. Lead figure, "WENDY," 38'' high. Antique reproduction, can be piped for water from shell.

Note: Also available in bronze.

GARDEN PIECES

CANTERBURY BRONZE OR ETERNITY LEAD

No. 2890. Lead figure, 22" high,

2889-B Lead figure on lead bird bath base. 17" high. Can be had with different arrangement of animals

No. 2889. Lead figure, 14" high,

No. 2889-A. Lead figure, piped for water, with flutes, 14" high.

No. 1249. Stone and lead fountain, 26" diameter x 26" high; can be piped, and water can come from the pipes. NOTE: The figure can be purchased separately and is No. 2889, is made of lead only. Self-contained recirculating pump can be used.

No. 2581. Lead figure, famous small Verrocciccio, 15½" high, piped.

No. 1665. Boy with vase, Lead, 25" high, Base 15" dia.

No. 2449. Lead figure, Boy Riding Dolphin, can be piped, 14" high.

Note: Also available in bronze.

© 1974
Kenneth Lynch & Sons
Wilton, Conn. 06897

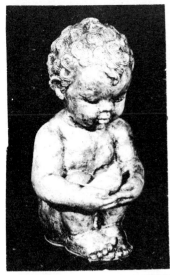

No. 968. Stone "BIRD-HOLDER", 14″ high,

No. 967. Stone "BIRD-WARMER", 14″ high,

No. 964. Stone "GAZER" 15½″ high.

No. 963. Stone birdbath, feeder or fountain, can be piped 26″ high,

No. 965. Stone "BOY ON FISH" by Anne Kopper, 20″ high, 21″ long. Can be piped.

No. 969. Stone "YOUNG ST. FRANCIS", 23″ high,

No. 966. Stone "CUBS" 14″ high.

No. 973. Stone "PELICAN" 21″ high.

No. 1240. Stone Bird Bath with "BIRDHOLDER" figure by Anne Kopper. Figure is No. 968, stone, 14″ high, with bronze wings added. Bird is of lead. Bowl is approximately 30″ diameter.

© 1974
Kenneth Lynch & Sons
Wilton, Conn. 06897

No. 2472 and 2472-A. The above figures are piped for water and furnished with stone base. Bronze or Lead

No. 2472-A. Lead figure of "PAN," piped for water, 28" high. This is one of the best treatments of this subject we have ever seen. It is by Mr. Robert Amendola, sculptor.

Now available in Bronze

WARNING: These figures have been illegally copied. They have been offered in New York City auction rooms and bring about the same price as the genuine shown here. The spurious copies are made of a cheap white metal which breaks easily and deteriorates in the sun and weather. Non-genuine if not stamped "Eternity Lead, Kenneth Lynch & Sons, R. Amendola, Sculptor."

GARDEN PIECES
CANTERBURY BRONZE OR ETERNITY LEAD

No. 2220. Lead figure of Pan, beautiful detail, can be piped, 6½" high.

Note: Also available in bronze.

No. 2427. Pan by Joseph Kuthmayer, 41" high. Note: THIS IS A LIFE SIZE FIGURE.

Now available in Bronze or Lead.

No. 2003. Lead figure, piped, 26" high.

Now Available in Bronze

No. 2003. Set of four satyr musicians available in either lead or bronze. They are from English models and they are very much admired by collectors of this material. They are 26" high and, of course, should be used on stone pedestals.

No. 2880. Lead figure, "MUSICIAN," 18" high. Note: These two figures are antique reproductions. Now Available in Bronze

NOTE: On Nos. 2879 and 2880, the lead is 18" high; however, with the stone bases, which must be used, it gets them up nearer to 24" in height. The flutes can be piped. These are not the most beautiful examples of their period, but rather the reproduction of work of a country craftsman. Late 17th century.

© 1974
Kenneth Lynch & Sons
Wilton, Conn. 06897

No. 1038. Stone figure on ball, 39″ high, 13¾″ square.

No. 1039. Stone figure on ball, 39″ high, 13¾″ square.

No. 1035. Stone figure on ball, 39″ high, 13¾″ square.

This Figure has been revised. It is now holding a Tambourine.

No. 1043. Stone figure on ball, 39″ high overall; base is 13¾″ sq.

No. 2454. Lead figure, piped for water, 16″ high.

Now Available in Bronze

No. 5509. Stone figure, 42″ high with acorns. Summer or early Fall. An altogether delightful piece of workmanship.

No. 5508. Stone figure with grapes 42″ high. Beautifully detailed, could possibly be called Autumn or late Summer.

© 1974.
Kenneth Lynch & Sons
Wilton, Conn. 06897

No. 1710. Stone. Caesar. 23'' high. Base is 5'' square.

No. 1708 Stone Bust of Hermes. 30'' high x 9'' diameter.

No. 1727. Stone Bust of Beethoven. 18'' high x 6'' diameter base.

No. 1711. Stone. Bust of David. 30'' high x 22'' across shoulders. Base is 9'' diameter.

© 1974.
Kenneth Lynch & Sons
Wilton, Conn. 06897

TEDDY ROOSEVELT

No. 5423. Head of Teddy Roosevelt in Roughrider uniform circa 1900. This remarkable piece of sculpture was a gift of the Proctor family (A.P. Proctor, Sculptor) to Kenneth Lynch & Sons for having stored Mr. Proctor's collection of work for so many years at no cost to them.

The story is that Mr. Lynch, Sr., and other members of the family served with Colonel Roosevelt and there is considerable interest in this piece of work. It is 22" high and 17" wide overall and it is available in bronze, lead or stone.

No. 5567. Cast stone head of a poet. Perhaps the aged Sophocles. From Constantinople. Second century B.C. it is thought. Courtesy of the British Museum. This piece is in the full round in good detail. Furnished in very darkened stone. Suitable for use out of doors or mounting on a pedestal. Furnished with bronze mounting rod. Life size

No. 5566. Stone casting bust of Antonia. Daughter of Marcus Antonius and Octavia, mother of the emperor Claudius. Early first century A.D. 22½" high. By permission of the British Museum. Suitable for use out of doors and furnished with stainless steel anchor.

A statue of St. Francis without the devotional aspect becomes a pagan thing. After much investigation on the part of, and help from the Franciscan Fathers and the Jesuit Fathers, we have decided that the "Canticle of the Sun" is the most fitting and devotional prayer that could accompany a St. Francis figure.

Most high omnipotent Lord, Thine are the praises, the glory, the honor, and all benediction.

To Thee alone, Most High, do they belong, And no one is able to praise You as You deserve.

Praised be Thou, my Lord, with all Thy creatures, Especially the honored Brother Sun, Who makes the day and illumines us through Thee.

And he is beautiful and radiant with great splendor, And bears the signification of Thee, Most High One.

Praised be Thou, my Lord, for Brother Wind, And for the air, cloudy and clear and every weather, By which Thou givest sustenance to Thy creatures.

Praised be Thou, my Lord, for Sister Water.

Which is very useful and humble and precious and chaste.

Praised be Thou, my Lord, for Brother Fire, By whom Thou lightest the night, And he is beautiful and jocund and robust and strong.

Praised be Thou, my Lord, for our sister Mother Earth, Who sustains and governs us, And produces various fruits with colored flowers and herbage.

Praise and bless my Lord and give Him thanks And serve Him with great humility.

Praised be Thou, O'Lord, for those who give pardon for Thy Love And endure infirmity and tribulation.

Blessed be those, who endure in peace, who will be, Most High, crowned by Thee!

I pray to Thee in thanksgiving for the tranquility of the garden And all the wondrous things of nature.

No. 2221. Lead St. Francis Plaque, used with No. 2209 Shrine. The reverse side has beautifully inscribed, "The Canticle of the Sun", as shown above. 7½" wide x 12" high. Now Available in Bronze

No. 2209. Lead St. Francis Shrine or Birdfeeder. 16: high by 12" wide. There is a small basin on the obverse side which acts as a foot to make it stand and which can be used as a bird feeder or to hold a votive candle. On the reverse side is the complete " Canticle of the Sun" as shown above. Can be furnished with loop on top for hanging in tree. Note: This piece is sold at a special price to encourage this devotion. Now available in Bronze

ST. FRANCIS

No. 1261. Stone, 36″ high, "ST. FRANCIS HOLDING SHELL." Can be used as bird feeder or as fountain with water coming from shell.

No. 118. St. Francis, cast stone, 30″ tall, antique finish.

No. 517. Stone "ST. FRANCIS." This is the original Panzeroni model. Three sizes: 26″, 40″ and 48″ high.

No. 1548. St. Francis by Robert Amendola, cast lead with antiqued stone base which serves as bird feeder. 27″ high.

Also available in bronze.

No. 2441-A. St. Francis on shell bird bath, 19″ high overall, shell is 15″ wide, lead. Available in Bronze

© 1974
Kenneth Lynch & Sons
Wilton, Conn. 06897

No. 39. St. Francis cast stone - 17¼" high.

St. Francis, cast stone, antique finish,
Size No. 132: 13½" high
Size No. 137: 18" high.

No. 8. St. Francis, cast stone, 24" high.

No. 2441. St. Francis, lead, 19" high, 7" base.

Now Available in Bronze

No. 1261. Stone St. Francis holding Shell. This can be used as a bird feeder. Or it can be used as a fountain with water coming from the shell. Many design compositions could be made using one of these figures as the central feature on the edge of a pool where birds and animals would drink. This exceptionally wonderful piece of sculpture is offered in three sizes: 30" high, 38" high and 48" high. This was one of our most recommended pieces of garden sculpture.

© 1974
Kenneth Lynch & Sons
Wilton, Conn. 06897

DEVOTIONAL PIECES

No. 2151.
Head of Christ, lead
or stone, 9" by 14".
Also available in bronze.

No. 2893. Lead "MADONNA,"
from European collection, 30"
high, 7 1/4" base.
Also available in bronze.

No. 1138. Stone "MADONNA,"
32" high, base 11" square.
NOTE: See Pedestal Section
for base which is 19 3/4" high.

No. 1139. Stone Madonna,
41" high, base 14" x 14"

No. 1279. Stone "ST.
JOSEPH," 53" high.

No. 290. Madonna, cast
stone, antique finish, 27"
high.

© 1974
Kenneth Lynch & Sons
Wilton, Conn. 06897

No. 1136. Stone "ST. FIACRE, THE VENERABLE," 48" high.

No. 989. Stone "ST. ANTHONY," 32" high.

No. 560. St. Fiacre, cast lead or cast stone, 19" tall, furnished either as wall hanging or to stand.

Note: Also available in bronze.

No. 191. St. Fiacre, younger version, 31" high, 8" by 10" base, by George Mitchell. Cast stone.

© 1974
Kenneth Lynch & Sons
Wilton, Conn. 06897

No. 1137. Stone "ST. FIACRE THE YOUNGER," 48" high.

No. 190. St. Fiacre, older version by George Mitchell, 32" high, 8" by 10" base. Cast stone.

DEVOTIONAL PIECES

No. 1720. Stone, St. Francis. 30'' high. 7½'' square base.

No. 1718. Stone, St. Francis. 42'' high. 10'' square base.

No. 1712. Stone, St. Joseph. 21'' high. 6'' square base.

No. 1717. Stone, St. Anthony. 36'' high. 10'' octagonal base.

© 1974.
Kenneth Lynch & Sons
Wilton, Conn. 06897

No. 1715. Stone, St. Mary.
38'' high. 9'' octagonal base.

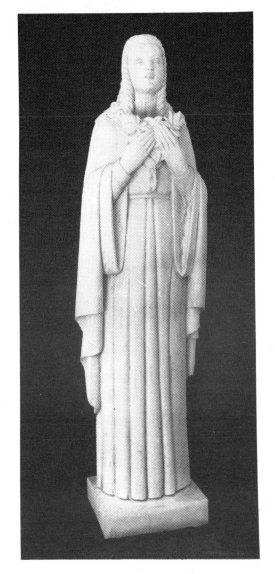

No. 1716. Stone, St. Theresa.
52'' high. 11'' square base.

Actually the features on these figures are most attractive. Please ask for photographs.

No. 1728. Stone Angel Head.
12'' high, 12'' wide,
5½ projection.

© 1974.
Kenneth Lynch & Sons
Wilton, Conn. 06897

No. 713. Quan Yin with Base attached. 54½'' high, 12''
wide, 10'' deep. Stone

No. 714. Lotus Base — Available also as Planter. 15''
high, 12'' wide, 10'' deep. Stone

No. 786. Seated Buddha. 43½''
high, 23½'' wide, 17½'' deep.

No. 718. Stone base. 14½''
high, 21'' wide, 13½'' deep.

No. 539. Buddha, cast
stone, 21½'' high.

No. 529. Buddha, cast stone, 18''
high.

No. 534. Hotei, 24'' high.
Cast stone.

No. 1429. Reproduction of carved wood figure of Cambodian Temple Dancer, but now made in cast stone. She is standing on a lotus base. Antique finish. 48" high x 13 1/2" base. A very excellent garden piece.

No. 547. Kuan Yin, 34" high, cast stone, antique finish.

No. 700. Goddess of Flowers. 54" high, 21" wide, 13" deep.

No. 710. Rectangular Base Planter (Small). 14" high, 13" wide, 21" deep.

No. 701. Temple Urn. 15½" high, 28" wide, 13" deep.

No. 1527. Bamboo design lead planters in three sizes: 16½" long by 3" in dia.; 11½" long by 2 1/4" in dia.; 7½" long by 2" in dia.

Note: Also available in bronze.

© 1974
Kenneth Lynch & Sons
Wilton, Conn. 06897

No. 535. Cast Stone Bowl. Two sizes: 17" dia. and 24" dia.

No. 1428. Indonesian Figure Wall Plaque, with small basin, flat back. Made in cast stone and can be piped. Two sizes: small, 31 1/2" high x 17" wide; larger size, 49" tall x 11 1/4" wide.

No. 546. Kuan Yin, cast stone, 42" high, antique finish.

No. 707. Standing Buddha. 56" high, 14" wide, 14" deep. Stone,

No. 710. Rectangular Base Planter (Small). 14" high, 13" wide, 21" deep.

No. 709. Fret Table - Small Top. 16" high, 22" wide, 22" deep.

No. 1174. Japanese Stone Water Basin, 24" high x 21" diameter.

No. 723. Buddha and Ginko Tree Plaque (Pierced). 33" high, 29" wide, 3½" deep. Stone

No. 545. Kuan Yin, two sizes: 40" high and 53" high, cast stone antique finish.

© 1974
Kenneth Lynch & Sons
Wilton, Conn. 06897

No. 706. Seated Quan. 42'' high, 24'' wide, 18'' deep.

No. 724-A. Pagoda. 67'' high, 19'' wide, 19'' deep.

No. 702. Goddess of Love. 58'' high, 15'' wide, 10½'' deep.

No. 715. Seated Quan - Hooks for hanging if desired. 30'' high, 12'' wide, 6½'' deep.

No. 716. Planter. 7'' high, 22'' wide, 11½'' deep.

No. 544. Kuan Yin, 24'' tall, cast stone.

No. 549. Kwang Planter, 18½'' by 21'' x 15'', cast stone.

GRECIAN SCULPTURE

No. 846. Grecian Goddess Athena Plaque. 56" high, 32½" wide, 5" deep. Stone

No. 801. Cherub Fragment Plaque. 19" high, 44" wide, 4 3/4" deep. Stone

No. 866. Grecian Frieze. 16" high, 52" wide, 5" deep. Stone

ORIENTAL PIECES

No. 1286. Garden Seat, Japanese geta design, 18" wide, 30" long, 14 1/2" high.

No. 536. Bowl, cast stone, 21" in dia.

No. 1525. Cast lead antique, bamboo shaped vases. Two sizes: 5" dia. by 11" high; 3½" dia. by 11" high. NOTE: CAN ALSO BE MADE SHORTER.

No. 704. Fret Urn. 16" high, 16" wide, 16" deep. Stone

No. 1285. Japanese stone garden seat, 36" long, 18" wide, 16" high.

No. 305. Japanese Lantern,
cast stone, antique finish, 27"
high, 22" dia.   Also 18" Dia.

JAPANESE STONE LANTERNS

Kenneth Lynch & Sons is greatly indebted to the artists, designers and the monks at both Kyoto and Nara, Japan, for their help in doing research on these lanterns. The designs are practically limitless and, as you can see, we show many.

The Japanese are very good stone workers. We have seen as many as 50 of these lanterns in front of one shrine.

No. 533. Pagoda, cast stone, three sizes:' 4 ft. 5 ft. and 7 ft. high.

The stone lantern was one type of lantern used in the ancient times as a lighting facility which later developed into a decoration for gardens.

A variety of materials **were** used to make lanterns in the ancient times. The lanterns with the frames of cast-iron, bronze and other materials were often used for interior lighting while the stone lanterns for exterior lighting.

The stones used for these lanterns included granite, andesite, tufa and lamble. Candle or seed oil provided the source of light to the stone lanterns.

The type of stone lanterns vary according to their original utility. The stone lantern was originally "votive" lantern or lantern offered to Shinto or Buddhist deities. Later, it began to be used as a road lamp and coastal lighthouse and then as a decoration in gardens as the Japanese traditional gardening art developed since the medieval age.

There are 21 types of stone lantern belonging to the "votive" lanterns. Some of the types are called Hannyaji, Tono-mine, Genkoji, Nishinoya, Sangatsudo, Eizanji, Semi, Maru, Tomyoji, Uzumasa, Tomadera and etc.

The shape of stone lanterns also varies according to the traditional types. For example, the Genkoji type is usually hexagonal, while the Nishinoya type is square.

As to decorative stone lanterns, there are 14 types such as Yukimi, Oribe, Zendoji, Kasuga and so forth. The raison d'etre of stone lanterns is only for decoration today and electric lamps have replaced candle and seed oil as the source of light in most cases.

No. 532. Rankei, cast stone, 18" by 24"; 18" by 36"; and 24" by 48".

No. 1521. Japanese lantern, aluminum with antique finish, three sizes: 25" dia. by 20" high: 22" dia. by 15" high; 18" dia. by 12½" high.

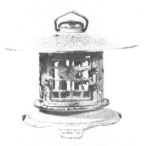

No. 1519. Japanese lantern, 11" in dia. 8" high, aluminum with antique finish.

No. 1233. Stone Lantern, 48" diameter.
NOTE: The top was carefully carved
with little ridges to support both moss
and bird food. Because these ridges
retain moisture, the moss will grow
like a nice green blanket.

No. 1173. Stone Lantern, 36"
high x 30" wide (sode gata).

No. 1172. Stone Lantern, 18" high 10 1/2"
wide.

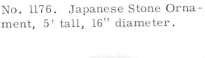

No. 1176. Japanese Stone Ornament, 5' tall, 16" diameter.

No. 1170. Stone Lantern,
40" high x 36" diameter.

No. 1232. Stone Lantern, 48"
square. The top of this lantern
was designed to retain water,
moss and bird food. Any base
can be used, but the one shown
is our No. 96.

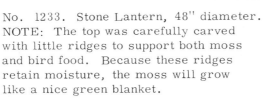

No. 1169. Stone Lantern, 4' diameter
x 4' 9" high, antique finish.

©1974
Kenneth Lynch & Sons
Wilton, Conn. 06897

Japanese lantern, cast stone, antique finish, five sizes:
Size 293: 30" high by 25" dia.
Size 294: 25" high by 19" dia.
Size 295: 18" high by 15" dia.
Size 296: 14" high by 12" dia.

No. 304. Japanese lantern, cast stone, antique finish, 38" high.

No. 538. Japanese lantern, cast stone, 50" high.

Japanese lantern, cast stone, five sizes, antique finish.
Size 298: 26" high by 26" in dia.
Size 299: 26" high by 19" in dia.
Size 300: 19" high by 16" in dia.
Size 301: 15" high by 12½" in dia.

No. 1178. Stone, 5' tall, 24" wide.

No. 5246
Cast stone lantern. Top 24" x 18".
Overall height 26"

No. 5245
Cast stone lantern 18" x 8" top x 14" high.

No. 5237
Cast stone lantern 18" across base
by 14" high

No. 5239
Cast stone lantern 18" in diameter
x 10" high.

No. 5241
Cast stone lantern 18" diameter top
x 15" high.

No. 5247
Electrified Japanese Lantern. 17" diameter
top, 16" high overall. Unbreakable. This
lantern is made of Japanese lava stone mixed
with resin. It is a very neatly finished piece
of work, such as the Japanese would use either
on a terrace, in a garden or even in a bedroom.
Comes electrified, ready-to-use.

No. 5242
Cast stone lantern 18" diameter
x 14" high.

No. 5243
Cast stone lantern 18" diameter x 10" high.
Note the base is No. 92 and is 10" x 10" x 10".

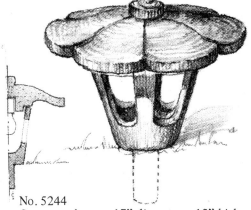

No. 5244
Cast stone lantern 17" diameter x 12" high

No. 543. Japanese lantern, 23" high overall, cast stone. NOTE: ALSO VERY DESIRABLE WHEN USED WITH ROOF AND FIRST SECTION.

No. 1179. Stone Monument, minimum 6' tall with a 24" base. It can go as high as 8'.

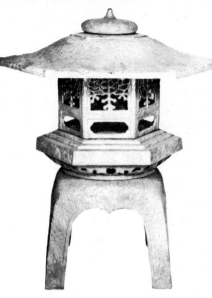

No. 1523. Japanese lantern, aluminum with antique finish, 24½" high by 19" in dia.

No. 724-A. Pagoda 67" high, 19" wide, 19" deep.

No. 1287. Stone Lantern, Bird Feeder and Shelter, 48" high x 25" diameter.

No. 1522. Japanese lantern, aluminum with antique finish, 9" high by 9" square.

No. 1177. Stone Bird Feeder, 5" tall, 16" diameter.

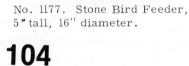

No. 1171. Stone Bird Feeder, 30" long x 18" high.

© 1974.
Kenneth Lynch & Sons
Wilton, Conn. 06897

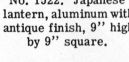

No. 1000 Stone Clydesdale is one of the truly great pieces of horse sculpture available. Everyone loves these great gentle beasts and any country place would be proud to have a pair of these on its gate-posts. This is first-class sculpture done by a knowledgeable craftsman. Note the treatment of the mane and tail. Certainly this is one of the best loved pieces Kenneth Lynch & Sons has ever produced. It weighs about 400 lbs and is all reinforced with stainless steel armature.

42" high, base 23" x 46".

No. 1633. Young Pegasus, by Gifford Proctor, Bronze or Lead 37-3/4'' on cast stone base.

No. 1632. Colt, by Gifford Proctor, Bronze or Lead 37-3/4'' high on cast stone base.

© 1974.
Kenneth Lynch & Sons
Wilton, Conn. 06897

No. 6125. Horse. This great piece of sculpture is available in bronze only. It will be made in limited edition. Above you see photographs of the original models by Mr. Gifford M. Proctor, F.A.A.R.—N.S.S. The size is as follows: The base is 6'3¾" x 22½" x 4½". The height from the underside of the base to the top of the horse's head is 6'1½". This is a lost wax casting in the finest of bronze, all Roman jointed.

No. 4987. Pair of French Carousel type Horses probably 17th century. This one is a mare and is wearing a decorative collar with fleur-de-lis and Maltese Crosses alternating. The small strap which hangs pendant-wise from the decorative collar possibly could have held a bauble of some kind. These are unquestionably designed to grace the entrance of an estate and are sold in pairs. The size is 25" high overall and the base is 16" wide x 37" long. Furnished complete with anchors. Restored from the antique by a great sculptor who is interested in horses. Available in stone.

© 1974
Kenneth Lynch & Sons
Wilton, Conn. 06897

No. 493. Large horse plaque, 5 ft. long, 3'-6'' high, furnished in ARMOR STONE©, easy to hang.

No. 746. Tang Horse Plaque. 38'' high, 45'' wide, 3½'' deep.

No. 2167. Leaden plaque of heavy draft stallion from an original by Albrecht Duer. 4-5/8'' by 7½''.

Note: Also available in bronze.

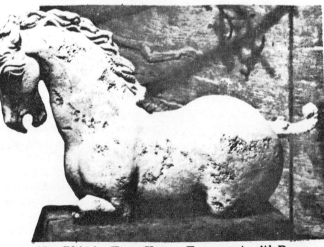

No. 731-A. Tang Horse Fragment with Base. 19-16½'' high, 20'' wide, 9½'' deep. Stone.

© 1974
Kenneth Lynch & Sons
Wilton, Conn. 06897

What greater artistic privelege could one have than to be permitted to reproduce this magnificent horse head from the East Pediment of the Parthenon?

BY GERRIE LEWIS — AMENDOLA

No. 1331. Horse Head from model shown above. Available in bronze, lead and stone. All of these piped for water when so desired. Furnished complete with anchors. An heroic, magnificent, breathtaking piece of sculpture. Size 27" high x 32" long.

No. 1016. Horse Head, 14" high, 16" long. Stone.

From the east pediment of the Parthenon comes this sculpture of a horse's head, panting and exhausted after a night of drawing the moon goddess, Selene, across the skies in her celestial chariot. It is one of the masterpieces of realistic Greek sculpture some time between 438 and 431 B.C.

Although the Parthenon sculptures were executed by many artists, the design of this classical masterpiece was most probably conceived by the sculptor Phidias.

The original is of marble and is housed in the Elgin Room of the British Museum, London. Reproduced with permission of the Trustees. Height: 27". Length: 32"

No. 740. Persian Horse Head. 27" high, 27" wide, 11" deep. Stone.

No. 640. 19th century horsehead with flowing main and oak leaves at base of neck. Cast stone, 32 1/4" high, 13" wide.

No. 4994. Stone Horse Head from our 19th century collection. It is 28" at longest measurement. The base against the wall is 24" x 10". It is not impossible that this piece would be improved with an added back member, probably oval in shape.

No. 364. Cast stone horse-head, 12½" high and 12½" projection.

No. 3411. Aluminum hitching post from a century old pattern; about 14" high, can be mounted on post or pipe.

©1974
Kenneth Lynch & Sons
Wilton, Conn. 06897

No. 1000-U. Cast stone Unicorn with lead horn and
lead ears, 54" long x 40" high; base is 24" x 46".
Horn can be made removable. Horn and ears also in bronze.

No. 1632.-U. All lead
Unicorn Colt, 30" long
x 22 1/2" high.

Note: Also available in bronze.

No. 4526-U. Resting Unicorn,
all lead, 11" long, 7 1/2" high.
Antique reproduction.
Note: Also Available in Bronze.

No. 2942-U. Lead
Unicorn. His horn
can be piped for
water, 26" long x
17" high.
Note: Also Available in Bronze.

No. 640-U. Stone Unicorn with lead horn,
32 1/2". High x 13" wide x 22" Projection.

No. 1016-U. Greek Unicorn head, 21" projection,
16 1/2" high. The head is cast stone; the horn is
available in Bronze or Lead.

No. 364-U. Stone Unicorn with lead horn,
12 1/2" high x 20" Projection. Horn also in bronze.

No. 1632-HU. All lead Unicorn head, 18"
projection. Colt-like features.
Now available in Bronze.

©1974
Kenneth Lynch & Sons
Wilton, Conn. 06897

UNICORNS

We made a unicorn
fountain with the unicorn
by a pool resting. Horn
dripping water.

This illustration used through the courtesy of the
Metropolitan Museum of Art is from the famous
tapestry on display at the Cloisters. The Unicorn has
generally been accepted as a symbol of purity. It is
also, however, an extremely decorative piece of
sculpture.

No. 4987-U. Cast stone Unicorns with
very delicate features. It is felt that
in the case of this particular model
the horn should be gilded as possibly
should be the collar on the Unicorn.
Furnished complete with anchors.
size is 25" high overall and the base is 16"
wide x 37" long.

No. 2738U. Cast Lead or Bronze
25" Long x 19½" high.

No. 731-AU. Stone Unicorn with lead horn and lead
tail, 24" long x 16 1/2" high over all.
Horn and tail also in bronze.

THE CENTAUR

CANTERBURY BRONZE OR ETERNITY LEAD

In this book you will find three Centaurs ranging in size from small bronzes to life size pieces. Mr. Lynch's personal research on this sculpture subject has been enormous and represents a revival of interest in the history of these great creatures who are alledged to have come from the area of Macedonia and were illustrated in art for almost fifteen hundred years. Mr. Lynch has almost completed a book for children entitled, "The Little Centaur" which narrates the story of the birth, raising and training of one of the most intelligent of all Centaurs who developed into beautiful manhood and was a credit to his kind. "The Little Centaur" will be published by the Canterbury Publishing Company of Canterbury, Connecticut.

No. 1601. Castlead—41 1/4"
high on a cast stone base 12"
x 24".

"CENTAUR" A most beautiful piece of sculpture. The young Centaur is looking in amazement at his guest. The Centaurs were children of Dia and Ixion. Half man and half horse, much admired for their physical prowess.

By Gifford M. Proctor, F. A. A. R. -N. S. S.

©1974
Kenneth Lynch & Sons
Wilton, Conn. 06897

No. 6426. Centaur. This great piece of sculpture is available in bronze only. It will be made in limited edition. Above you see photographs of the original models by Mr. Gifford M. Proctor, F.A.A.R.—N.S.S. The size is as follows: The base is 6'¾" x 22½" x 4½". The total overall height to the very top of the bow is 7'10". The height from the underside of the base to the top of the Centaur's head is 6'5". The Trustees of the Art Committee of the Craft Center Museum have recommended that this Centaur be made available without the bow but strumming a lyre and this would be a very simple matter for Mr. Proctor. This is a lost wax casting in the finest of bronze, all Roman jointed.

THE CENTAUR

No. 5540. Bronze Centaur, 8½" tall. This wonderfully modeled, happy looking piece of small sculpture has long been the property of the Craft Center Museum and it is available for reproduction in a limited number of pieces. It is available in bronze only. It is part of the Lynch collection of Centaur models.

© 1974
Kenneth Lynch & Sons
Wilton, Conn. 06897

A substantial collection of lions is offered. These popular beasts are constantly being modeled and carved. However, this takes time. Shown on these pages are excellent models readily available.

No. 1359. Stone Lion of unusually fine detail. It is, 34" High, 54" Long and 19" Wide. Base is 14" Wide x 42" Long left and right.

No. 1087. Stone Lion, 36" long, 26" high, base 14" x 36".

No. 1151. Stone Lion with ball, 28" high on base 26" x 12". Left and Right.

No. 1307. Lioness, stone, 28" high x 60" long.

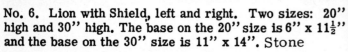

No. 6. Lion with Shield, left and right. Two sizes: 20" high and 30" high. The base on the 20" size is 6" x 11½" and the base on the 30" size is 11" x 14". Stone

No. 1358. Stone Lion 48″ high furnished right and left. Exceptionally fine detail and excellent modeling.

No. 1308. Stone Lion 26½" High, 46" Long and 20" Wide, base is 45½" long x 20" Wide.

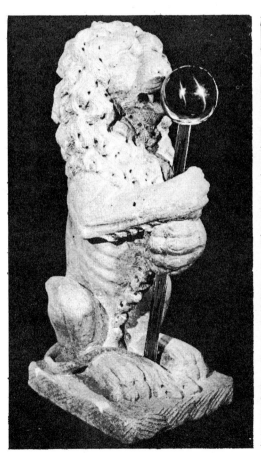

No. 2063. St. Steven's lion, cast lead, 15" high. Perfect reproduction of famous original.

ALSO IN BRONZE

No. 1085. Lion, bronze, lead and stone, but in all cases with bronze staff and orb. 36" high, base 12" x 15".

NOTE: Orb and staff can be verde antique instead of gold leaf and bright.

© 1974
Kenneth Lynch & Sons
Wilton, Conn. 06897

No. 1719. Stone Lion. 45" high x 18" octagonal base.

No. 1709. Stone Foo Dog. 23" high. Base 11" x 22".

DOGS

No. 909. Poodle, Cast Stone 22½" High.

ALSO IN BRONZE

No. 2232. Pair of lead logs, 24" high.

No. 272. Dog with basket, 24" high, made of cast stone. NOTE: HANDLES OF BASKET ARE MADE OF LEAD. THEY WILL NOT BREAK.

No. 244. Stone dog, lead collar

No. 2588. Poodle, cast stone, 21" high, copyright.

No. 1147. Stone dogs, 28" high on base 11" x 15".

No. 1349. Foo Dogs, stone. Available in two sizes: 24" high and 13" high. Left and right.

STONE DOG

No. 1900. Fairfield Stone Dog designed for many purposes. This stone dog is completely reinforced and weighs approximately 600 lbs. On this page you will see a sketch of the dog with dimensions shown. These dimensions are reasonably accurate. This nostalgic piece was found in an antique shop near Philadelphia and carries a plate on the front which says, "J.W. Fiske". The plate is made of lead. It is normally furnished in a light antique color, weathered-looking. However, he can be poly-chromed by the buyer. On these pages you will see illustrations of this dog and the various uses that were recommended for him. Starting in 1900 and running through 1914. In the square column on which the dog is standing, there is a steel pipe reinforcing 2" in diameter and it is threaded to receive other devices which can increase the height of the column. Perhaps you will be the one to think up new things for this fine friend of man.

No. 1906. Post and Knob.

© 1974
Kenneth Lynch & Sons
Wilton, Conn. 06897

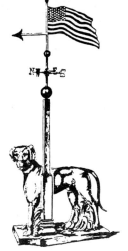

No. 1912. Dog and Flag Weathervane.

No. 1903. Dog and Lamp.

No. 1905. For Flag Gate.
With 1 Dog
With 2 Dogs

No. 1908. Dog with Bar in Socket. Swings like a gate.

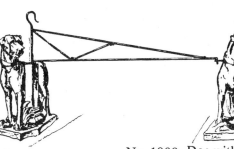

No. 1908. Dog with Bar in Socket. Swings like a gate.

SIGN

No. 1910. Dog with a sign.

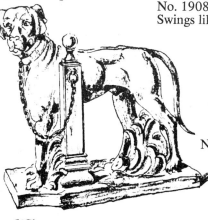

No. 1902. Dog chained to Post.

No. 1904. Dog with Mail Box

No. 1911. To support a table in a garden.

No. 1914. Dog as Sidewalk hedge guardian.

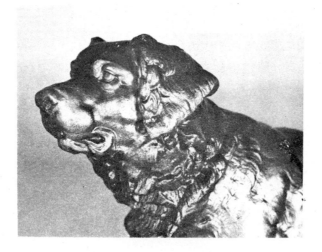

No. 6138. A Newfoundland dog made of Fairfield stone. Extremely strong. Reinforced with stainless steel. This fine antique reproduction is 51'' long x 38'' high. The base is 39'' long x 16¼'' and 3'' thick. It comes furnished with anchors so that it cannot be moved.

©1974
Kenneth Lynch & Sons
Wilton, Conn. 06897

No. 1899. Stone dog. 50'' long x 32'' high. Base is 50'' long x 20'' wide x 3'' thick. This is an antique reproduction and we think the artist was trying to do a setter. However, we leave this for you to judge. He comes complete with stainless steel reinforcing and anchors for fastening him down.   . P.S. He is also available in fiberglass on a wood base

No. 6136. Dalmatian Dog. Made of stone. 27'' long, 16'' high x 13'' wide. The base is 30'' long x 16'' wide x 4'' thick. He is reinforced with stainless steel and comes with stainless steel anchors for fastening. This is an antique reproduction and has a great charm.

No. 6134 Stone Dog. So familiar all over the world. He is listening for you. We are indebted to Mr. Ted Coolidge for this beautiful large model. He is strongly armatured, made of Fairfield Stone. The base is 18'' wide x 36'' long. He is 39'' high from the underside of the base to the top of his head.

No. 4712. Dog. Furnished in bronze or lead. The size of the base is 22" x 14" and is 5½" thick. The entire piece of sculpture is approximately 36" high.

No. 4713. Dog. Furnished in bronze or lead. The size of the base is 22" x 14" and is 5½" thick. the entire piece of sculpture is approximately 36" high.

No. 4699. Stone Dogs. 46" high with a base 21" x 19".

©1974
Kenneth Lynch & Sons
Wilton, Conn. 06897

No. 2468. Large Dogs Head 10'' x 12'' can be piped. Available in Bronze, Lead or Stone.

No. 494. Kitten, 6½'' high, lead or stone, by G. Amendola. **ALSO IN BRONZE**

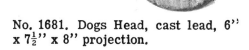

No. 1681. Dogs Head, cast lead, 6'' x 7½'' x 8'' projection.

ALSO IN BRONZE

No. 5564. Crouching Cat. This French version of this very appealing subject is offered in bronze, lead or stone. It is 15'' long x 7'' wide x 8'' high.

No. 270. Elephant, 44″ long by 20″ wide by 28″ high. This piece was a forty-year favorite with children in Denmark and it is shippable in cast stone.

This wonderful stone elephant is now available in a larger size companion to our large hippopotamus. It is 55″ long, 25″ wide x 35″ high. All of these pieces should be considered for elevation and blocking can be put under them to make them appear taller. **Can be piped,**

©1974
Kenneth Lynch & Sons
Wilton, Conn. 06897

No. 4701. stone elephant, 50" long overall and 36" to top of trunk. The base is 18" x 35". It can be piped.

No. 1145. Stone Elephants, garden seats, left and right. 20" high on base 10" x 14".

No. 551. Elephant-Burma, antique stone, height 22", length 24".

ANIMAL STATUARY

No. 2825. Stone Hippopotamus, 5' long, 28" high, 40" x 24" at base. Can be piped. Furnished with lead ears; very suitable as fountain piece or play area piece. Extra good piece of sculpture. **Can be piped,**

No. 278. Hippo, 20" long, cast stone, 20" long, 10" wide, 10" high, piped upwards at end of nose.

No. 374. Terra cotta or cast stone, 3-1/2" x 7" or 8" x 12".

© 1974
Kenneth Lynch & Sons
Wilton, Conn. 06897

No. 165. 13" high, base 6" by 12½" cast stone.

No. 273. Lucifer, modeled from pet of that name, by the eminent sculptor Joseph Boulton, 27" high, a base of 12", cast stone only.

No. 2498. Rabbit, lead or cast stone, by Olympio Brindisi, 7" high, 10 1/4" long.

ALSO IN BRONZE

No. 166. 8-1/4" high with base 7-3/4" x 5-3/4" stone.

No. 2298. Rabbit, lead, by Gustave Lindstrom, 10" high, 12" long. **ALSO IN BRONZE**

No. 121. 11" long, cast stone.

No. 122. 8" long, stone.

No. 2481. Rabbit. Bronze, Lead, Stone. Most beautiful of models. 4¼" long x 3" high.

No. 167. 7-3/4" high with base 6-3/4" x 4" stone.

No. 123. 6" long, cast stone or lead.

ALSO IN BRONZE

No. 2380. Squirrel,
lead or stone, 11" high,
old English model.

ALSO IN BRONZE

No. 2140. Cast
lead, 16½'' high
by J. Kuthmayer.

ALSO IN BRONZE

No. 2529. Lead Squirrel by Mr.
Joseph Boulton, 9'' wide, 8 1/2''
high, 5'' diameter base. This is
a signed piece and looks great on
the top of a gatepost or it is particularly desirable any place
where you can get close enough
to see it for it is a most elegant
piece of work. Mr. Boulton says
this is just the way squirrels get
when it is raining.
Note: Also Available in Bronze.

No. 2149.
Squirrel
lead 6''
high, by
Joseph
Kuttmayer.

ALSO IN BRONZE

No. 2275.
Stone Squirrel,
17'' high.

No. 1108. Stone Squirrels,
18'' high.

© 1974.
Kenneth Lynch & Sons
Wilton, Conn. 06897

No. 2945. Lead Poodle with Saddle, 19" long x 12" high.

Now available in Bronze

No. 698. Pool Carousel of four figures. Each figure is approximately 18" long and 14" high. The figures are made of fine Eternity lead and are modeled in a style which makes them extremely attractive. The Carousel should be built from 48" to 54" in diameter, depending upon the situation. It is made to revolve slowly by a water jet coming from an additional pump submerged in the pool. It is intended to be used in a shallow pool about 6' in diameter. Water could be made to rise from other jets by using a second pump. Lights can be introduced as well. This is a most attractive piece of pool decoration.

No. 2943. Lead Swan, can be piped. Can also be used as feeder or planter. 17 1/2" long x 13 1/4" high.

Available in Bronze

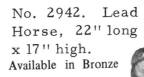

No. 2942. Lead Horse, 22" long x 17" high.
Available in Bronze

No. 2944. Lead Lion, 19" long x 11" high.

Available in Bronze

©1974
Kenneth Lynch & Sons
Wilton, Conn. 06897

No. 94. Cast stone, piped, 28" high, 30" long, base 18" x 30".

No. 971. Lead Otter, beautifully modeled by Claire Low, 24¾" high. Works well where water can splash on it.

Also available in Bronze or Cast Stone.

No. 1329. Sea Lion, stone, 24" high x 19" long x 10" wide. Can be piped.

No. 742. Stone "SUNG GOAT," 15 1/2" high x 16" long x 8" wide.

No. 2311. Bull, lead or stone, 20" long x 10" high.
Available in Bronze

No. 1168. Kangaroo, stone, 21 1/2" high x 32 1/2" long. NOTE: Ears are made of lead.

No. 756. Sung Goat, 16" high x 14" long stone. NOTE: The table shown with the Goat is No. 755.

©1974
Kenneth Lynch & Sons
Wilton, Conn. 06897

No. 60. Monkey, cast stone, 23'' high on a base 10'' x 10''.

No. 429. Monkeys, can be piped, terra cotta or cast stone, 16'' by 20''.

No. 61. Monkey, cast stone, 22'' high on a base 10'' x 10''

No. 1180. Skunk. Very realistic. Furnished in lead and in cast stone; 15'' high, 14'' long. Smaller size available in cast stone only; 9½'' high by 10'' long.

No. 428. Monkey, 14'' by 17'', can be piped, terra cotta or cast stone.

No. 30. Bear, cast stone, 22'' high.

No. 276. Baby seal, piped. Cast, stone or lead. Helen Boulton, Sculptor. A most excellent piece of work. Size: 22'' long, 16'' high and 14'' wide.

ALSO IN BRONZE

No. 2194. Fox, lead, 15'' by 30''. This is one of our very best models.

ALSO IN BRONZE

No. 2152. Monkey, 23½'' from foot to hand, by J. Johnstone - cast lead.

ALSO IN BRONZE

© 1974
Kenneth Lynch & Sons
Wilton, Conn. 06897

No. 4792. Lead deer with special antlers added. The deer is 31" high to top of ears. The size of the base is 32" long by 5" high. The antlers extend another 15" from the top of the head. This is an extremely decorative piece of sculpture and being made of lead, it needs either support or reinforcing. In England the pair was supported by wires which were attached to a brick wall directly behind the deer. The pair was used in a great entry way. While some effort has been made to reinforce these antlers, success would depend upon their not being disturbed. It is not impossible that if the deer were to be seen from one side that a bronze support member could follow up behind the deer. Elaborate ideas of topiary arrangements using the antlers have been very successful by making a very simple frame and fastening it to the deer. This has been done and it looks very good. This deer can also be furnished in bronze.

No. 2474. & No. 2473. Pair of deer, lead or bronze, 31" to top of ears, not including antlers. Stone bases, 5" high and 32" long. An unusually fine piece of workmanship. Lead in stock-- bronze on special order.

©1974
Kenneth Lynch & Sons
Wilton, Conn. 06897

No. 917. Cast Stone Deer 19½'' High x 24'' Long. Note: Also Available in Bronze.

No. 4793. Special arrangement of our Lead Deer **No. 2474** with floral antlers added. Very popular in England years ago. Size 31 in. to top of ears. The base is 32 in. long. The Deer is also offered in bronze on special order. The height of the floral antlers is optional and, of course, being done on special order we can make this to suit the customers requirements. However, as shown in the drawing the overall height is approximately 5 ft. 6 in. Note: Also Available in Bronze.

No. 4607. Deer, 37 1/2'' high x 30'' long, lead or bronze.
NOTE: This is the finer of the two models found in Italy. When made of lead, the legs are reinforced with bronze; however, additional reinforcement directly under sto-stomach is offered at no extra charge.

No. 2178. Giant Frog by Joseph Kuthmayer, cast lead, 15" high. Will take up to 1 1/2" pipe, oval. Lead or Stone

    Note: Also Available in Bronze.

No. 164. Frog, cast stone, 15" long 8" high.

No. 386. Japanese Frog, cast stone, mother frog with baby on back. 6", 9" & 18" high.

No. 14. Frog, cast stone, 9" high, base 8" by 7".

2166
LEAD FROG
By
Josef Kuthmayer
legs and fingers are delicately free.
A very fine piece of work.
5" high Piped.
Note: Also Available in Bronze.

No. 2173. Lead Frog, 7" long.

Note: Also Available in Bronze.

No. 2579. Frog on lily pad, piped for water when requested. Also used as ash tray. Made of lead only. 6 1/4" x 2" high.

No. 2165. Lead Frog 5 1/2" long.

Note: Also Available in Bronze.

© 1974
Kenneth Lynch & Sons
Wilton, Conn. 06897

No. 2030. Lead Frog, 4½'' high by 6½'' by 7½''.
No. 2031. Same design. 7½'' high by 11'' by 11''.

Now Available in Bronze

No. 2824. Leap Frog, 20'' high, furnished in cast stone. A staggered line of these makes a wonderful play arrangement.

Note: Also Available in Bronze.

No. 2250. King Frog on Ball for wall mounting water jets, cast lead or cast stone, 7½'' high.

No. 66. King Frog on base, 7½'' high, 6-3/4'' in dia. Cast lead or stone.
No. 66A. Matching Queen, no crown.

Also available in bronze.

No. 987. Stone Frog, piped. Joseph Boulton, sculptor. 9'' high, 8'' diameter at base.

No. 2176. Frog on lily pad, by Joseph Kuthmayer, leaf 5 1/2'' dia. Overall height 5 1/2'' lead.
Now Available in Bronze.

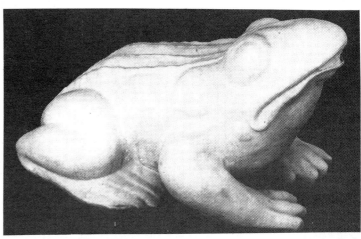

No. 2179. Italian Frog, cast lead, 3-3/4'' wide, 3'' long x 1-3/4'' high.

No. 13. Cast stone, 8'' high, base 10'' by 9''.

No. 1731. Stone Frog. 22'' long x 12'' high x 14'' wide.

Kenneth Lynch & Sons
Wilton, Conn. 06897

No. 4943. Stone dolphin 36" high on a base 16" x 14". We asked the sculptor to do something extra grotesque and this is what he produced; and it looks wonderful. This dolphin is furnished on a 2" thick square base which measures 17" x 15" and is drilled for water.

No. 4944. Stone dolphin piped for water. This massive beautifully carved piece is 21" high on a base 10" x 16" and is drilled for water. This is an extra good grotesque dolphin such as one sees very much in France and Italy. In unusually fine detail. This dolphin is furnished on a 2" thick stone base which measures 12" x 18".

No. 2025. Lead dolphin, English model, 15" high.

Note: Also available in bronze.

No. 2159. Lead dolphin, drilled for water, English model, 10" high.

Note: Also available in bronze.

No. 2100. Lead dolphin, 21½" high.

Note: Also available in bronze.

DOLPHINS

No. 2164. Cast lead Dolphin, 17" high, by John Donnelly.

Note: Also Available in Bronze.

No. 2062-A. 31" wide and 8" high. The plaque is 23" wide x 28" high cast stone.

No. 1611. Cast, lead or stone, by Gifford M. Proctor, F.A.A.R., N.S.S. NOTE: ALSO FURNISHED CAST INTO ANY SHAPE BACKPLATE, ETC. Size: 15-3/4" high by 11 1/4" wide.

Note: Also available in bronze.

No. 2163. Dolphin on Wave, cast lead, 8" high, 4 1/2" wide. By Olympio Brindisi.

Note: Also Available in Bronze.

No. 2062. Lead wall dolphins with twisted tails, 18½" high x 17" wide, English reproduction. NOTE: CAN BE FURNISHED IN CAST STONE WHEN MOUNTED ON BACKPLATE AS ILLUSTRATION ABOVE.

Note: Also available in bronze.

No. 75. 38" high, stone, on a base 14 1/4" x 14 1/4", can carry large pipe.

No. 2158. Very finely modeled dolphin, cast, lead or stone, by Joseph Kuthmayer© 7" x 9".

Now available in Bronze.

© 1974
Kenneth Lynch & Sons
Wilton, Conn. 06897

No. 211. Dolphin, cast stone, shown in Attitudes A, B, and C, 39'' long. Can be piped. Can be arranged on weighted stanchions with brass pipes connected to adjustable devices to hold the dolphins at any angle for various effects.

No. 211-D. Boy on dolphin on wave. Dolphin and wave are cast stone; boy is cast lead, 41'' long.

No. 1336. Cast Stone Dolphins on Wave. Furnished as shown on stone base. About 54'' long.

No. 4989. Dolphin available in bronze or lead, 8'' long, 5 3/4'' wide. The relief is 2¼''. The original was from a beautiful diminutive fountain • in a lady's garden in France.

No. 3. Dolphin, cast stone, 21-1/2'' high, 12'' x 10-1/2'' base, piped. Illustrated on No. 12 pump case pedestal 10'' high x 14-1/4'' dia.

No. 1334. Dolphin. Exquisite detail, furnished in bronze or lead. Antique reproduction, 14'' high x 7½'' wide.

No. 1335. Dolphin, cast stone, piped for water. 14'' long x 13'' high.

© 1974
Kenneth Lynch & Sons
Wilton, Conn. 06897

No. 2162. 7" wide by 5½" high, cast lead.

Note: Also Available in Bronze.

No. 2160. Cast lead dolphin, 17" high, low relief.

Now Available in Bronze.

No. 2847. Dolphin by Joseph Boulton, 27" long. Bronze, lead or stone. Can be piped as large as 2". A strong, lively, beautiful piece of Sculpture by a great master. No photograph could do it justice.

No. 2191. Grotesque dolphin head, probably originally from France. Will take large pipe for water. Is approximately 10" wide and 10" projection. Lead or stone. available in Bronze

No. 1005. Stone Dolphin fountain jet with three jets, one from each dolphin. 16 1/2" high.

No. 887. Bronze, lead. 21" high, 7" x 6" oval base. Furnished as pedestal or piped for fountain jets.

© 1974
Kenneth Lynch & Sons
Wilton, Conn. 06897

No. 2846. Boy Riding Dolphin, lead, 27" long, 18" high overall. NOTE: This dolphin can take a very large pipe. NOTE: This figure is also furnished with the dolphin in stone.

Now Available in Bronze

No. 2845. Dolphin, 27" long, 18" high at tail, can take very large pipe. Furnished in lead or stone.

Now Available in Bronze.

FISH

No. 316. Fish on snail shell, cast stone, 15½" x 11".

All fish fountains can be piped and some of them take pipes quite large. We will try to install pipes as specified.

No. 2032. Cast stone or lead fish, 12 1/4" high, 14" long, 10½" x 10½" base, & 11" high 11" long, 9½ x 4½ base. Now available in Bronze

No. 438. Cast, stone or lead. 10 1/4" high.

No. 652. FISH ON SHELL Background, fountain head 15" x 14". Lead or bronze. Piped.

No. 441. Fish waterjet, 7" x 14", cast stone or lead. Now available in Bronze

No. 64. Cast stone fishes, both piped, 22½" high; base 13" x 9".

No. 310. Cast stone fish design; one fish leaping over the other. This comes piped with jets in the fish's teeth, plus one in his nose. This is a very lively piece of sculpture, 18" high, 8" x 8" base.

No. 2470. Double fish fountain, 28" high, 18" wide. Cast lead; all bronze or lead fishes with cast stone base by special order. Piped.
Now available in Bronze

No. 2790. Fish Water Spout or Ash Receiver. Two Sizes: 3 1/4" long, 4½" long. Lead or Bronze

©1974
Kenneth Lynch & Sons
Wilton, Conn. 06897

No. 2741. Cast lead starfish, 12" long, 8" high. Shown in drape position for pool edge but can be made in any shape.

Note: Also Available in Bronze.

No. 2471. Bronze or lead, 10" x 18," piped. By G. Lewis.

No. 4509. Bronze Fish Fountain, piped, 16 1/4" high.

No. 2456. Fish fountain, 14" high, base 4" by 7", cast lead

Note: Also Available in Bronze.

No. 2742-A

No. 2742-B

No. 2742-C

No. 2742-A, B, C. Lead Fishes by Geraldine Lewis, 23" long; can spout water.

Note: Also available in bronze.

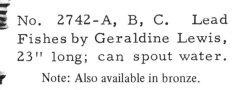

No. 2742-C. Lead Fish on stone wave, 23" long x 20" high.

Note: Also Available in Bronze.

No. 2742-A and C. Lead Fishes on stone waves, 36" long x 30" high.

Note: Also Available in Bronze.

Composition showing No. 2742-A, B, and C rigged up on a wave-like formation, 34" high x 52" long. All piped for water and squirting vigorously under considerable pressure. More figures could be added to the design if it was felt desirable. Lead Fishes Cast Stone Waves.

Note: Also Available in Bronze.

© 1974
Kenneth Lynch & Sons
Wilton, Conn. 06897

No. 2742-A, B and C. These beautiful lead fishes are remarkable pieces of sculpture and can be piped. These can be worked in any arrangement which you can draw.

SEA HORSES

No. 2425. Dolphin on Wave, 9" x 7". Lead or Bronze. Can be piped.

No. 2122. Cast lead seahorse, 16" high, piped; finely sculptured model by Joseph Kuthmayer.
Also Available in Bronze.

No. 28. Seahorse pool fountain, cast stone, 24" high on a 10" oval base, piped.
Also Available in Bronze.

No. 561. Boy on Seahorse. Cast lead or cast stone seahorse. In all cases, boy is made of lead. 31" high, can be piped. Note: Also Available in Bronze.

No. 2101. Seahorse wall fountain, cast lead, by Josef Kuthmayer, 15" high, 12½" wide.
Note: Also Available in Bronze.

No. 2121. Cast lead seahorse, 15" high by Kuthmayer. Piped.
Also Available in Bronze.

No. 986. Stone Seahorse wall plaque, 21" overall.

© 1974
Kenneth Lynch & Sons
Wilton, Conn. 06897

SNAILS

Everybody seems to like our snail collection. We offer them in cast lead and cast stone with lead horns.

No. 643. Boy astride snail. Snail is 30" long, 10" high and can be purchased riderless. This figure is approximately 26" high and 30" long when completed. Snail is No. 4611. Note: Also Available in Bronze.

No. 642. Boy dancing on snail. Snail is 30" long. Boy is 28" high. Furnished in bronze, lead, or stone snail with lead boy.

No. 2483. Decorative snail shell in bronze, lead or stone. 5 1/4" by 4" by 3" thick.

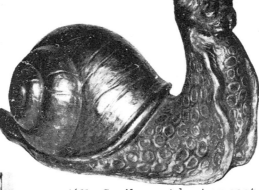

No. 4611. Snail, cast lead or cast stone with lead horns, 20" high x 30" long. Note: Also Available in Bronze.

No. 2822. Boy driving snail. Cast lead. 21 1/2" high. Should be on stone block about 3" high. Note: Also Available in Bronze.

No. 180. Cast stone snail with lead horns, 7" high, 21" long.

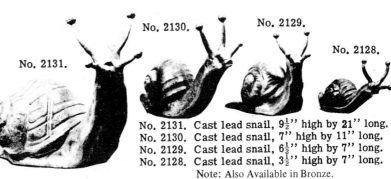

No. 2131.   No. 2130.   No. 2129.   No. 2128.

No. 2131. Cast lead snail, $9\frac{1}{2}$" high by 21" long.
No. 2130. Cast lead snail, 7" high by 11" long.
No. 2129. Cast lead snail, $6\frac{1}{2}$" high by 7" long.
No. 2128. Cast lead snail, $3\frac{1}{2}$" high by 7" long.
Note: Also Available in Bronze.

No. 2810. Turtle 57½'' Nose to tail. Cast Stone or Armorstone
Will take large pipe.

No. 2458. Cast lead investigating turtle, 13''
piped.
No. 2459. Cast lead investigating turtle, 7''
piped.
(NOTE: THIS TURTLE CAN BE FURNISH-
ED WITH HEAD BACK IN CLOSER TO
SHELL.) Also Available in Bronze.

No. 319. Stone Turtle, 23'' Long, 15'' Wide, 10'' High. Will
take Large Pipe. Also in 48'' Long.

No. 335. Cast stone turtle.
Two sizes: 13'' x 8'' and
7½'' x 5'', can be piped.

No. 2233. Small lead turtle, beautiful
workmanship, 4'' long, piped with upper
shell fastened securely to body, or,
upper shell removable to use as ash
tray, stamp case, etc.

Now available in Bronze.

No. 2143. Cast lead turtle,
piped, 9'' long.

Also Available in Bronze.

© 1974
Kenneth Lynch & Sons
Wilton, Conn. 06897

No. 2715. Fish Sculpture.
Vertical tilt to any angle. Piped.
Stone or bronze in four sizes:
68'' high - body 32'' x 20''
50'' high - body 20'' x 18''
42'' high - body 14'' x 14''
34'' high - body 12'' x 19''

These models can
support a strong, lively
water display.

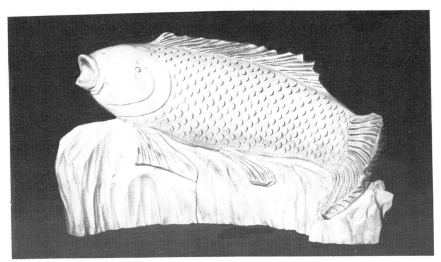

No. 2716. Fish Sculpture. Horizontal tilt to any
angle. Piped. Stone or Bronze. 25'' long x 15''
high x 14'' wide.

© 1974.
Kenneth Lynch & Sons
Wilton. Conn. 06897

ARCHITECTURAL EAGLES

No. 5490. Eagle. A most unusual design. Flat back but can also be furnished double faced. The size is 56″ wing spread x 37″ high. We recently remodeled this piece using a badly damaged antique model which we had in our warehouse. It is believed that we made the original in the very early 19th century. It was made of zinc and there were still traces of polychroming on it, the wings being brown, gold and black; the head apparently had some black, white and red on it with red, white and blue shield, etc. This piece was restored for a famous architect and did wonders for a very simple modern building. The original was in zinc; however, we offer it in bronze, lead or stamped zinc. This is a truly magnificent piece of native American art. Available to you at a tiny fraction of the price of any of the earlier reproductions and they are exactly the same in detail.

Now available in Bronze, Copper, Lead, Stainless Steel (lead coated), Zinc in two sizes. 56″ wing spread by 37″ high, or 28″ wing spread by 16″ high.

No. 6002. Eagle. 40″ wide x 10½″ high. Available in bronze, lead or stamped zinc.

© 1974
Kenneth Lynch & Sons
Wilton, Conn. 06897

No. 2618.
Eagle: This is the famous Chesapeake furnished in two sizes: 6 ft. x 25'' and 4 ft. x 17''. Beautifully carved and decorated. Furnished in wood only. Flat Back.

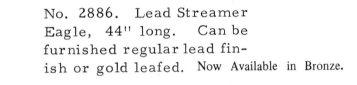

No. 2886. Lead Streamer Eagle, 44'' long. Can be furnished regular lead finish or gold leafed. Now Available in Bronze.

No. 2582.
Eagle: 13'' wide x 11½'' high. Antique reproduction. Bronze, lead. Flat Back.

No. 2619.
Eagle: The Louisburg. Furnished in two sizes: 3 ft. 8'' by 15½'' and 24 3/4'' x 9''. Boldly carved in wood only. Flat Back.

No. 2614.
Eagle: 13½'' wide x 6'' high. Antique reproduction. Furnished in carved wood. Flat Back.

No. 2266.
Eagle: Very sharp but bold relief furnished in two sizes: 11'' high by 11½'' wide and 6'' wide by 5½'' high. Furnished in cast lead only. Very sharp detail. Flat Back.

No. 2580.
Eagle: 13½'' high x 13'' wide. Base is 8 x 9''. Cast stone only. Full Bodied.

No. 2617.
Eagle: 34'' wide x 10½'' high. Boldly modeled full relief Furnished in carved wood or cast lead. Flat Back.

No. 2245.
Eagle: 16½'' wide by 12'' high. Contemporary furnished in bronze, lead, aluminum. Full Bodied.

No. 282.
Stone Eagles, right and left, 28'' high x 27'' wide.

No. 2613.
Eagles: lead or bronze, beautifully chased; 6'' high, 9'' wide. French reporductions.

No. 2616.
Eagle: Antique reproduction. 27'' wide x 9'' high. Furnished in carved wood, bronze, lead, or aluminum. Flat Back.

No. 4033.
Eagles: 4¼'' high x 5½'' wide. Antique reproduction from Philadelphia. Originally used as Snow Birds. Furnished in bronze or lead. Flat Back.

No. 2181.
Eagle: 24'' wide x 5'' high. Rather low relief but exquisitely executed. Antique reproduction. Bronze, lead and aluminum. Flat Back.

© 1974
Kenneth Lynch & Sons
Wilton, Conn. 06897

Lead Eagles are used particularly in America and England. #2196 and #2415 are two of the largest and most impressive lead Eagles ever produced. #2266 and #2613 have probably the finest detail of any Eagle.

No. 2196.
Eagle: 45'' wide by 19'' high. Right and left. This is a majestic piece of work, beautifully executed in cast lead only from the original English Antique. Full Bodied.

Now Available in Bronze.

No. 2415.
Eagles: Right and left. 19'' high by 17½'' wide furnished in cast lead only from the original model by the late Raphiel Menconi for James C. MacKenzie, A.I.A. This is one of the best pieces of work available. Full Bodied.

Now Available in Bronze.

No. 106 and 107. Stone Eagles, right and left, 24'' high x 16 1/2'' wide.

No. 2621.
Lead Eagle: 4½'' x 5'' low relief. Flat Back.
Now Available in Bronze.

No. 2183.
Eagle: 11'' high by 8'' wide. Lead reproduction of Old Fire Mark. Plaque.
Now Available in Bronze.

No. 2244.
Eagle: 30'' wide by 14'' high. Contemporary furnished in bronze, lead, aluminum, or cast stone. Full Bodied.

ARCHITECTURAL EAGLES

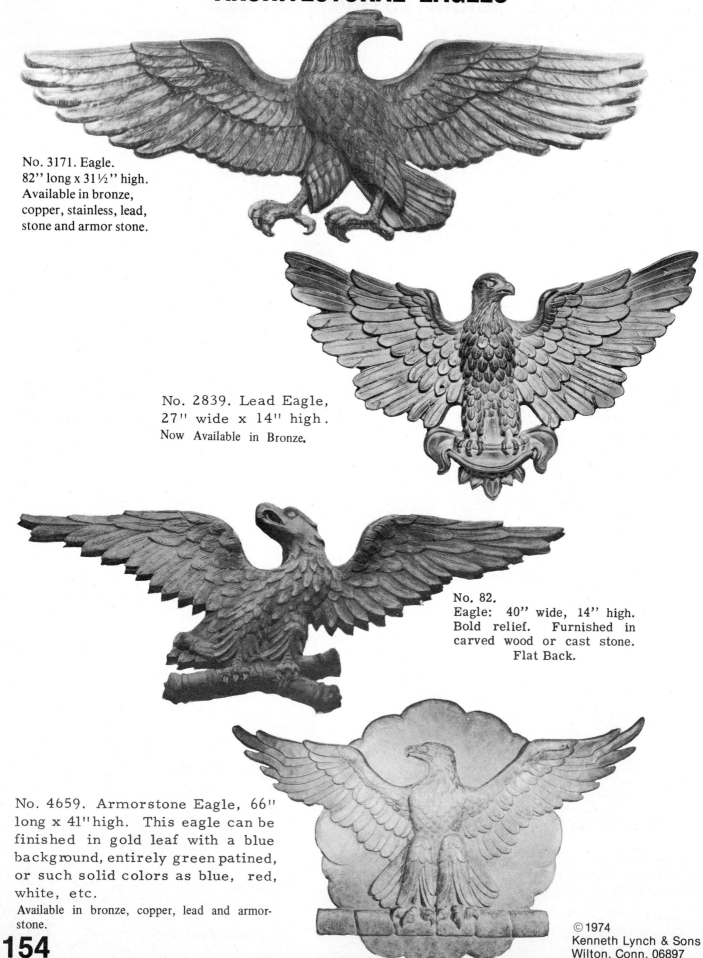

No. 3171. Eagle.
82'' long x 31½'' high.
Available in bronze,
copper, stainless, lead,
stone and armor stone.

No. 2839. Lead Eagle,
27'' wide x 14'' high.
Now Available in Bronze.

No. 82.
Eagle: 40'' wide, 14'' high.
Bold relief. Furnished in
carved wood or cast stone.
Flat Back.

No. 4659. Armorstone Eagle, 66''
long x 41''high. This eagle can be
finished in gold leaf with a blue
background, entirely green patined,
or such solid colors as blue, red,
white, etc.
Available in bronze, copper, lead and armorstone.

© 1974
Kenneth Lynch & Sons
Wilton, Conn. 06897

No. 2077. Lead Ravens, 19" head to tail, very fine pieces for gate post finials. bronze or lead.

No. 2288. Cockatoo, 18" tall, cast lead. Right and left. This is an authentic reproduction of an important English piece.

Now Available in Bronze.

No. 2861. Penguin. Bronze or lead by Helen Bolton, 22" high. Helen Bolton, the wife of Joseph, is also an accomplished artist and we have several pieces of her work available.

A pair of these at an entry way elevated to read against sky or trees! Look. Wonderful!

No. 998. The massive stone owl by Joseph Boulton. This piece of sculpture is breathtakingly beautiful. It is the most impressive piece of animal sculpture we have in our collection. The talons, the beak and the horns are made of Eternity Lead. It is 45" tall. This is a signed piece limited edition.

© 1974.
Kenneth Lynch & Sons
Wilton, Conn. 06897

No. 975. The Great Sentinel Owl. by Mr. Joseph Bolton, 36" high. Furnished in bronze, lead or cast stone with lead claws and lead beak. This is truly a most magnificent and heroic piece of work. Signed by the artist. Limited edition. Furnished complete with anchors, etc. for installation. This is easily one of the most impressive pieces of sculpture in the entire world.

No. 2888. Lead Owl, 21 1/2" high, by Joseph Boulton. NOTE: The owl is the only bird that can turn his head 360° and Mr. Boulton has done a two-faced owl known as the Janus; one face is smiling and the other is grim.

Available in lead or stone.

JOSEPH BOULTON. This master sculptor has accomplished so much in his long and interesting life that we have employed Mr. John Reilly to do a special booklet on him for his work is far too great and requires much more telling about than could be done in this space. This booklet will be sent to you free of charge.

Mr. Boulton was born in Goodknight, Tex., and lived on the prairies, in the desert and in the wilderness.

Kenneth Lynch & Sons has always felt it a great privilege to work for Mr. Boulton.

©1974
Kenneth Lynch & Sons
Wilton, Conn. 06897

No. 4213. Bronze Owl by Joseph Bolton. 8" high. This piece should be on a marble base approximately 6" x 6" and we have made this owl in statuary woodsy brown with some gold looking through the finish and have used it on a verde antique base. These bases are readily available at modest cost.

No. 1292. Mother Owl with young under wing, by Joseph Boulton. Furnished in cast stone with lead talons and beak. 30" high on a 16" dia. base.

This is a large owl. Baby is nesting under Mother. Extra good detail by a great master.

No. 4992. Bronze Owl by Joseph Bolton. It is 9" high with a 5" diameter base. It should be mounted on a piece of marble 6" in cube. This is a companion piece to the Owl shown above, and this likewise is a fine collector's item. It is a signed piece with the author's permission and a limited edition. It is recommended that they be bought in pairs.

©1974
Kenneth Lynch & Sons
Wilton, Conn. 06897

No. 1726. Stone Owl. 23'' high x **8''** diameter base.

No. 1726A. Stone Owl. 18'' high x 9'' diameter base.

No. 1725. Stone Pelican. 31'' high x 22'' long x 12'' diameter base.

© 1974.
Kenneth Lynch & Sons
Wilton, Conn. 06897

No. 2892.   Lead Bird, 59" high x 44" wing spread.   Can
be piped.   Reproduction of 19th century American fountain
piece.   This is a very valuable collector's item.

Also available in bronze.

No. 2736.
Crane. Lead body with bronze legs. Two sizes and four attitudes.

Large Size Attitude A - 26"   Large Size Attitude C - 31"
Small Size Attitude A - 11"   Small Size Attitude C - 14"
Large Size Attitude B - 43"   Large Size Attitude D - 36'
Small Size Attitude B - 25"   Small Size Attitude D - 14"

© 1974.
Kenneth Lynch & Sons
Wilton, Conn. 06897

ROOSTERS

CANTERBURY BRONZE OR ETERNITY LEAD

No. 2434.
Chanticleer.
14'' high. Lead.
Now Available in Bronze.

No. 2197.
French Rooster. 26'' high. Lead or
cast stone. Generally sold in pairs.
Now available in Bronze.

No. 2197.
French Rooster. 26'' high. Lead or
cast stone. Generally sold in pairs.
Now Available in Bronze.

No. 101.
Rooster. 23½'' high. Cast
stone.

No. 2577.
Rooster. By Felix. 17'' high.
Cast stone.

© 1974
Kenneth Lynch & Sons
Wilton, Conn. 06897

No. 1625.
Rooster. By Gifford Proctor. Two
sizes: 18'' high and 24'' high. Cast
lead. Now available in Bronze.

No. 2435.
Rooster. 9½''
high. Lead.
Now available in Bronze.

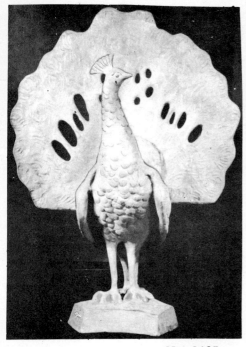

**No. 2405.
English Peacock. Cast lead.
Right and left. 24" high.**
Now available in Bronze.

No. 2405. Lead Peacock,
side view showing tail
socket for either lead
tail or iron topiary tail.
Now available in Bronze.

No. 1330 Stone Turkey, two
sizes, 20" high and 24" high.

No. 2405. Lead Pea-
cock with topiary
tail, 36" high. Note:
Topiary tail is part
of basket planted in
ground and peacock
merely stands in
front of topiary tail.
Bird can be brought
indoors separately
and topiary tail can
be easily dug out of
ground and basket
removed to green-
house for winter.

No. 2060. Lead Turkey by Geraldine
Lewis, 25 1/4" high x13" wide. NOTE:
These turkeys can be furnished with
the heads looking to the right or left
or straight ahead. NOTE: The tail
is removable so that a topiary frame
may also be used.

No. 2405. Lead Pea-
cock with iron topiary
tail, 36" high. Note:
tail fits into socket on
bird.

Now available in Bronze

No. 4197. Topiary
Peacock Tail to be
used with our lead
Peacocks as shown
in the adjoining
sketch. The tail is
3' tall.

© 1974.
Kenneth Lynch & Sons
Wilton, Conn. 06897

No. 2142.
Lead Fantail Pigeon.   English model.   11'' high.
Now available in Bronze.

No. 1554.
Bee. $4\frac{1}{2}$'' x $3\frac{1}{2}$'' Bronze or
lead. Low relief.

No. 4535.   Owl by G. Lewis
lead only.   Two sizes: 8''
and 11'' over-all measurement.

No. 2184.
Fantail Pigeon.   Bronze or lead.   5'' high.
Also used as book ends.

No. 2421.
Baby Pigeon. 3-3/4'' high. Bronze or lead.
NOTE: THIS IS A COLLECTOR'S ITEM.

BIRDS
CANTERBURY BRONZE OR ETERNITY LEAD

No. 2124.
Bird. Lead. 3'' long.

No. 2126.
Bird. Lead. 3'' long.

No. 2125.
Bird. Lead. 3'' long.

Now available in Bronze.

No. 2258.
Bird. 6'' long - 5'' wide.
Bronze or lead.

No. 2734.
Bird Alighting. 3'' head to
tail. Bronze or lead.

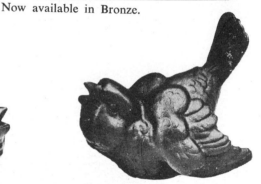

No. 2735.
Bird Nesting. 3'' head to
tail. Bronze or lead.

No. 4618. Two lead Birds mounted
on lead plate. Size of lead plate is
8'' x 3''.

No. 2255.
Bird. Bronze or lead.
5½'' long.

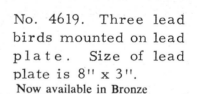

No. 4619. Three lead
birds mounted on lead
plate. Size of lead
plate is 8'' x 3''.
Now available in Bronze

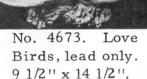

No. 4673. Love
Birds, lead only.
9 1/2'' x 14 1/2''.

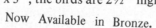

No. 2960. Lead Birds on lead
plate which can be bent over edge
of bird bath. Size of lead plate is
8'' x 3''; the birds are 2½'' high.

Now Available in Bronze.

No. 155.
Pair of Birds. 5'' high. Cast
stone.

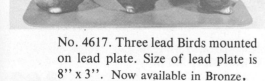

No. 4617. Three lead Birds mounted
on lead plate. Size of lead plate is
8'' x 3''. Now available in Bronze.

© 1974
Kenneth Lynch & Sons
Wilton, Conn. 06897

No. 2248. Goose, 22'' wide, 22'' back to front, 22'' high – Lead. Piped. Now Available in Bronze.

No. 2246. 26'' wide. 30'' back to front, 17'' high, lead. Piped. Now Available in Bronze.

No. 2247. 25'' wide, 30'' back to front, 17'' high, lead. Piped. Now Available in Bronze.

No. 685. Lead duck, 5 1/2'' high, 5 1/4'' long. Now Available in Bronze.

No. 686. Lead or stone duck, 12 1/2'' high, 14'' long. Now available in Bronze or Lead.

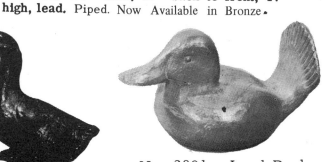

No. 2891. Lead Duck, 4 1/4'' high x 7'' long. Carved by John Lacey. Now available in Bronze or Lead.

No. 2471-B. Lead, 15'' high.

2475

2475

No. 2475. Duck and ducklings fountain, cast lead, 26'' high from top to bottom. It is illustrated in a basin made of 1503 border pattern.

No. 2270.
Bird. By Joseph Boulton. 5''
high. Bronze or lead.

No. 2141. Penguin - Lead
14½'' high - By Borcelleni.
Now available in Bronze.

No. 2262.
Bird. By Joseph Boulton.
4-3/4'' high. Bronze or lead.

No. 415.
Pelican. 15½'' tall - 11½''
long. Cast stone.

No. 4616. Lead
Bird, 3 3/4'' x
2 1/2''.

No. 285.
Duck Fountain. Piped.
17'' high. Bronze, lead
or stone.

No. 2138.
Lead Bird, 5 1/2'' high.
Will perch on edge of any
flat surface, tank, bird
feeder, etc.

No. 542. Pigeon-
10'' long. Cast lead.
Now available in Bronze.

© 1974.
Kenneth Lynch & Sons
Wilton, Conn. 06897

BIRDS
CANTERBURY BRONZE OR ETERNITY LEAD

ST. RAPHAEL, FRANCE. An unusual garden ornament found in a garden near St. Raphael.

No. 4832. Lead or bronze goose. 18″ high.

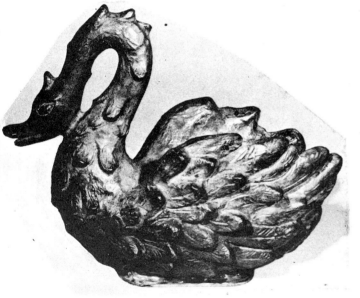

No. 2943. Lead or bronze swan. 17½″ long x 13½″ high.

No. 207. Duck. Stone. 14″ high.

No. 2461. Lead Goose Boy, piped, 25½″ high.
Now Available in Bronze.

No. 2137. Lead duckling, piped on request, 5″ high, 8″ long.
Now Available in Bronze.

No. 2471-A. Lead 5″ high, 7″ long.
Now Available in Bronze

PLAQUES
CANTERBURY BRONZE OR ETERNITY LEAD

No. 2802. Cello player wall plaque. Bold Relief. 10-3/4" x 9". Lead or bronze.

No. 2951. Lead Plaque, "PONY EXPRESS RIDER," 17 1/2" diameter.
Note: Also available in bronze.

No. 935. St. George & Dragon, Cast Lead Bas Relief 14½ x 16 1/4.
Note: Also Available in Bronze.

No. 2898. Lead Rosette water supply, 12" x 12".

Now available in Bronze.

No. 2849. Lead back for fountain, 12 3/4" x 25 1/2". Water can be made to flow from any part of this design. This can also be incorporated as a motif in a stone design.

No. 2848. Lead architectural design, suitable for fountain back, etc. 10 3/4" x 16 1/4". Can be incorporated into other design and can also be furnished in stone.

Note: Also Available in Bronze.

No. 2852. water supply for fountain, 9 1/2" x 11 1/2".

available in Bronze or Lead.

No. 2855. Lead water supply for fountain, 10 3/4" x 17 3/4".
Now available in Bronze

No. 2851. water supply for fountain, 7 1/2" x 10 1/2". available in Bronze or Lead.

No. 2854. Lead water supply for fountain, 10 3/4" x 17 3/4".
Now available in Bronze

© 1974
Kenneth Lynch & Sons
Wilton, Conn. 06897

PLAQUES

CANTERBURY BRONZE OR ETERNITY LEAD

No. 2957. "FRONTIER" plaque, 28" high x 42" wide. Available in stone or lead.

Note: Also Available in Bronze.

No. 2952. Wall Plaque titled "STAMPEDE," 31 1/2" long x 24" high. This can be furnished either in bronze, lead or stone.

No. 2857. water supply for fountain, 10 3/4" x 17 3/4". **Bronze or lead.**

No. 2853. water supply for fountain, 7 1/2" x 9 1/2". **Bronze or lead.**

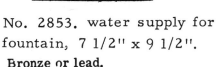

No. 2856. water supply for fountain, 10 3/4" x 17 3/4". **Bronze or lead.**

PLAQUES   AWARDS   HONOR ROLLS   TESTIMONIALS   BAS RELIEF   PORTRAITS   LETTERS

THREE SIMPLE STEPS

1.—Merely tell us the purpose of your tablet and the inscription, if possible. If you have not decided on the size we will suggest a few appropriate sizes for your consideration. The features of a few designs can be combined into your tablet without any difficulty.

2.—As soon as we receive your order, work on the creation of your tablet will begin. Before the molten bronze is cast a final proof showing the exact arrangement of the inscription will be sent for your approval. This gives you added assurance of complete satisfaction.

3.—The finished tablet is then shipped to you complete with all fastenings ready for installation. You will be well pleased with the beautiful, painstakingly prepared tablet which has undergone four rigid inspections in order to fulfill your needs.

If a sculptured portrait is requested, we will work from photographs you send, and we will submit models for your approval. This assures a good likeness. Should you wish any assistance in choosing the most suitable design for your tablet, our designers will be happy to help you.

There Is Neither Obligation Nor Additional Charge For This Friendly Helpful Service.

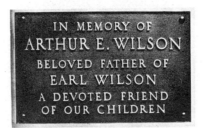

© 1974
Kenneth Lynch & Sons
Wilton, Conn. 06897

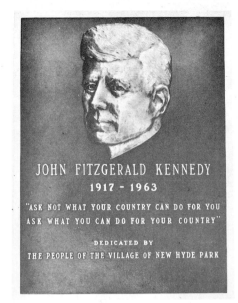

© 1974
Kenneth Lynch & Sons
Wilton, Conn. 06897

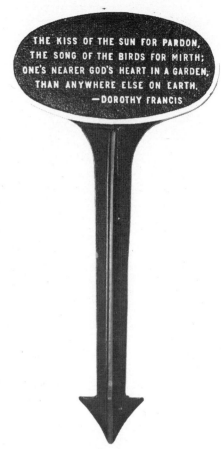

No. 4524. Garden Plaque in cast stone. Modeled and signed by Mr. Joseph Boulton. It is made of reinforced cast stone and it is 38" in diameter x 2½" thick. This massive and beautiful ornament can be used against a wall, elevated or down low, or it can be used in the ground itself and it was actually used as a marrying plaque in a church in New Hampshire.

No. 5460. Aluminum garden plaque painted black with gilded letters. It includes a small piece of pipe to act as a stake. The size is 14" wide x 7½" high.

No. 5570. Garden Plaque made of lead. This lead is soft and will follow the contour of a rack or a tree as it can stand considerable contour bending. It has a beautiful soft finish of garden lead. It is intended for those who want something extra fine. The size is 8" x 14". It can be fastened with screws or nails which would be furnished.

Available in Bronze.

© 1974
Kenneth Lynch & Sons
Wilton, Conn. 06897

No. 104. Armorini. (looking left), cast stone, 22" high by
14" wide for wall hanging. Antique reproduction.
No. 105. Armorini. (looking right), same as No. 104.

No. 251. & No. 252. Armorini, Cast Stone Antique finish,
24" x 13".

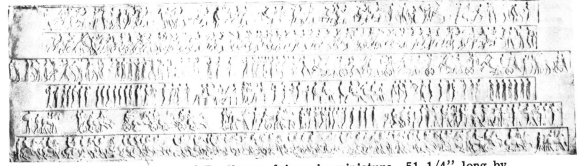

No. 552. Plaque of Parthenon frieze in miniature, 51 1/4" long by
13 1/4" wide, fine cast stone, antique finish.

LANTERN

No. 5010   Heavy brass. Exact copy of old French Station wall light with old
Paris medallion on front.

Height 22''   Spread 11 3/4''   Depth 11''

Available in smaller size

Height 18''   Spread 9 3/8''   Depth 8 3/4''

The handles are generally Lead Antique but they can be Gilded or Bronze.

No. 514. Massive Stone Urn. 53" high, 37½" in diameter. This is truly the largest and most decorative urn we have ever seen. The handles are made of eternity lead and are beautifully chased and detailed and are massive in every way. Reproduced for a famous architect who carefully supervised the modeling and casting so as to achieve a perfect result for a distinguished client, who has generously given us permission to share this magnificent piece of work with you.

No. 2422. Lead Urn with cover, 12" in dia., 9" high.

No. 818. Cast stone French vase, 28" high, 19" wide and 11" deep.

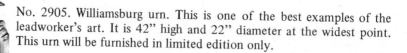

No. 2905. Williamsburg urn. This is one of the best examples of the leadworker's art. It is 42" high and 22" diameter at the widest point. This urn will be furnished in limited edition only.

These large, beautiful urns were done for the Equitable Life Insurance Company at Washington, D. C. and are a reproduction of famous urns at Williamsburg, Virginia.

No. 2416-M. Charles II Series, lead, 21" high, 24" across the handles.

No. 2416-S. Charles II Series, lead, 17" high, 21" across the handles.

No. 1684. Lead English Vase, 19" high, 22" across the handles.

No. 2906. Lead Urn designed by Charles F. Gillette, Landscape Architect. This massive urn is 45" high, 24" diameter with 17" square base, and weighs almost 1,000 pounds. This is very impressive. It is all reinforced with bronze.

Now available in Lead and Bronze.

No. 2416-L. Charles II Series, lead, 16" high, 32" across handles.

No. 565. Lead urn with handles, 25" high, 17-3/4" wide. Also furnished in cast stone with lead handles.

No. 4641. Lead Urn, correct bell shape. Pierced through for light, etc. 18" high.

© 1974
Kenneth Lynch & Sons
Wilton, Conn. 06897

No. 2959. Detail of lead urn which is 30" diameter x 35" high down to the first square base.

The illustration above shows the beautiful fountain designed by F. Nelson Breed, AIA.

The pool was 11 feet in diameter and the overall height was 7 feet 7". Water was introduced from all four sides of the pedestal and was recirculated from pump mechanism within the pedestal. The urn is No. 2959 and Mr. Breed worked diligently with our modeller to achieve the above result. This master architect did much to introduce the necessary refinement and discipline needed to produce this lovely fountain.

No. 1529. Lead urn, 26½" high, 30½" wide.

No. 1530. Lead urn, 30" high, 17" wide.

No. 1528. 36" high, base 12" sq. lead urn.

URNS

No. 113. Lattice Urn, 18" high, 10" diameter base. This is a very much loved and admired piece and we have carefully preserved the detail for many years. Stone.

No. 1344. Stone Lattice Urn with cover. Extra large size 36" high x 28" diameter.

No. 597. Urn, made of cast stone, garnished with lead garlands and lead figures, 36" high, 29" wide across the figures. The base is 11" square. Also furnished in all lead.

No. 567. Richly ornamented lead urn, 32" high, 22½" dia.

No. 141. Cast stone, 26" high, top dia. 18", base 9½" sq.
Also, 33" high, 25" dia. by 12-3/4" sq. base.

No. 563. Cast stone urn, 23" high by 18" dia.

No. 2198. Lead basket urn, 15" dia. 8" high. NOTE: WE ALSO MAKE THIS IN CAST STONE.

No. 185. 14" high, cast stone.

No. 569. Oval urn, 14" high, 27" long, 17½" wide, cast stone.

URNS

No. 2842. Lead Urn designed by Charles F. Gillette, 26" high. It is draped with hand-wrought roses.

Now available in Bronze.

No. 596. Lead Urn, 30" high 9" square base. Linen-shaped swags with lion heads on opposite sides.

Now available in Bronze.

No. 564. Lead Urns, 22 1/4" high, 14" diameter. A most severe and beautiful design. This can also be furnished in bronze and stone.

© 1974
Kenneth Lynch & Sons
Wilton, Conn. 06897

No. 813. Florentine Urn. Furnished in cast stone, cast lead and cast bronze. It is 33" high, 19" diameter at widest point. This urn has also been used truncated and sliced in half. This is a very fine piece of modeling.

No. 571. Cast stone urn, 15" high by 12½" dia.

No. 2423. Lead Vatican vase with cover, 15" wide, 15½" high.
Also available in bronze.

No. 2948. Lead Urn designed by Charles F. Gillette, Landscape Architect. 30" high with 15 1/4" square base. Very beautiful floral swags.

Note: Also available in bronze.

No. 2909. Lead Urn, 31" high, 18" diameter. The vase is 20 1/2" high. This is from the original Adams pattern.

No. 2039. Lead Adams Urn, 24" high, 15" dia.

No. 1063. Stone Planter Urn. 20'' high, 29 1/2'' diameter, 15'' square base.

No. 1351. Stone Urn, 31'' wide x 20'' dia. x 20'' high.

No. 2417. Lead vase, 18'' high, 13'' dia. at top.

No. 209. Cast stone 20½'' high, 17'' dia. 7½'' square base.

No. 815. Pompeian Urn, cast stone, 19'' high, 25½'' wide, 25½'' deep.

No. 210. Cast stone, 28'' high, 20'' dia. top. Base 11-3/8'' square.

No. 566. Shell urn, 17 1/4'' high by 16½'' long. Cast stone.

No. 1353. Stone Shell-like Urn. 26'' long, 15'' wide, 13'' high.

©1974
Kenneth Lynch & Sons
Wilton, Conn. 06897

No. 1175. Stone urn. Height 36''; diameter 18''. Base 13'' square.

No. 1088. Stone vase-like finial 48" high, 22" largest diameter, 17" square base. NOTE: The ped is 20" high.

No. 307. Cast stone finial, 33'' high.

No. 1086. Stone decorative finial, 44" high, 13" square base.

No. 1047. Stone finial ornamant, 39" high, 20" diameter, 12" square base.

No. 1122. Stone vase-like finial adorned with swags and shells, 52" high, 24" diameter at largest point, the base is 20" square and 20" making the whole arrangement 72" high overall. They can, however, be purchased separately

No. 1150. Stone vase-like finial, 44" high, 21" largest diameter, base 13" square.

No. 1149. Stone Finial Ornament, 44" high, 21" largest cross-measurement, base 13" x 13".

No. 568. Cast stone urn finial, 41½" high, 17" at greatest diameter.

No. 1048. Stone decorative finials, 47" high, 23" diameter at largest point, 13 1/4" square base.

No. 1054. Stone decorative finial, 47" high, 23½ diameter, 18" base.

No. 690. Stone Obelisk. 3 sizes: 100" high with 18" square base, 80" high with 18" square base, 58" high with 12" square base.

No. 1084. Stone decorative finial urn form, 44" high, base 12" square.

FINIALS

Note: All finials are reinforced internally. All finials can be equipped with a coupling flush with the bottom. Be sure to request this. All finials can be furnished with an installation anchor at no extra charge. Many customers are merely installing with a dab of epoxy cement as opposed to using iron anchors and generally this is very satisfactory. Just make certain the surface is clean. If you are going to ask for iron anchors make sure the hole for them is drilled in the correct location. Generally the anchors are 3/4" in diameter and you should have an 1½" hole. Stone finials are very rugged indeed in spite of their graceful addition to an entrance way.

No. 6093. Cast stone. 28" high base 12" square.

No. 6092. Cast stone. 34" high, base 12" square.

No. 6091. Cast stone. 19" high base 8" dia. Check 6½" dia.

No. 6008. Cast stone. 17" high. base 8" dia. Check 6½" dia.

No. 6090. Cast stone. 13½" high, base 8" dia, Check 6½" dia.

© 1974.
Kenneth Lynch & Sons
Wilton, Conn. 06897

No. 1612. Lead pineapple, 12" high, 6" dia Base 5" x 5".

No. 694. Pineapple, cast stone, 13½" high, 5½" dia. Piped.

No. 2962. Lead Pinecone by G. Lewis, 8" high x 8" diameter. Can be made much higher by adding segments. Special drawings available on this Pine Cone, developed to any size you desire.

No. 84. Stone Pineapple, 22 1/2" high, 11" square base.

No. 358. Cast stone, 33½" high, base 11½" x 11½".

No. 80. Cast stone, 36" tall.

No. 692. Stone Pineapple finials. Heights are
12''-16''-20''-25''-30'' 36''

No. 2227A. Lead Pineapple
with wrought bronze leaves,
22'' high overall.

No. 109. Cast stone,
25'' high, 10½'' dia. Base
is 7'' x 7''.

No. 1127. Stone Pineapples, 24'' high.

No. 224. Cast stone
pineapple, 12'' high.
Piped.

No. 112. Cast stone
pineapple, 16'' high,
7½'' dia.

No. 2831. Pineapple furnished
two ways; all stone or lead Pineapple with stone base. As shown
on the left, it is 18'' high and base
is 10'' square.

Special

Special

No. 6057. Balls. Bronze, Brass, Lead, Copper, Stone from 1'' diameter to 72'' diameter. Please inquire. Balls in Halves - Price upon application. From one to one thousand. Shipped Nested. Quote will always be for two halves (per ball).

No. 1977. Stone ball finial. The base is 23'' x 23'' square. Total height 19¾'' and the ball is 15'' in diameter. Completely reinforced and comes with a special anchor.

Many other sizes available.

This stone block is made any size to fit your column, generally 3 to 4'' thick and overhangs the masonry.

No. 691. Ball Finials, cast stone, many sizes available beginning at 10'' in dia. These units are assembled and the points are made of lead.

No. 689. Ball & Point Finial - cast stone ball, lead finial, ball diameters, 10'', 14'' and 18'', heighth 2½ times ball diameter.

No. 5517. CLASSIC STYLE BALL FINAL. 25'' Height overall, Ball 12'' diameter, Base 13½'' x 13½'' High.

No. 688. Shell, cast stone, 23" high, $12\frac{1}{2}$" dia.

No. 4547. Acorn finial. Cast Iron or Aluminum, with or without Ring. 8½" high x 6½" diameter, fits *over* 4½" diameter post or inside 5" diameter hole.

No. 4517-B.

Gate Post Tops. Thse tops are designed to fit nominal 4 x 4's and can be nailed or screwed in place using non ferrous screws. They are beautiful cast lead

No. 2077. Lead Ravens, 19" head to tail, very fine pieces for gate post finials.

See also page 155. Bird section, detailed illustration.

STONE POSTS

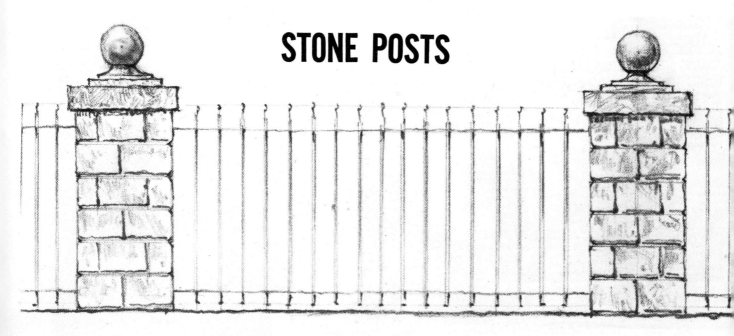

No. 1737. Stone Ball Caps. Many sizes up to 48" square base with 30" ball. Consult us for details.

© 1974.
Kenneth Lynch & Sons
Wilton, Conn. 06897

No. 1134. Fruit
Basket, 16″ high,
18″ at the largest
diameter, base 11″.
Stone.

No. 1094. Stone shell-like
container filled with fruits
and flowers, 28″ high, 10½″
square base.

No. 34. Fruit basket, 14″ high, 16½″ dia. 6½″ base dia. Cast
stone, antiqued.
No. 35. 12½″ high, 11½″ dia. base, 7″ x 7″, Cast stone.
No. 390. Cast stone fruit basket, 15″ high, 17″ in diameter.

No. 1046. Stone Fruit Basket,
20″ high, 12″ diameter, 8″ diameter base.

No. 1129. Stone Fruit Baskets, 28″ high, base 12″ x 12″.
Pedestals shown are 20″ high
with 15″ x 15″ base.

No. 519. Cast stone, 21'' high, 14'' in dia.
No. 520. 29'' high, cast stone.
No. 521. Cast stone, 18'' high.

No. 1133. Stone Shell filled with other products of the sea. Delightfully carved in the form of shells, etc. 24'' high, 24'' large diameter, base 14''x14''.

No. 2424. Lead fruit basket, 14'' high, 13'' in dia.

No. 1128. Stone Fruit Basket, 20'' high, 10'' square base. NOTE: Pedestals are 20'' high x 16'' square.

No. 1049. Stone Fruit Basket, 20'' high, 12½'' diameter, 10'' square base.

No. 1130. Stone Fruit Basket, 20'' high, base 14'' x 14''.

© 1974.
Kenneth Lynch & Sons
Wilton, Conn. 06897

No. 192. Fruit basket, 23''
high, 18½'' dia. 8'' x 8'' base,
cast stone.

No. 1132. Stone Fruit Baskets, 28'' high, 19'' large diameter,
base 10'' x 10''.

No. 1131. Stone Fruit Basket, 28'' high, 20'' large diameter,
base 14'' x 14''.

No. 33. Cast stone, 16''
high, 16½'' wide, 8''
base.

No. 1163. Stone
Fruit Basket, 16''
high, 12'' diameter,
7'' base.

No. 1135. Stone Fruit Baskets, 16'' high, 16'' largest diameter,
base 9''.

©1974
Kenneth Lynch & Sons
Wilton, Conn. 06897

No. 1299.
Stone Planter,
21'' dia. x 26''
high.

No. 401. Stone.
Turned Vase. Height 3', diameter 3' 2''.

No. 187. 16'' x 16'' x
$14\frac{1}{2}$'' high, cast stone.

No. 1302. Stone
Planter, 26 3/4''
dia. x 16'' high.

No. 402. Stone.
Turned Vase. Height 3', diameter 2' 7''. Base excluded.

© 1974
Kenneth Lynch & Sons
Wilton, Conn. 06897

No: 1295.
Stone Planter,
16 1/2″ dia. x
8″ high.

No. 411. Stone.
Turned Vase. Height 1′ 6″, diameter 2′.

No. 371. Cast stone,
18-5/8″ dia. $9\frac{1}{2}$″ high.

No. 399. Stone.
Turned Vase. Height 1′ 8″, diameter 2′ 2″.

No. 1296. Stone
Planter, 19 1/2″
wide x 11″ high.
Carl Milles.

No.38. Cast stone, 9″
high, top dia. $13\frac{1}{2}$″.

No. 599. Cast stone. 22" dia. by 19 1/2" high.

No. 163. Celtic urn. Cast stone. 9" high by 12-1/2" dia.

No. 160. Cast stone, 11" high, 14" dia. top.

No. 356. Cast stone, 14" dia. 6" high.

No. 145. 12½" high, top dia. 12½" cast stone.

No. 600. Cast stone. 21" dia. by 18" high.

No. 243. Cast stone, 7" high, 9 1/4" in dia.

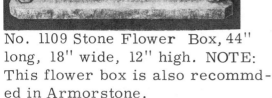

No. 1109 Stone Flower Box, 44"
long, 18" wide, 12" high. NOTE:
This flower box is also recommd-
ed in Armorstone.

No. 357. Cast Stone, Lead,
Armorstone © 45½" Long x
12" High x 12" Wide.

No 1097. Stone Planter, 60"
long, 18" wide, 12" high.
NOTE: This planter is also
offered in Armorstone.

No. 369. Cast Stone, Lead, Armorstone © 50" Long. 13" High. 12½"
Wide.

No. 1098. Stone Planter, 44"
long, 18" wide, 12" high. #605
NOTE: This planter is also
offered in Armorstone.

No. 1303. Stone Box,
9 1/2" x 9 1/2" x 21 1/2"
long. Excellent small
planter.

No. 95. Cast Stone or
Armorstone © - 9 3/4"
Wide x 34½" Long x
12 1/2" high.

No. 509. Cast Stone or
Armorstone © - 10" High
8 1/4" Wide, Any Length
up to 60".

No. 917A. Stone Planter 6' long,
10" high, 12" wide. NOTE: This
planter is offered in Armorstone
and is very satisfactory in this
material.

© 1974
Kenneth Lynch & Sons
Wilton, Conn. 06897

No. 331. Planter, 31'' high by 23½'' in dia., cast stone, very heavy and strong.
This planter can be cast in solid stone, to be used as either a drinking fountain or bird font.

No. 1045. Stone Planter, 29'' high, 19'' diameter, 12 1/2'' square base.

No. 325. Cast stone, 22'' high, 14'' dia.

No. 2726. Stone planter or sand jar. 18'' high, 14'' dia.

No. 1113. Stone Planter, 30'' diameter, 36'' high, 24'' diameter, base. NOTE: This planter is also offered in Armorstone.

No. 204. Cast stone, 10 1/4'' high, 22½'' dia.

No. 128. Oval cast stone, 8'' high, 22'' long and 11½'' wide.

No. 591. Square shrub planter and seat combination, made in many sizes to order. Cast stone.

No. 162. 15½'' dia., 9'' high, cast stone.

No. 159. Cast stone, 19½'' in dia. 9-3/4'' high.

No. 1306. Strawberry Jar, 17''high, 12''dia.

No. 143. Stone Planter, 15½'' high, top dia. 20''.

No. 205. 20½'' high, top dia. 18'', bottom dia. 10 1/4'', cast stone.

No. 1297. Stone Planter, 41 1/2'' dia. x 30 1/2'' high.

No. 1294. Stone Planter with molded feet on square base, 18'' x 18'' x 17'' high.

No. 1300. Stone Planter, 22'' dia. x 16'' high. Also available in Armor-stone.

No. 1305. Stone Box, 15'' wide, 20'' high with 7''projec-tion.

No. 1299. Stone Planter, 21'' dia. x 26'' high.

No. 1166. Stone Vase, 15'' high x 6½'' diameter.

©1974
Kenneth Lynch & Sons
Wilton, Conn. 06897

Lead work started with the Lynches more than 100 years ago, making everything from lead window cames (for stained glass) to great boat keels. Lead pools, statuary and planters from the Lynch shops have long been collector's items and at this writing the Lynches are the last remaining workers in genuine Eternity Lead. The family interest in this work has encouraged them to rescue old models and moulds from such prestigious names from the past as Hoyt, Miller and Doing, Hope, Bromsgrove, Crowther (U.S.) Allen. These priceless treasures now rest with the Trustees and their product is yours to enjoy. The Lynch company will always have a lead yard.

These three pieces, No. 2223, No. 2709 and No. 2708 are a labor of love on the part of the leadworkers in the Lynch Company. They are collectors' items, make wonderful gifts and are specially priced.

No. 2223. Lead vase, 3-3/4" high, 3-1/2" in dia. A most exquisite piece of workmanship.

No. 2708. MINIATURE lead Cistern with Marine motif by Josef Kuthmayer. 4 1/8" in diameter, 3 1/4" high. A collectors item. (Read Haddon Hall Information).

HADDON HALL MINIATURE -- No. 2709.

For many years we have had requests from customers for a desk size cistern. In order to do this right it virtually had to be a piece of jewelry, therefore, we selected as a model one of the greatest cisterns of all. The one from Haddon Hall England and our best pattern maker made an exact scale reproduction of this. It is cast in lead exactly the way the original was done, with infinite care and fine detail.

This wonderful reproduction, which incidently was made by special permission, makes a fine collectors item, a planter, or a desk box for pencils. A pair of them would serve beautifully as bookends. The size is 4 1/2" long, 2 1/2" high, 3" front to back.

©1974
Kenneth Lynch & Sons
Wilton, Conn. 06897

No. 2710. Lead Cistern. 48" long, 40" high, 16" front to back. Sizes changeable.

No. 2156. Lead Cistern made from border design #2156. 18½" high, 19" projection, 52" long. This design can be made into any shape tank--round, square, etc., any size but height remains constant.

No. 2719. Lead border. 7 1/4" high.

No. 2717. Lead Border Design. 3 1/4" high.

Below — Group of small lead tanks made from border designs No. 2717 and 2719.

Left to Right:-
No. 1613. Lead Tank. 6" x 6" 3 1/4" high.
No. 1614. Lead Tank. 12" diameter, 7 1/4" high.
No. 1615. Lead Tank. 3" square, 3 1/4" high.

Left to Right:-
No. 1616. Lead Tank. 10" diameter, 3 1/4" high.
No. 1617. Lead Tank. 4" diameter, 7 1/4" high.
No. 1618. Lead Tank. 3 1/4" diameter, 3 1/4" high.

No. 1619. Lead Tank. 4" wide, 9" long, 7 1/4" high.

No. 1620. Lead Tank. 8½" diameter, 7 1/4" high.

No. 1615. Lead Tank. 3" square, 3 1/4" high.

No. 1617. Lead Tank. 4" diameter, 7 1/4" high.

No. 1621. Lead Tank. 9" long, 3" wide, 3/4" high.

No. 1616. Lead Tank. 10" diameter, 3 1/4" high.

"Eternity Lead"

No. 2371. Large lead planter. 48" long - 20" high - 15" wide at center. Other sizes available.

No. 357. Lead Flower Box, 45 1/2" long, 12" high x 12" wide. Also stone.

No. 2438. Lead Cistern. 24" high - 36" wide - 22" extreme depth.

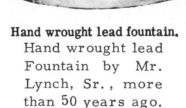

Hand wrought lead fountain. Hand wrought lead Fountain by Mr. Lynch, Sr., more than 50 years ago.

$2,800
26"59.

No. 2369. Lead Flower Tub. 26" square. Other sizes can be furnished.

No. 2707. Lead Cistern. Antique reproduction. 48" long, 40" high, 16" front to rear.

No. 2705. Lead Cistern with special spout. 36" wide by 20" high by 16" front to back. Size changeable.

No. 2834. Lead Pots with gadroon tops, tapered sides. 3 sizes: 4" high x 5 1/2" dia., 5" high x 7 1/2" dia., 6 3/4" high x 8 1/2" dia.

No. 2840. Lead, 6 3/4" high x 8 1/2" dia. Any ornament can be used.

No. 2714. Lead Cistern. 26" wide, 34" high, 18" front to back.

© 1974.
Kenneth Lynch & Sons
Wilton, Conn. 06897

No. 2238. Reproduction of English Antique. Bold relief, 12" high by any length.

No. 2174. Children and Deer Placque. Lead facia reproduction. English antique. 7½" high.

No. 1504. Lead Border Design. 7" high.

For more borders and ornaments in sheet metal send for Book 7474.

No. 2117. Lead border design. 6" high.

No. 2364. Lead border design. 6½" high.

No. 2354. Lead border design. 4" high.

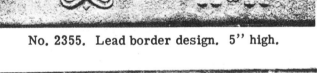

No. 2355. Lead border design. 5" high.

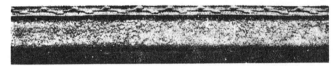

No. 2353. Lead border design. 3½" high.

No. 2360. Lead border design. 6" and 9" high.

No. 2358. Lead border design. 5" high.

No. 2363. Lead border design. 6 3/4" high.

No. 2356. Lead border design. 5" high.

No. 2359. Lead border design. 6" high.

No. 2362. Lead border design. 5½" high.

No. 2361. Lead border design. 5½" high.

©1974
Kenneth Lynch & Sons
Wilton, Conn. 06897

ETERNITY LEAD — BORDERS

You can have any special size or shape to fit any particular condition. We shall be pleased to co-operate with you fully. HEIGHTS ARE LIMITED TO THE MEASUREMENTS GIVEN UNDER RESPECTIVE DESIGNS.

No. 2111. Lead Border Design. 5 3/4" high.

No. 2116. Fascia 14" high.

No. 2115. Lead border design. 8" high.

No. 2352. Lead border design. $4\frac{1}{2}$" high.

No. 2118. Lead border design. 5 3/4" high.

No. 2870. 3" wide.

No. 2871. 3 1/2" wide.

No. 1622. Planter with bronze brackets. 6 ft. long - $6\frac{1}{2}$" high - 6" front to back.

No. 1623. Planter with bronze brackets. 6 ft. long - $6\frac{1}{2}$" high - 6" front to back.

For more borders and ornaments in sheet metal send for Book 7474.

No. 2346. Lead border, bold relief 5" high. Suitable only for square or rectangular tanks or round tanks over 30" diameter.

No. 2113. Lead border design. 8" high.

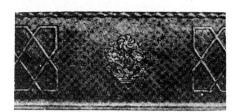

No. 2378. Fascia. 16" high.

No. 2114. Lead border design. $3\frac{1}{2}$" high.

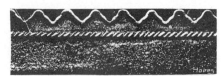

No. 2357. Lead border design. 5" high.

No. 2108. Lead border design. 4 1/4" high.

The Designs shown on these pages CAN BE MADE IN ANY SIZE OF RECTANGULAR, SQUARE, ROUND, HEXAGONAL, SEMI-CIRCULAR OR TAPERED SQUARE. HEIGHTS ARE LIMITED TO THE MEASUREMENTS GIVEN UNDER RESPECTIVE DESIGNS.

No. 1502. Lead Border Design, made into tanks of any size. The illustration is 8" high x 20" diameter.

For more borders and ornaments in sheet metal send for Book 7474.

No. 2938. Lead Border Design with shells, 8" high, can be made to any diameter. Illustration is 20" diameter.

No. 2938. Lead Border Design, 8" high.

No. 1502. Lead Border Design, 8" high.

No. 1572. Border Design. 6" and 8" high.

No. 2896. Lead Border design, 9 3/4" high.

No. 2348. Lead border design. 4" high.

No. 2366. Lead border design. 9" high.

No. 2894. Lead Border Design, 18" high.

No. 2112. Lead border design. 6" high.

No. 2367. Lead border design. 9" high.

No. 2195. Wave border of unusual merit in two sizes: 3" high, 5 1/4" high.

No. 4551. Lead Grape Facia, 6" high, any length.

©1974
Kenneth Lynch & Sons
Wilton, Conn. 06897

LEAD BORDERS

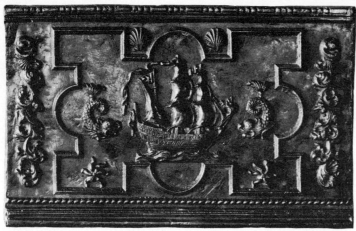

No. 2171. Lead border design. Ship and Dolphin. 18" high.

No. 2168. Lead border design. Rebecca At The Well. 12½" high.

No. 2238. Reproduction of English Antique. Bold relief, 12" high by any length.

No. 4910. Lead facia suitable for pool edging and planter and cistern edging. It is 9" high.

No. 2368. Lead border design. 9" high.

No. 1624. English Lead Facia design. Avaailable in 3 heights 16"-18"-22". These will make planter tubs 16" to 48" in diameter.

No. 2899. Lead Border 20" high. Bold beautiful design.

No. 2120. Lead border design. 2 3/4" high.

No. 2347. Border design - lead. 6" high.

No. 2350. Lead border design. 4" high.

© 1974
Kenneth Lynch & Sons
Wilton, Conn. 06897

ETERNITY LEAD

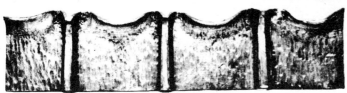

#1503 lead border design. Made any length. Available in four heights 4″ - 6″ - 8″ - 12″.

18″ diameter tank made from border design No. 1503. WE can form lead into any shape. Tanks, pools, cisterns, bird baths, etc., can be made to fit your individual taste.

No. 1503. Made to special shape, either 6″ or 8″ high. The pool itself is Armorstone and has our No. 1503 Border on the front. Is all the same color.

No. 1503. Lead Border design made into tanks of any size, 4″ 6″ and 8″ high. One of the most popular sizes is 19″ x 27″

No. 1503. Special Lead Tank, 12″ high.

#9038
1″x3/16″
5/16″x3/16″
3/8″x1/4″
5/8″x3/8″
3/4″x3/8″
7/8″x3/8″
1″x3/8″
Other sizes available

LEAD MOULDINGS

No. 2901. Lead Rope and Twine Design, 1 3/4″ wide.

No. 2897. Lead Rope Design, 1 1/4″ wide.

No. 2873. 2″ wide.

No. 2872. 1 1/4″ wide.

No. 2866. 3 1/2″ wide x 2″ high relief.

No. 2867. 3″ wide x 2 1/4″ high relief.

No. 2868. 2 3/4″ wide x 3″ relief.

No. 2869. 5″ wide x 3″ relief.

#9039
5/16″x1/8″
3/8″x1/8″
1/2″x1/4″
1/2″x3/16″
5/8″x1/8″
Other sizes available

#9040
3/8″x1/8″
5/8″x3/16″
7/8″x1/4″
1-1/8″x1/4″
1-1/2″x1/4″

#9041
5/16″x3/16″
1/2″x3/16″
3/4″x1/4″

ETERNITY LEAD & STONE

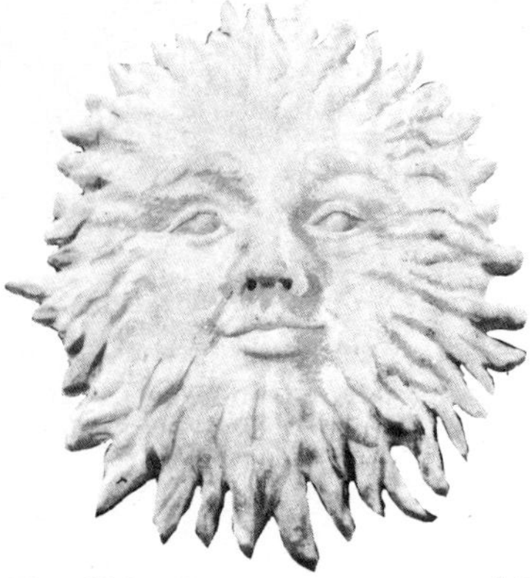

No. 195. Cast stone Sun, $17\frac{1}{2}$'' high, 16'' wide.

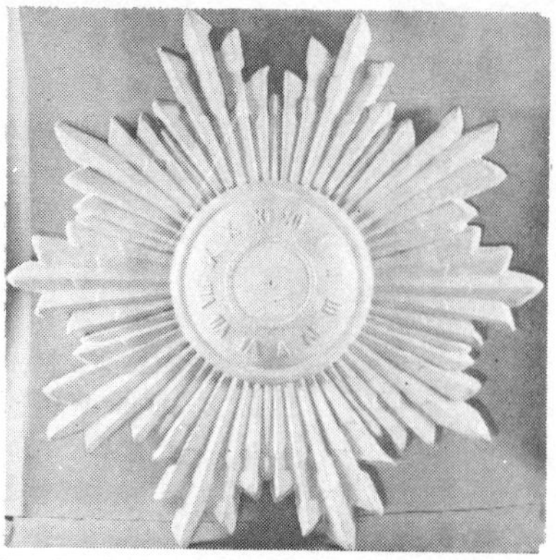

#50 Sunburst, 34'' dia., cast stone. Center can be changed to Sunface, Sundial, etc.

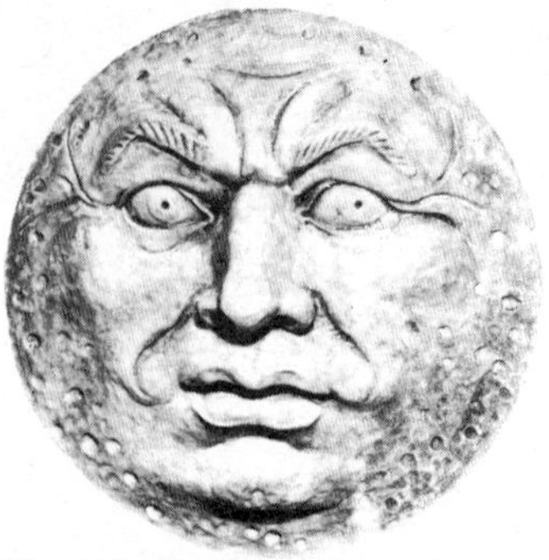

No. 144. Cast stone or Hydro-stone Moon, 15'' in dia.

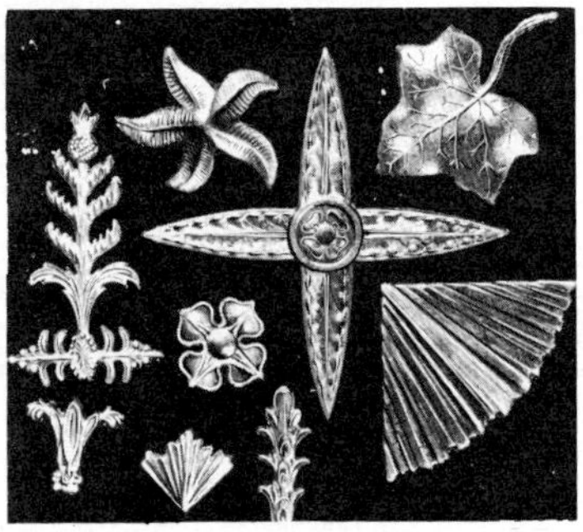

Plate #7

9100A—Starfish, bold relief, 3¼" dia.
9100B—Maple leaf 3½" wide.
9145—Crossed leaf 7".
9145A—Thistle 3" wide 5¼" high.
9145B—Leaf chain 3" long.
9145C—Rosette, 2" dia.
9145D—Flat sunburst, solid 3¾" radius.
9145E—Flat sunburst, solid 1½" radius.
9145F—Leaf, 1⅞" wide, 1⅞" high.

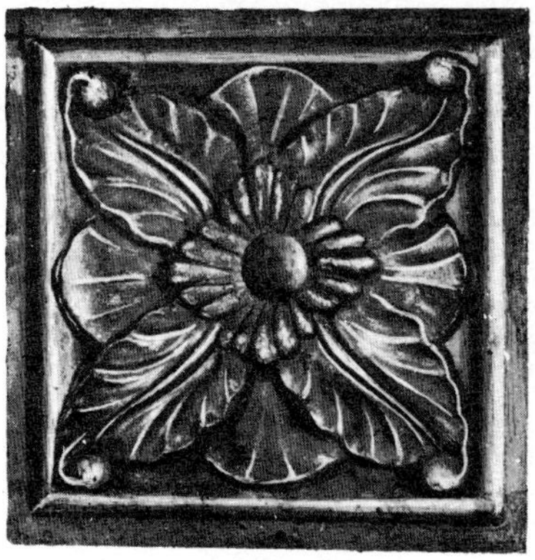

Plate #8

2469—Rosette wall fountain, very bold relief, water pours from very center. 10" square.

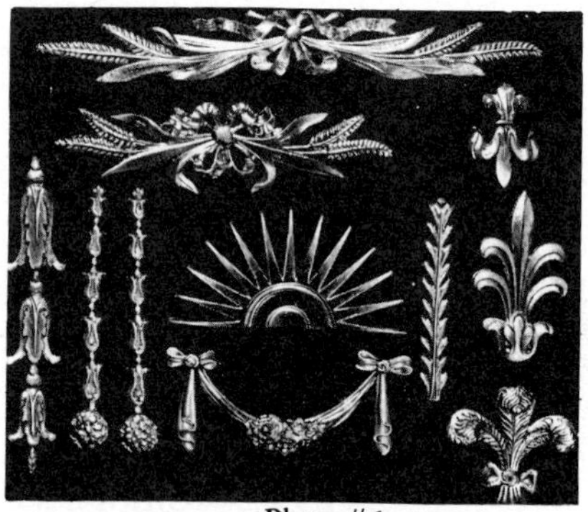

Plate #6

9199—Wheat & bow 13" long x 1½"
8½" long x 2½"
9177—Sunburst 6" diam.
9217—Rosette & leaf chain 6½" long, tapering flat back, Fan lights.
9215—Leaf chain 8" long tapering.
9204—Garland, flat back, 6⅛" wide·
3" high
9213—Leaf, 5" long ⅝" wide.
9612A—Leaf, 4¼" high x
2½" wide, right & left.
9150—Fleur de lis 2¾" high.
9193—Plumes, 3½" wide,
3⅛" high.

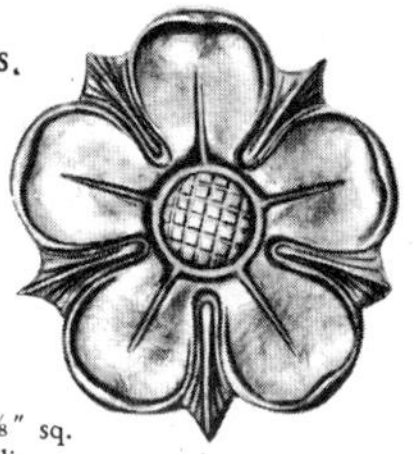

No.1518. Rosette: Lead and stone rosettes of this type are available from stock models from $1\frac{1}{2}$'' in diameter to 8'' in diameter.

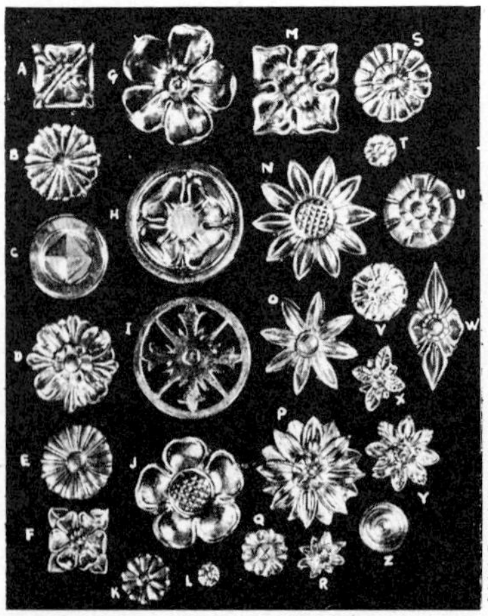

A 1-⅝" sq.
B 2" dia.
C 2-⅛" dia.
D 2-¼" dia.
E 2" dia.
F 1-½" sq.
G 3" dia.
H 3" dia.
I 3" dia.
J 2-¾" dia.
K 1-¼" dia.
M 2-⅛" sq.
N 3-⅛" dia.
O 2-½" dia.
P 3" dia.
L ½" dia.
S 2" dia.
T ¾" dia.
U 1-¾" dia.
V 1-¾" dia.
W 3⅛" dia x 1½"
X 1-¾" x 1-½"
Y 2" dia.
Q 1-¼" dia.
R 1-½" dia.
Z 1-¼" dia.

9200 A to Z sizes as marked.

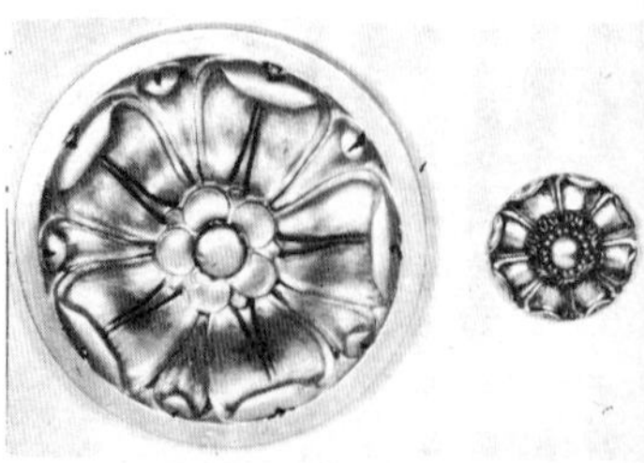

No. 683. Rosettes; are 4 1/4'' and 12'' dia. Hydrostone, cast stone, lead or bronze. We have many other rosettes of this type and design.

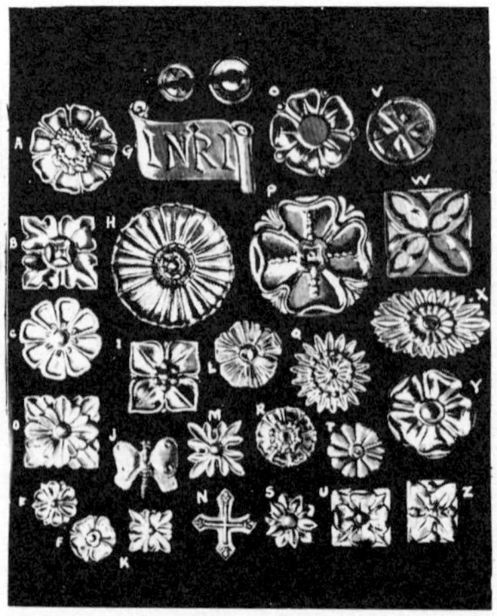

A 2" dia.
B 1-¾" x 1-⅝"
C 1¼" dia.
D 1-¾" sq.
E 1" dia.
G 2-¾" x 1-¼"
H 2-¾" dia.
I 1-⅝" sq.
J 1-¼" x 1-½"
K 1" sq.
N-1-½"
O 2" dia.
P 3" dia.
L 1-½" dia.
M 1-¼" sq.
R 1-⅜" dia.
S 1-¼" dia.
U 1-⅜" sq.
V 1-½" dia.
W 2" sq.
Q 2-⅞" dia.
X 2-¾" x 1-
T 1-⅜" dia.
Y 2" dia.
Z 1½" x 1-¼"

9201 A to Z—sizes as marked.

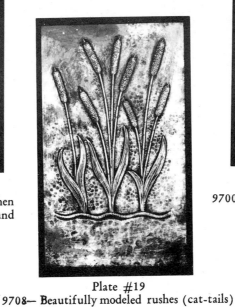

Plate #18
9707—Side panel of flower box which when assembled makes a tapered box 13″ deep and 11″ wide at base and 13″ wide at top.

Plate #10
9700—Large square leaf 8″x8″x⅜″ thick. Can be piped

#9701
Old English setting simulating flower pot and vines, 7″ wide, 7¼″ high.

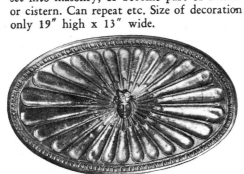

Plate #19
9708— Beautifully modeled rushes (cat-tails) panel, can be arranged to make decorative motif for wall with fountain added etc. or set into masonry, or become part of a tank or cistern. Can repeat etc. Size of decoration only 19″ high x 13″ wide.

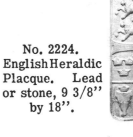

No. 2224. English Heraldic Placque. Lead or stone, 9 3/8″ by 18″.

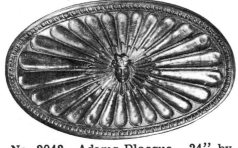

No. 2042. Adams Placque. 24″ by 14½″. Lead or stone.

No. 2185. Sun. Lead, 5½″ diameter.

Plate #8
2469—Rosette wall fountain, very bold relief, water pours from very center. 10″ square.

No. 1517. Lead Sun. 13″ diameter.

No. 1511. 12″ square.

No. 1512. Lead or stone. 11 3/4″ square.

No. 1514. Lead or stone. 18″ square.

No. 1513. Lead or stone. 12″ square.

No. 2704. Lead Cistern. Antique reproduction. Date and initials can be changed. 3' 8" in diameter, 2' 6" high.

NOTE: The tank with cattails is our design No. 9708 shown on page 39.

No. 2198. Lead basket urn, 15" dia. 8" high. NOTE: WE ALSO MAKE THIS IN CAST STONE.

No. 2370-A. Lead flower tub 19" square at top, 19" high. Other sizes furnished.

No. 1090. Circular Stone Well Housing, ready to receive an iron harness with pulley. The well stone is 60" diameter x 4" thick; the housing is 40" diameter, x 32" high. Suitable well harnesses are offered to go with this piece.

No. 1044. Stone circular Well Housing. The base is a stone 40" in diameter x 4" thick; the decorative well housing is 31 1/2" in diameter x 31" high. The wrought iron can be as shown or any other design selected from those shown in this catalog.

No. 2672. Wrought Iron Well Rigging, made to fit your stone work; generally 6' high x 3' to 4' wide.

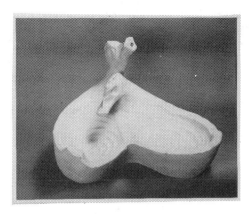

No. 284. Bird font and feeder - stone. 13" high x 16" wide. Can be piped for fountain.

No. 974. Stone Bird bath by Joseph Boulton. 22" diameter, 5" high. Strong, rugged; can sit on rocks or any pedestal.

 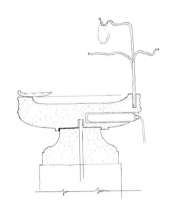

No. 4799. Heated Bird bath 21" in diameter by 12" high. This is a deluxe piece of garden equipment. The bronze branch is designed for a special hook for suet and the shell can contain feed. If you will notice the cross section, you will see that this is furnished with an anchor so that it cannot be knocked over and the heating element fits into a socket specially cast in place. This has been successfully used now for more then 40 years.

No. 4778 Stone bowl of crisp new design. It is now available 16" in diameter by 8" deep. Will be made available in any other sizes upon request. It is used very widely as a springtime planter and also as a bird bath when stones are placed in the bottom for the "nonswimmers." Made of Fairfield stone and packed two pieces per mulch filled drum. The bottom has a good substantial flat area which overcomes rocking and spinning.

Kenneth Lynch & Sons
Wilton, Conn. 06897

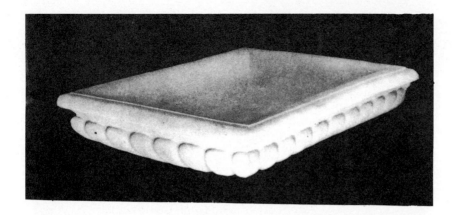

No. 832. Architectural stone bird bath, fine detail. 31'' long X 23½'' Wide X 6¼'' High. Can be used on ground or up on a pedestal.

No. 831. Stone bird bath, reproduction of English antique found at Claydon House, size 14'' Wide 20'' Long 5'' High

No. 527. Stone bird bath, 21'' dia.

No. 88. Bird feeder or font, 28'' overall heighth, bowl is 24'' in dia., cast stone, antique finish.

No. 974. Stone Bird bath by Joseph Boulton. 22'' diameter, 5'' high. Strong, rugged; can sit on rocks or any pedestal.

© 1974
Kenneth Lynch & Sons
Wilton, Conn. 06897

No. 524. Stone, Lily pad bird feeder, 28'' diameter. This piece was carved specially to hold bird seed and is most unusual.

No. 202. Stone bird bath, 32'' dia. by 7½'' high.
No. 202A. 32'' dia. by 3½'' high. Same as No. 202 except 4'' cut off for flat bottom.

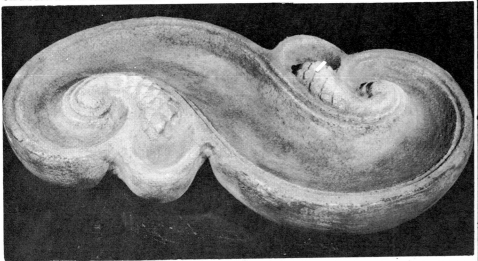

No. 279. Bird bath, cast stone, large, luxurious, 34'' long, 18'' wide, 7'' high.

No. 9. Antique Cast Stone Bird Bath. 68'' high overall, approx. 31'' diameter.

No. 579. Fountain unit or bird font, has pump receptacle, cast stone, very decorative, 29'' dia., 32½'' high.

No. 578. Bird font or fountain, 45'' tall, 36'' in dia. cast stone, designed to take pump, small pedestal and central ornament.

No. 140. Cast stone, 28½'' wide, 21'' projection, 7'' deep. Shown elevated on small block.

BIRD BATHS

Lead, English shell bird baths with figures. Shell is 15" dia. in all cases.
Dimensions for height are given with each figure.

No. 2517. Two birds, 11" high.

No. 2518. Pigeon, 12" high.

No. 2102. Lead Shell, 15" diameter. Serves many purposes in and around garden, mainly as bird feeder or bird bath.

No. 2410S. Shell bird bath on lead rock with squirrel and bird, 15" dia.

No. 2024. English lead antique reproduction bird feeder or font, 15" in dia., 14" high to top of bird. Looks very attractive on stone block to get more elevation.

No. 2401. Lead shell bird bath on legs, English model, 15" in dia.

No. 2410. Lead Shell Bird Bath, English model. Two sizes: 15" diameter x 9" high and 21" diameter x 11" high.

No. 2520. Three songsters. 11" high.

No. 2410B. Lead Bird Bath, English model. Large size 21" diameter.

No. 2519. Pan & Pipes, 15" high.

No. 2007A. Lead shell bird bath on special stone, fluted, ornamented, base, 36" wide, English model.

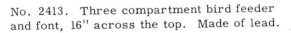

No. 2413. Three compartment bird feeder and font, 16" across the top. Made of lead.

No. 2516. Catbird, 15" high.

No. 1065. Stone Font or Birdbath, 36" diameter x 30" high.

No. 528. Stone Font, very suitable for bird bath, classic design, 31" high x 26" diameter. Pedestal base can be bought separately.

No. 1342. Stone Bird Bath, English model, 18" high x 16" diameter. The base is 12 1/2" square.

No. 2826. Lead shell and frog, 24" wide, furnished so it can be piped for water or a recirculating pump. NOTE: BASE IS #526 AND IS 14" ON THE DIAGONAL AND CAN BE USED WITH ANY SHELL. BASE IS CAST STONE.

No. 2402C. Bird bath, cast lead, old English model, 15" in dia.

No. 2402. English lead basin bird bath on legs, 15" in dia.

No. 2402B. English lead basin on ornamented foot, 15" in dia.

No. 1551-C. Lead Bird bath and feeder, 13" x 15" x 19 1/2" high. NOTE: Available in stone also.

No. 1551-B. Lead Bird bath and feeder, 13" x 15" x 10" high. NOTE: Is available in stone also.

©1974
Kenneth Lynch & Sons
Wilton, Conn. 06897

No. 1142. Stone Shell on pedestal, 31" high 28" wide.

No. 41. Stone Shell, 18¾" diameter. Can be had with or without birds. Approximately 24" high over all.

No. 241. Bird bath, rustic cast stone, 24" high by 21" in dia.

No. 1343. Bird Bath, stone, 25 1/2" high. Base is 16" x 16".

No. 1066. Stone Birdbath or Font. 36" diameter x 36" high.

No. 217. Bird bath, 14" dia, stone.

No. 574. Birdbath Fountain, can use recirculating pump, 24" high, bottom, 31½" face to face, cast stone.

No. 117. Stone bird bath on dolphin pedestal, 22" high, 29" dia.

ABOUT TOPIARY WORK

All the great gardens in Europe have for centuries had amazing exhibitions of Topiary work. Great bushes and closely filled trees were grown and then an expert gardener who was part sculptor, would trim these into the shape of balls, pyramids, peacocks, roosters, etc., etc. Some of these figures took generations to grow.

Here in America we do not have time for this. Also being a mobile population, we had to devise a way to do these Topiary forms so they could be grown quickly and the gardener could use our forms as a guide to get the proper shape — but most important so they could be easily removed to another location. Therefore, in all cases, we offer a ground basket which is to be buried in the ground and filled with earth the regular way. If the owner did have to move and wanted to bring his Topiary plants with him, he would merely have to remove the basket and the tree all at once.

This is a very pratical idea and particularly so for nurserymen who want to do the planting on their own premises and deliver it to the customer already grown and trimmed.

One of our good friends in Greenwich, Conn. has sent us some photographs showing in remarkable detail the Topiary pieces developing — from the empty urn to the finished plant. Of course, this was done in an urn, but also can be done right in the earth if you never intend to move it to another place or if it is of a hardy type and does not need to be brought indoors in the winter. There is one nursery which guarantees as much as two feet of growth per week in the summertime.

You can certainly add a great deal of interest to your garden and you will find this very simple to do.

The sizes shown under the Topiary frames are sizes that we picked arbitrarily so that we could price them and are not necessarily the size you must accept If you feel you want a different size, tell us and we will let you know immediately whether or not we can make it to that size and what it will cost. The drawings are approximately to scale, and in all cases we will give only one dimension.

Empty Urn   ½ Grown   Full Grown

Here we show a Topiary arrangement with a basket at the bottom. This is designed so that it can be moved if the owner has to move to a new location. The basket is made of galvanized iron. It is also ideal for nurserymen who want to do the planting on their premises and deliver the finished product to the customer.

No. 4162. Rooster frame planted by Ms. Ernesta D. Ballard, Director, The Pennsylvania Horticultural Society. This rooster is being grown directly in the body of the bird on sphagnum moss without any connection with the ground below. Ms. Ballard did this so the bird could accompany her where topiaries are displayed. Growth down to and in the ground is, of course, recommended.

A new book on Topiary by S. Wilbourne will be available soon, write us.

TOPIARY

No. 4157. Top-iary form in by-ramid shape, shipped with our lattice urn all ready for plant-ing.

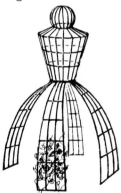

No 4134. Top-iary Bower, 8' tall.

No. 4129. Top-iary English De-sign, 8' tall.

No. 4132. Top-iary Design, 6' tall.

No. 4146. Top-iary design, 6' high.

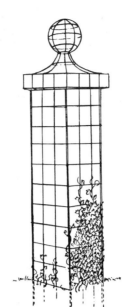

No. 4153. Top-iary Gate Post, 9' tall. So many people want gate posts and find them difficult to afford made of stone. We have offered this so-lution and it wo-rks out very well. It must be thickly and heav-ily planted and kept trimmed to look like anything.

No. 4147. Top-iary design, 6' high.

No. 4148. Top-iary design, 6' high.

No. 4155. Top-iary Obelisk, 8' tall.

No. 4137. Top-iary Obelisk, 6' tall.

No. 4133. 6' tall.

No. 4136. Top-iary Mushroom form, 6' tall.

No. 4154. Top-iary form, 8' tall.

No. 4130. Top-iary French Spiral, 6' tall.

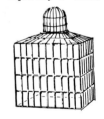

No. 4135. Top-iary Form, 5' tall.

No. 4131. Top-iary Design, 6' tall.

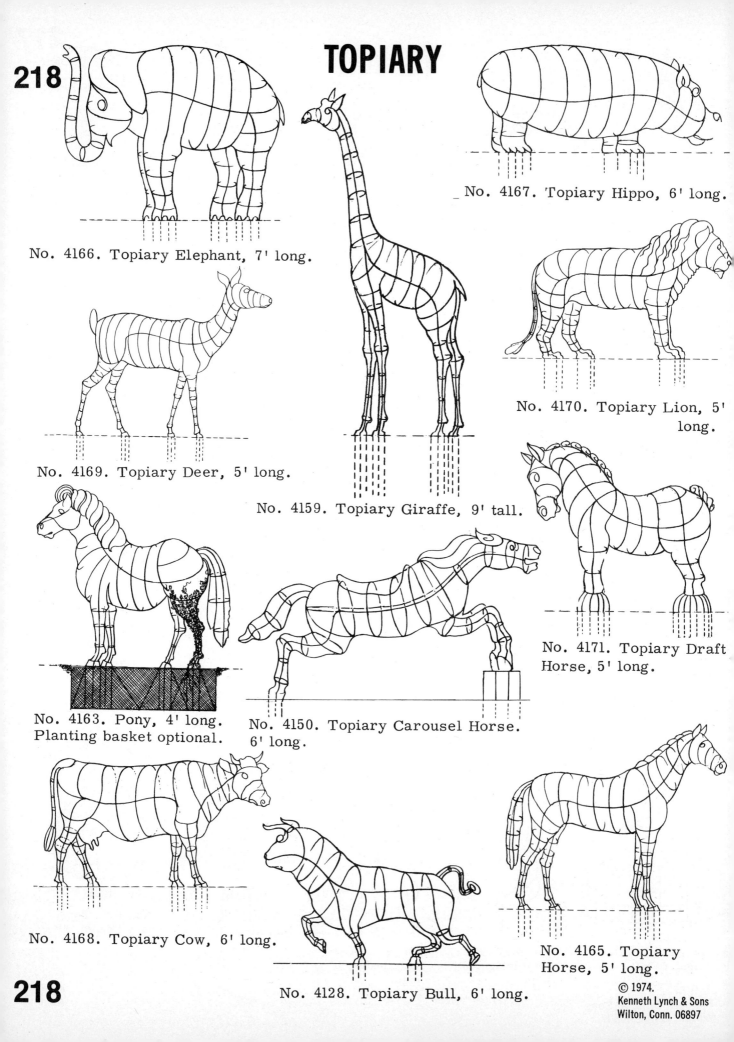

No. 4166. Topiary Elephant, 7' long.

No. 4167. Topiary Hippo, 6' long.

No. 4169. Topiary Deer, 5' long.

No. 4159. Topiary Giraffe, 9' tall.

No. 4170. Topiary Lion, 5' long.

No. 4163. Pony, 4' long. Planting basket optional.

No. 4150. Topiary Carousel Horse. 6' long.

No. 4171. Topiary Draft Horse, 5' long.

No. 4168. Topiary Cow, 6' long.

No. 4128. Topiary Bull, 6' long.

No. 4165. Topiary Horse, 5' long.

TOPIARY

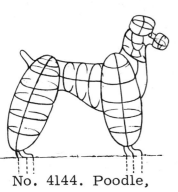

No. 4144. Poodle, 3' long.

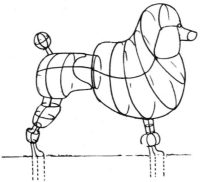

No. 4143. Poodle, 3' long.

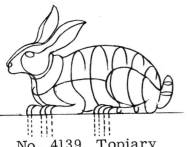

No. 4164. Dog, 3' long.

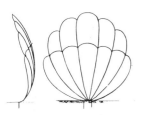

No. 4139. Topiary Rabbit, 4' long.

No. 4127. Topiary Pouter Pigeon, 4' tall.

No. 4197. Topiary Peacock Tail to be used with our lead Peacocks as shown in the adjoining sketch. The tail is 3' tall.

No. 2405. Lead Peacock with topiary tail, 36" high. Note: Topiary tail is part of basket planted in ground and peacock merely stands in front of topiary tail. Bird can be brought indoors separately and topiary tail can be easily dug out of ground and basket removed to greenhouse for winter.

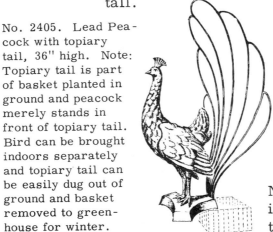

No. 4138. Topiary Rabbit, 4' tall.

No. 2405. Lead Peacock with iron topiary tail, 36" high. Note: tail fits into socket on bird.

No. 4162. Topiary Rooster, 4' high.

No. 4161. Peacock, 4' high. Note planting basket under.

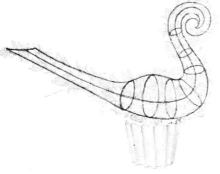

No. 4624. Topiary Bird Frame, 16" high x 32" long.

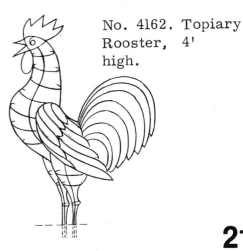

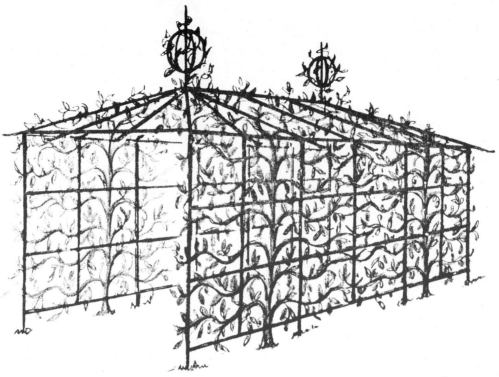

No. 4625. Topiary frame for grape arbor, etc., 10' wide x any length. Size for pricing 10' x 20'.

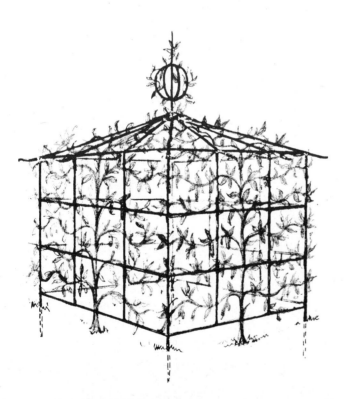

No. 4626. Topiary form for garden house with sphere on top. Bolts together Sized to order. size priced is 10' x 10'.

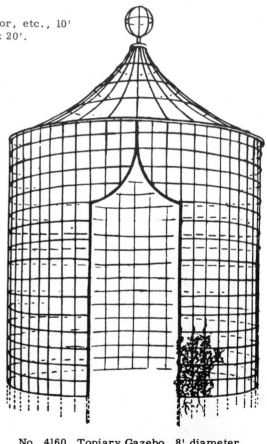

No. 4160. Topiary Gazebo, 8' diameter, 10' high to eave, 14' high to the very top.

© 1974.
Kenneth Lynch & Sons
Wilton, Conn. 06897

No. 4631. Espalier bronze Rain Tree, 3' wide, 6' high. Base is pump case. Pool is extra.

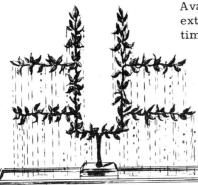

No. 4637. Espalier bronze Rain Tree, 6' wide, 8' high. Base is pump case. Pool is extra.

No. 893. Raintree, all bronze with cast stone base. Available 3', 4', 5', 6', 8', 10', high (with pump extra). Pool diameter should not be less than 1 1/2 times height of tree.

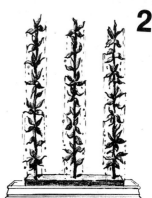

No. 4630. Espalier bronze Rain Tree, 4' wide, 6' high. Base is pump case. Pool is extra.

No. 4632. Espalier bronze Rain Tree, 3' wide, 6' high. Base is pump case. Pool is extra.

No. 4638. Espalier bronze Rain Tree, 8' wide, 6' high. Base is pump case. Pool is extra.

No. 4633. Espalier bronze Rain Tree, 6' wide, 6' high. Base is pump case. Pool is extra.

No. 4634. Espalier bronze Rain Tree, 6' wide, 6' high. Base is pump case. Pool is extra.

No. 4639. Espalier bronze Rain Tree pattern. Base is pump case. Pool is extra. Sized to suit condition, but as shown each individual tree is approximately 3' x 6'.

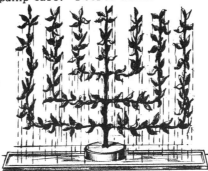

No. 4636. Espalier bronze Rain Tree, 8' wide, 6' high. Base is pump case. Pool is extra.

No. 4635. Espalier bronze Rain Tree, 6' wide, 6' high. Base is pump case. Pool is extra.

© 1974
Kenneth Lynch & Sons
Wilton, Conn. 06897

RAINTREES

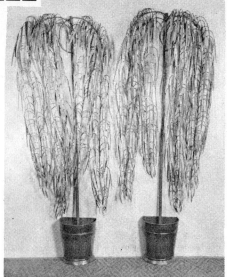

No. 4092. Weeping Willows, all bronze, green patine, piped for water; 6' high x 6' wide, other sizes to order. Bases are made of cast stone and, in most cases, one long base would be furnished instead of two.

No. 4094. Raintree Weeping Willow, all bronze, 6' tall.

No. 4097. Raintree Fountain, completely self-contained; recirculating; made entirely of Armorstone. 48" high x 28" wide.

No. 4093. Raintree, all bronze, grape design, piped for water.

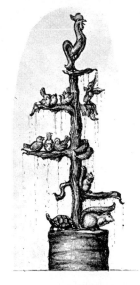

No. 4096. Lead Raintree, reinforced with bronze armature. Base is made of stone and is large enough to house a pump, recirculating the same water.

No. 4717. Special Raintree with lead pump case. The pump case is 16″ in diameter by 8″ high. The Raintree is 6′ high by 2′ 6″ wide and is designed to go in a half round pool and can be up against a wall remaining away from the wall a small amount. The pool would necessarily be at least 6′ wide and project not less then 30″.

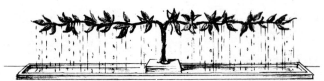

No. 4629. Espalier Rain Tree, verde bronze, with pump case. Pump and pool is extra. 6' wide.

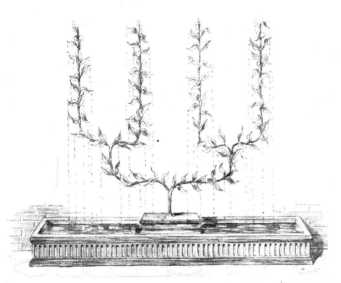

No. 4715. Special bronze Raintree using design No. 4633. It is 6′ wide x 6′ high, and should be connected back to a wall to overcome any vibration. The stone pool would be 8′ long by 10′ high 22″ wide. Other recommendations can be made on a pool.

No. 4097. Raintree Fountain, completely self-contained; recirculating; made entirely of Armorstone. 48″ high x 28″ wide.

No. 4719. Special Raintree and lead pool. The Raintree is 4′ 6″ high and the lead pool is made of border No. 2346 5″ high by 66″ in diameter. The pump is in the base of the Raintree.

No. 4716. Special bronze Raintree 6′ high overall and lead pool 3′ x 6′. The pool is ornamented with Zodiac ornaments and the pump is contained in the pump case. It is designed to go against a wall. However, it can be made to work in the full round and it can be made to be illuminated.

Kenneth Lynch & Sons
Wilton, Conn. 06897

RAINTREES

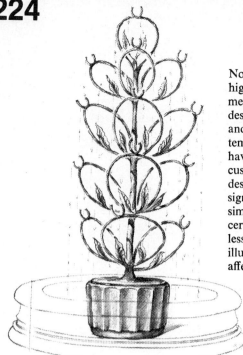

No. 4718. Special bronze raintree 60″ high overall by 24″ wide. The stone member at the bottom is a pump case designed to hold the recirculating pump and to stabilize the whole tree. This contemporary version of a raintree can have more or less ornament on it if the customer desires. Careful study of this design shows that on each level the designer made three large open loops to simulate great leaves. This tree would certainly require a pool at the base not less than 6′ in diameter and could be illuminated and achieve considerable affect.

No. 4720. Special Raintree and pump case. The Raintree is bronze is 6′ high and is approximately 4′ wide. The pump case is 20″ in diameter by 8″ high. This is designed to work from a pool and the pool should be if possible 8′ wide from left to right and project about 30″.

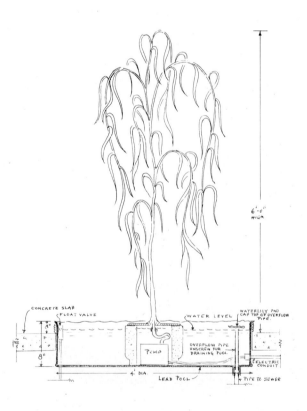

No. 4840. Illustration of Raintree No. 4094 bronze with special lead pool 4′ in diameter by 8″ deep. The Raintree is 6′ high, see accompanying sketch for application.

© 1974.
Kenneth Lynch & Sons
Wilton, Conn. 06897

POOL SYSTEMS

Pools can be made by at least seven different systems. We list them, mentioning their individual advantages and disadvantages, and showing a simple cross section so that you can see clearly what we are talking about.

You will note that we mention Armor Stone© throughout the discussions on this page. Armor Stone© is the copyrighted trade name for a material which we have developed which is made of very finely ground stone of any type we choose to use, and then the stone is reassembled in any shape we desire by the use of resin and reinforcing materials including fiberglass. A small sample will be sent to you upon request. We think it is the greatest material we have ever seen and on the right we illustrate what a finished piece of stone would look like.

POOL SYSTEM #1 is simply a large water container made of Armor Stone©. No curbing. Just set to grade and trim with flag stone or any other way you desire.

ADVANTAGES. Permanent, lightweight, easy to ship, comparatively inexpensive, simple, made to any size or shape.

DISADVANTAGES. Not as attractive as a pool with a curb. Must be careful not to collect mud, grass clippings because of no curb. It is a simple and inexpensive installation and looks like that; however, you can have Armor Stone© in a natural stone color or a weathered stone color so that it loses much of this appearance.

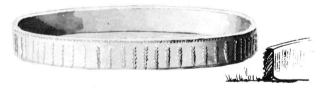

POOL SYSTEM #3. Lead facia combined with a pool of Armor Stone©. The Armor Stone© pool is made to any shape and size and then the decorative eternity lead facia is added by permanently securing the two together.

ADVANTAGES. Has all the advantages of the #2 system but is lighter and stronger. The Armor Stone© pool can have same lead color. Shipment is much easier to handle. Packing is considerably less expensive and it has most of the advantages of an all lead pool.

POOL SYSTEM #2 is made of all lead using any ornamental facia or border design, shown on our lead border pages; with an eternity lead bottom permanently burned on.

ADVANTAGES. Highly desirable. Very beautiful, very rich. Resaleable. Goes well with other things, indoors or out. Centuries of acceptance by architects and designers give it much prestige. Design and shape unlimited. Looks better with age.

DISADVANTAGES. Size is limited. Very heavy when size is large. 8 ft. in diameter largest practical size. Must be carefully and expensively packed and skidded. Requires equipment to handle when over 6 ft. in diameter. Must be carried on a pallet, otherwise will collapse. Size, cost, shape, final location should control buyer's decision.

DISADVANTAGES. Very few. Initial cost slightly greater (but final cost is less when you consider freight, packing and handling.) Lacks the resale value of an all lead piece. Customer may lack confidence in this material although we guarantee it without qualification and customer may have not as yet have been exposed to enough of this new material to grant it the acceptance it deserves.

POOL SYSTEM NO. 4

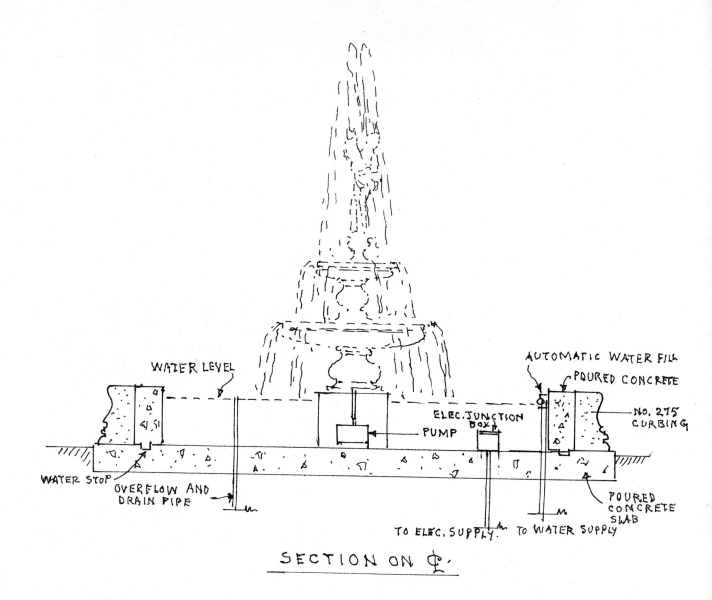

WATER LEVEL

AUTOMATIC WATER FILL

POURED CONCRETE

ELEC. JUNCTION BOX

PUMP

NO. 275 CURBING

WATER STOP

OVERFLOW AND DRAIN PIPE

TO ELEC. SUPPLY

TO WATER SUPPLY

POURED CONCRETE SLAB

SECTION ON ℄

Pool System No. 4.
Here we see a concrete slab with keyed plain curbing cast in place and our curbing set against it. The advantages of this system are:

      1. it is very strong,
      2. it provides extra protection against leakage.

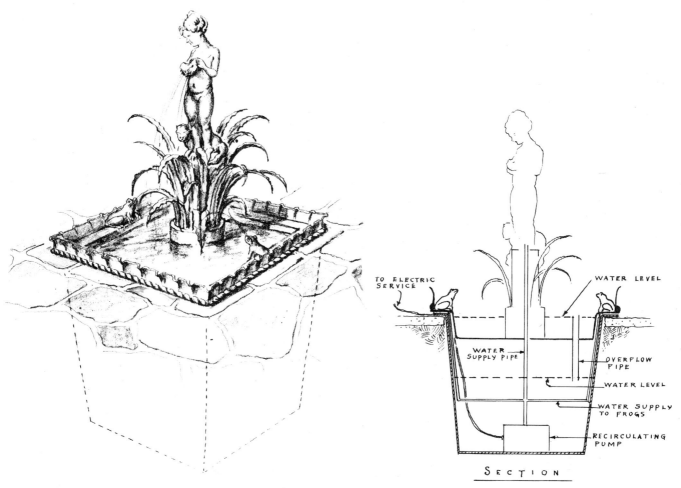

Labels on section diagram: TO ELECTRIC SERVICE, WATER LEVEL, WATER SUPPLY PIPE, OVERFLOW PIPE, WATER LEVEL, WATER SUPPLY TO FROGS, RECIRCULATING PUMP, SECTION

No. 4766. Special fountain arrangement using a lead "Otter Girl" No. 972 which is 25'' high.   The lead pool is 30 in. by 30 in. square and the two frogs are 4513. The leaf work in the pedestal are, of course, special. See accompanying section for mechanical diagram.

No. 4766. Special fountain arrangement using fiberglass pool below floor level with a lead border at the top. The "Otter Girl" is No. 972 41½ in. high

The above illustrated fountain arrangement can be used with any other figures of similar size. This is a diminutive arrangement and at the most the figure should be 18'' to 26''.

Note! The sump size is standard in system No. 5. The sump is 30'' square x 26'' deep. It can also be placed above grade and enclosed with stone or plantings.

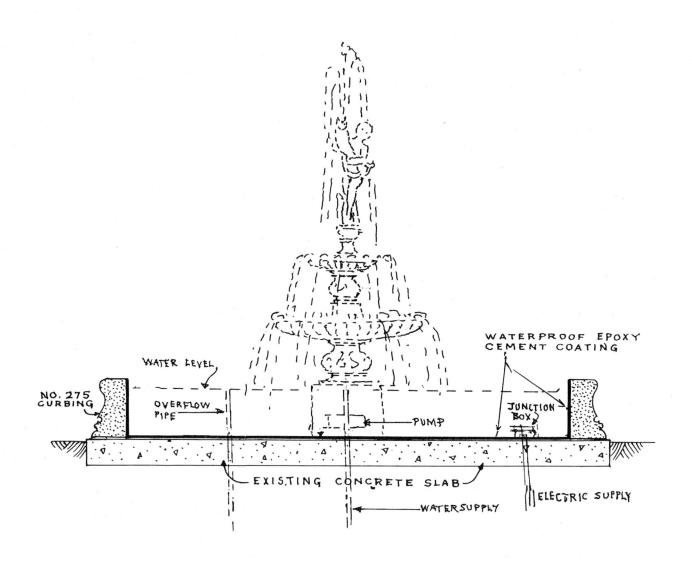

WATERPROOF EPOXY
CEMENT COATING

WATER LEVEL

NO. 275
CURBING

OVERFLOW
PIPE

JUNCTION
BOX

PUMP

EXISTING CONCRETE SLAB

ELECTRIC SUPPLY

WATER SUPPLY

Pool System No. 6. This is the very best system to use for a permanent installation.

Pool System No. 6. With Pool System No. 6 you take curbing section No. 275 and place it exactly the way you want it on your existing masonry deck or pool bottom.
See accompanying illustration of a craftsman placing pool parts.

© 1974.
Kenneth Lynch & Sons
Wilton, Conn. 06897

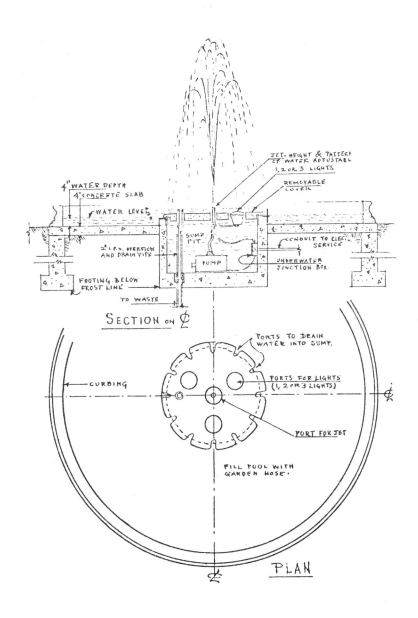

Pool System No. 7. Where an extremely shallow pool is desired, a concrete slab may be poured and a prefabricated sump installed in the center. The sump projects above the slab of the pool by 3″ thereby giving you enough water cover on the bottom. However, the main body of the water is collected in the sump where is installed the mechanical unit with pump, lights, etc. The cover of the sump is designed to permit light to come through, water jets to operate, however, there is not enough water in the pool for local laws to be concerned with (in some towns there are laws concerning the fencing of pools containing even as little as 14″ of water.) With the above system we do not see how any inspector could fail to pass it. Special drawings are available.

© 1974.
Kenneth Lynch & Sons
Wilton, Conn. 06897

POOL SYSTEM NO. 8

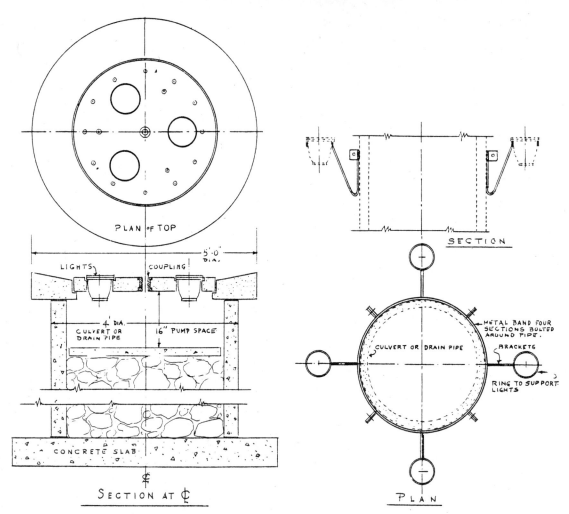

PLAN OF TOP

LIGHTS   COUPLING

5'-0"
DIA.

4' DIA.
CULVERT OR
DRAIN PIPE   16" PUMP SPACE

CONCRETE SLAB

SECTION AT ℄

SECTION

METAL BAND FOUR
SECTIONS BOLTED
AROUND PIPE.

CULVERT OR DRAIN PIPE   BRACKETS

RING TO SUPPORT
LIGHTS

PLAN

No. 5534. Cast Stone Top used on a piece of culvert pipe. The top is 60" in diameter and it is designed to be used on a piece of 48" culvert. When you are faced with the problem of producing a fountain in the center of a shallow pond, the ideal situation, if you can possibly do it, is to put a flat slab of concrete on the bottom of the pond. This could be either a piece of pre cast concrete or it could be cast and placed at a time when the pond is drained. However, it should be in level or as nearly as possible. The culvert should come to within 6" of the normal water level, and, of course, this is very easy to determine. In any event, the cast stone member on top of the vertical culvert section should be under water by a few inchs. The contractors who normally do this work install a slab or some similar member for the culvert to sit on and then they fill it with stone to within about 18" of the top. They then either introduce some gravel on top of the stone to give them a level area to work on or a pre-cast concrete slab. Then they purchase from us the slab No. 5534 shown above which is designed to have lights, fountain jets, etc., and the whole center piece is removable as you can see. Not long ago we were called up to make a ring-like device which went around the perimeter of one of these culvert members and this ring-like device was designed from pieces which could be bolted together and tightened and this gave another place where more lights could be attached. We have made a sketch of this situation so that you can see what we get. The space from the underside of No. 5534 to the top of the stones in the culvert, of course, could be greater should the pump be larger. We invite your correspondence.

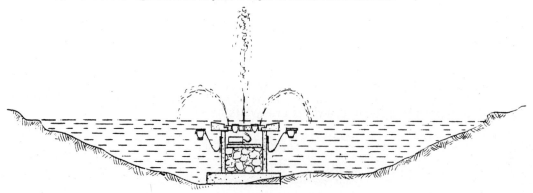

SECTION THRU A POND SHOWING
A TYPICAL INSTALLATION OF UNIT.

© 1974.
Kenneth Lynch & Sons
Wilton, Conn. 06897

POOL INFORMATION

The pool which contains the water is the most important element in a fountain. Much can be done with very little water, for on most fountains, there is never a great deal of water in the air so let us forget about the water which is aloft—it is not important.

Pools may be any shape whatever and as you will see in other places in this book, you can design beautifully shaped pools and they are extremely simple to build.

The water pattern which goes straight up in the air from the center of the pool, let us say 5 feet high, must have at the very minimum a 10 foot diameter pool.

This is a very good rule to follow that the pool must be a minimum diameter of double the height of the water.

The reason is obvious. First we have the wind blowing the water from one side to the other and water will bend with the wind, and then, of course, there is the splash for when a drop of water lands in a pool it will bounce any place within the whole 360° and this, likewise, can be blown. We find water bouncing as high as 2 feet or 3 feet depending upon the volume and the height.

When designing these pools one of the great considerations is the depth of the pool.

Certainly it is less expensive to build a shallow pool than it is to build a deep pool.

Pools as shallow as 6" would be acceptable; however, it may be necessary to have a depression in the center which is commonly called a sump and the sump is nothing more than a depressed part of the pool used to gather water so that your pump will have the proper water coverage.

I have seen pools which were purposely built very shallow, that is with almost no water laying in the bottom. As a matter of fact the bottom of the pool became merely a drainage area to drain towards the sump.

This pool was at a children's hospital where they encouraged the children to get in the water; however, the real water collecting device was in the sump and the pool acted as a spray area with the water running down into the center.

In this case the sump was about 3 feet in diameter and 3 feet deep and it was enclosed just like a well. It had a cast stone cover on it and fastened to this cover was the nozzle spray device—it was all very simple.

Many variations of this can be used and the most acceptable seems to be a pool made with our curbing No. 275 which is 10" deep. This makes it possible to operate without a sump. Therefore, you can just put down a slab and put the curbing around it, do a very simple water-proofing job so that it is water tight and you then have a pool.

If you will look in the fountain section you will see many mechanical drawings showing such an installation.

In most communities there are laws about pools. Therefore, before proceeding you should check with local law. At this moment we believe that 8" of water is acceptable in most places without a fence.

Fences, of course, are intended for swimming pools and similar installations; however, for garden pools, fountains and ornamental pools a fence would be a handicap.

Here we show a sketch showing a very simple garden pool arrangement which should satisfy the strictest of laws (see illustration A) (note: caption Ill. A).

If you will study this drawing you will see that the sump member which is available in cast stone and which is water tight is installed in the ground in such a way so that when the slab is poured a keyway locks into this sump and it is very simple to caulk with epoxy when the whole bottom of the pool is being water-proofed.

If I were building such a pool I would first install the water sump and get it in absolute level and it is easy enough to tell if it is level by filling it with water. Next, I would do whatever is necessary according to the climate and cast the slab, and, of course, this must be reinforced with ordinary road mesh. Any competent mason will readily understand these instructions.

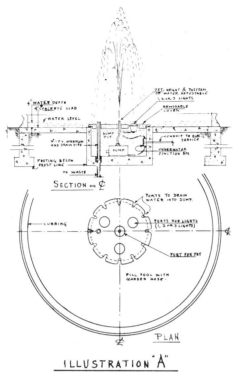

SECTION on ℄

PLAN

ILLUSTRATION "A"

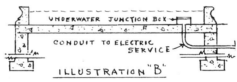

ILLUSTRATION "B"

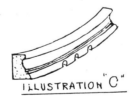

ILLUSTRATION "C"

Assuming that you have a situation that calls for the very minimum of water laying in the pool, and, of course, it is not going to be used for fish, then you could have as little as 2". However, in most cases curbing 10" high is very desirable and maintain about 8" of water in this at all times.

The various pipes, pumps, wires, etc., that go to pools are shown on the drawings and it is very clear.

Illustration A is designed merely to show the reader what can be done in an extreme situation with an absolute minimum of water in the bottom of the pool.

In one case an architect designed a large sump about 8 feet in diameter and 4 feet deep in order to give a very substantial amount of water for an elaborate pool he had designed and this was covered with a bronze grating which supported equipment which had to be at water level.

However, for the most part fountains are made with depths of water ranging from 6" to 24".

Illustration B.

Illustration B shows a good typical pool installation with the electrical service coming underground and being brought up in the pool before it is filled with water.

The electrical service, of course, is distributed through an underwater junction box equipped with cord seals, and, of course, these underwater junction boxes when properly assembled are absolutely water-proof. However, back at the source of power it is imperative that there be a dead cut-off or a complete cut-off of power before attempting to work on anything in the pool.

Most contractors drain the pool to begin with after having cut off the power and the smart ones put their own padlock on the handle of the switch which is at a remote location.

An alternative to this underwater set-up with the junction box arrangement is to use two or three wires coming through the curbing and if, when you are ordering the curbing, you let us know, we will make it with grooves in for the wires.

As the curbing is placed you will have some short pieces of copper tube to fit those grooves at the bottom of the curbing. See Sketch C. This will be put in the piece of curbing going in the direction towards your source of electricity. Merely set the curbing and feed the wire through it. Then when you are water-proofing the bottom of the pool, you will auto-matically seal this and you will have no leakage problem.

Now in order to join your pump and light to this, use an ordinary underwater connector with an epoxy package and these are readily available from electrical supply houses, pool supply houses and such people as Sears Roebuck. They are very inexpensive, they are made of plastic, they are about 1" in diameter and 4" long, they are clear and what happens inside is visible. You make the usual careful connection, assemble this device and fill it with epoxy and you have a water-tight connection.

Should it be necessary to break the connection, you merely cut the wire off at either end of this plastic underwater connector and start over again. It is all very simple.

This system precludes the problem of burying conduit and conduit is a sort of pipe that electricians use to protect wires.

There is regular underground burial wire which is readily available to bring the electricity to your pool.

Now the foregoing is for the simplest of installations.

When there are a multitude of lights, pumps, etc., then an electrical drawing must be made and this service is available.

FOUNTAIN DETAILS

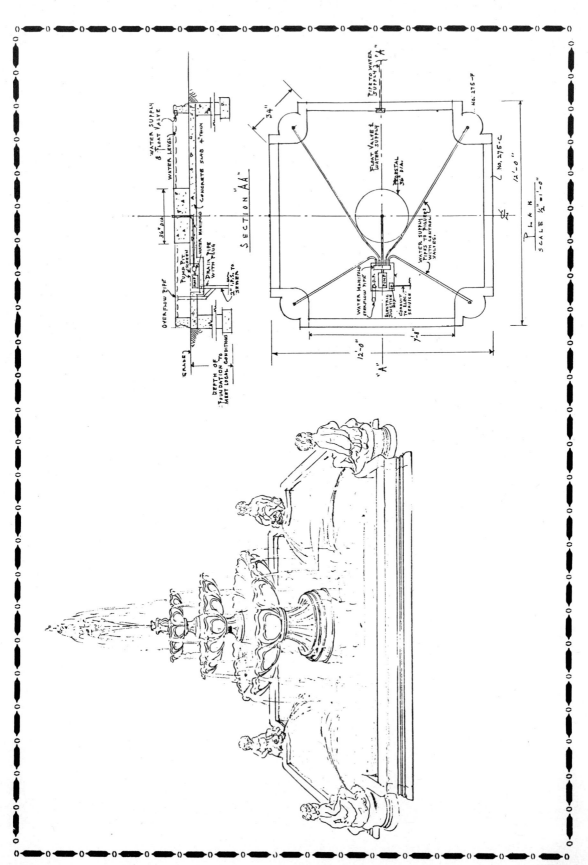

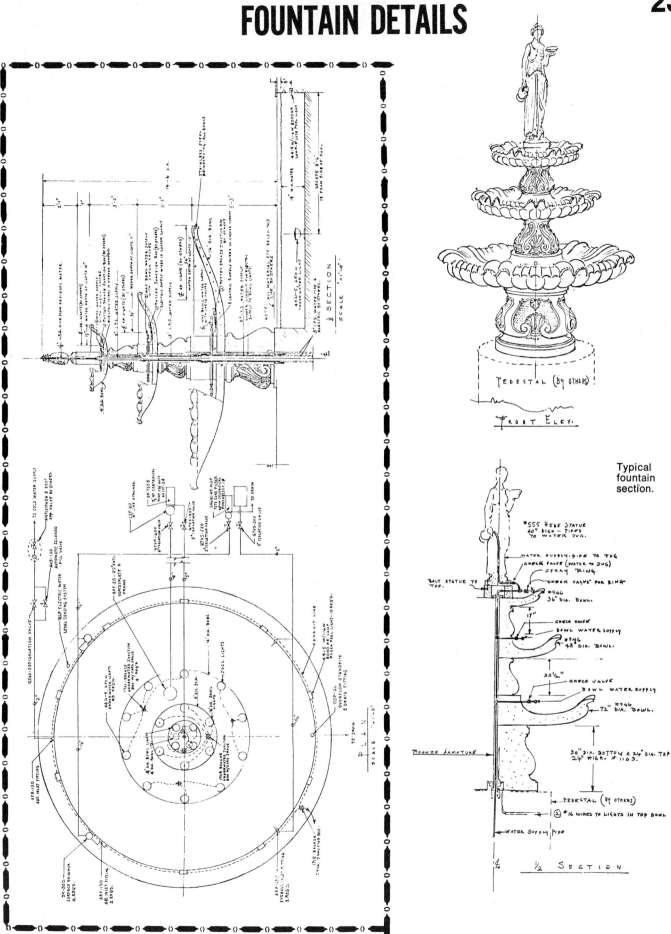

Typical fountain section.

Front Elev.

½ Section

POOLS

Shown on these pages is the greatest collection of pool shapes ever offered. They are made from curbing members No. 275 and could also be made from taller and broader members. The shapes shown are approximate. All pools must have a waterproof lining, bottoms and sides. By cementing the curbing members to a concrete slab with epoxy, then coating the entire interior with a waterproof material such as epoxy masonry to which can be added crushed marble or any other material finish you want. Any of these wonderful pool shapes can be developed very easily using our system. Consult other pages for additional shapes.

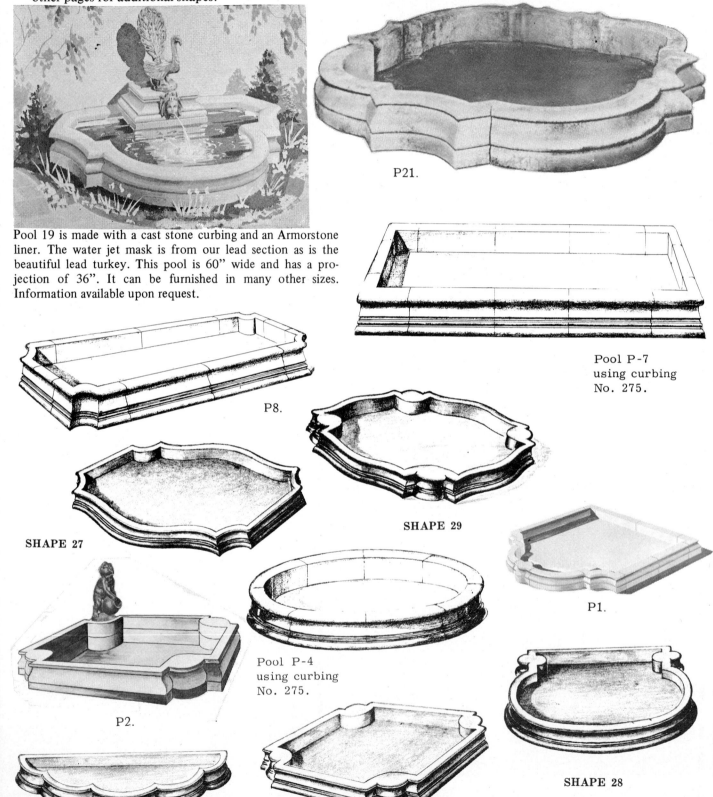

P21.

Pool 19 is made with a cast stone curbing and an Armorstone liner. The water jet mask is from our lead section as is the beautiful lead turkey. This pool is 60" wide and has a projection of 36". It can be furnished in many other sizes. Information available upon request.

Pool P-7
using curbing
No. 275.

P8.

SHAPE 29

SHAPE 27

P1.

Pool P-4
using curbing
No. 275.

P2.

SHAPE 28

SHAPE 38

SHAPE 26

© 1974.
Kenneth Lynch & Sons
Wilton, Conn. 06897

Pool shapes as shown here can be made from our stock curbing molds generally. A very popular shape is No. 36 and No. 2234. See notes concerning size.

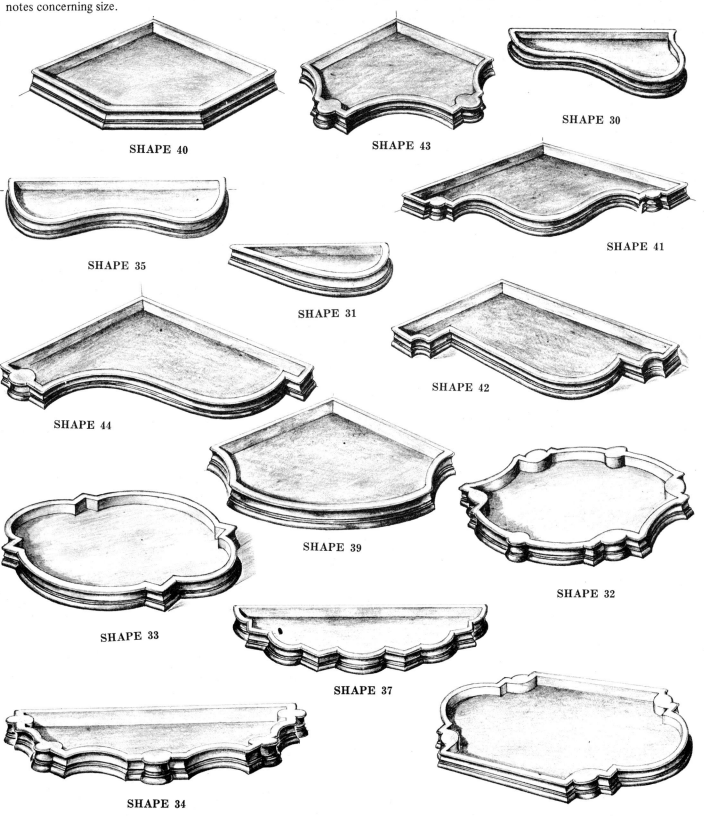

SHAPE 40

SHAPE 43

SHAPE 30

SHAPE 35

SHAPE 41

SHAPE 31

SHAPE 42

SHAPE 44

SHAPE 39

SHAPE 32

SHAPE 33

SHAPE 37

SHAPE 34

SHAPE 36

Very small pools are difficult to make. Larger pools are easier. Where water is involved the base pool should be a diameter equal to twice the height of the water jet. We invite your correspondence.
See special pool page for various pool systems.

POOL PLANS

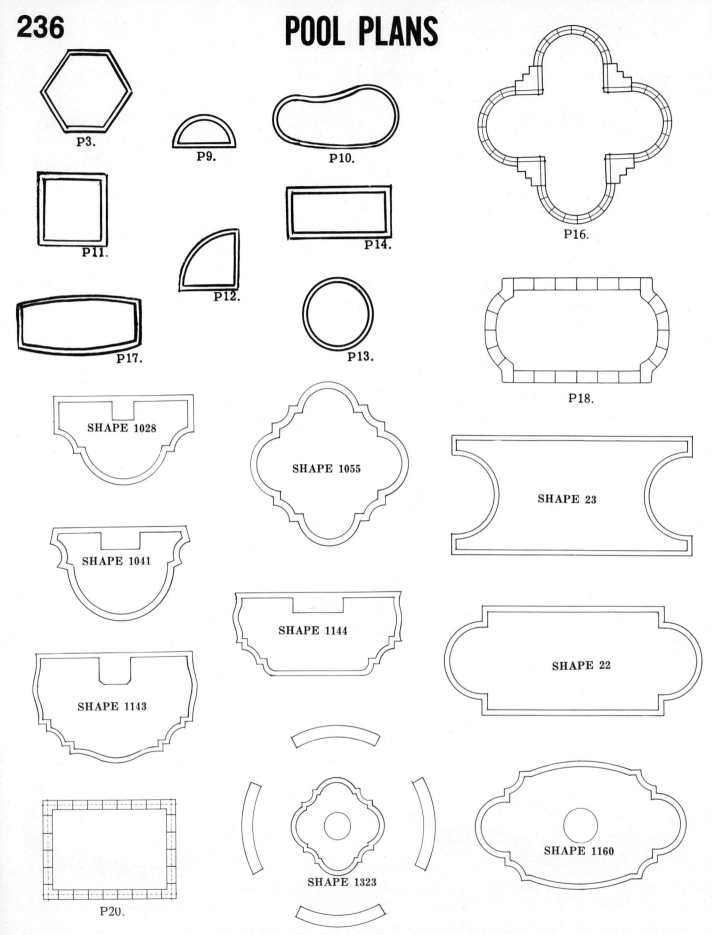

P3.

P9.

P10.

P16.

P11.

P12.

P14.

P17.

P13.

P18.

SHAPE 1028

SHAPE 1055

SHAPE 23

SHAPE 1041

SHAPE 1144

SHAPE 22

SHAPE 1143

SHAPE 1323

SHAPE 1160

P20.

© 1974
Kenneth Lynch & Sons
Wilton, Conn. 06897

CURBING ASSEMBLY

Stone curbing, sturdy, reinforced, is the foundation of most fountains. It is available in heights from 6″ through 24″. It is precut and prefitted to design thus eliminating any field labor. There is a tremendous collection of pool shapes available.

Pool Assembly

The above illustration is the reproduction of a photograph taken in our lofting area where pools are laid out and fitted prior to being shipped. In the very center you will see the base of a fountain which has been placed there more for identity than for any other reason. The fountain has been laid out with four segments by establishing a center line and a cross line, and these actually divide a circle which is the extreme outside of any projection in the design, and this, of course, is the perfect way to lay out a fountain. That is to lay out a fountain of this type. All of this material is pre-fitted in the lofting shop where a perfect layout is made and then the parts are cut on a diamond saw so that a nice fit is accomplished, and as each piece is cut it is put back into its correct position until finally all of the pieces have been fitted together.

If you use this system when assembling such fountains, in the field, you will, particularly after they have been so carefully cut and fitted here in our studio, achieve excellent results. The design shown above is our P21, but the same rule applies to almost any fountain.

Note that he has laid out a pair of cross lines which divide a circle into four equal parts, and, of course, the circle is the extreme outside of the pool.

All of the curbing members are laid exactly where they should be when the pool is finished.

Each piece is picked up and cemented in place with epoxy mortar separately, and it is joined to its neighbor at the same time. After the curbing has been set, and, of course, all of this must be absolutely level because water finds its own level every time, then the inside of the pool can be or covered with epoxy mixture which can be filled with a sand or crushed marble surface to suit.

This is the most desirable of all pool systems for a permanent installation. 10" is enough water for most ornamental pools, particularly if a sump for the pump is installed. However, 14" is much better where lighting is going to be used, and in recent years 14" curbing has become standard. You are invited to consult with us on this.

POOL CURBING

To select a Pool Curbing. Decide the shape. Refer to any pool design on any page when writing. Pools should hardly ever be under 8' in at least one direction. We will help you.

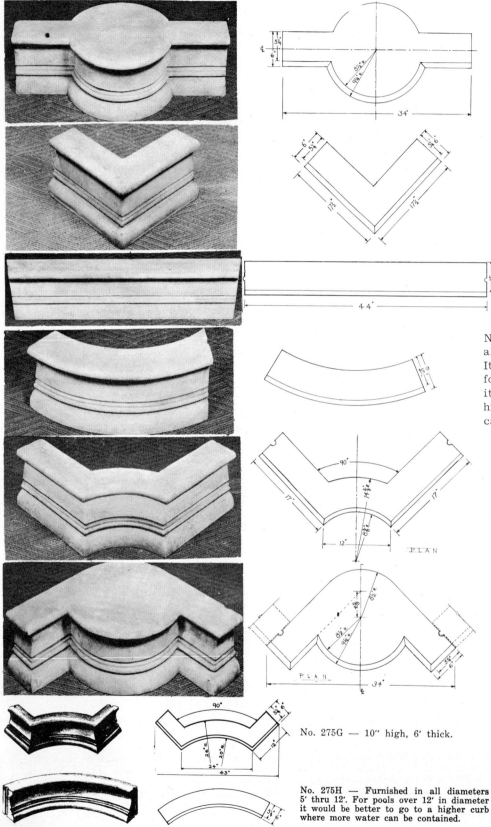

No. 275 - A. Stone curbing, 17'' diameter, 10'' high, 6'' thick.

No. 275-B. Stone curbing, 10'' high, 6'' thick, 17'' x 17'' (each leg).

No. 275-C. Stone curbing, 10'' high, 6'' thick, 44'' long.

No. 275-D. Furnished in all diameters 5' through 12'. It should be remembered that for pools over 12' in diameter it would be better to go to a higher curb where more water can be contained.

No. 275-E. Stone curbing, 6'' thick, 10'' high, 8 3/8'' radius, 17'' along sides.

No. 275-F. Stone curbing, .17'' diameter.

No. 275G — 10'' high, 6' thick.

No. 275H — Furnished in all diameters 5' thru 12'. For pools over 12' in diameter it would be better to go to a higher curb where more water can be contained.

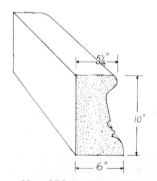

No. 275 Stone curbing. Made in shapes as shown above.

STONE POOL CURBING
CUSTOM MADE SECTIONS AND SIZES

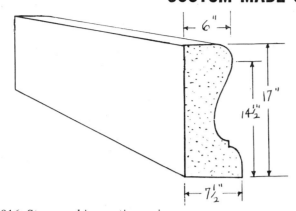

No. 4916. Stone curbing section series.

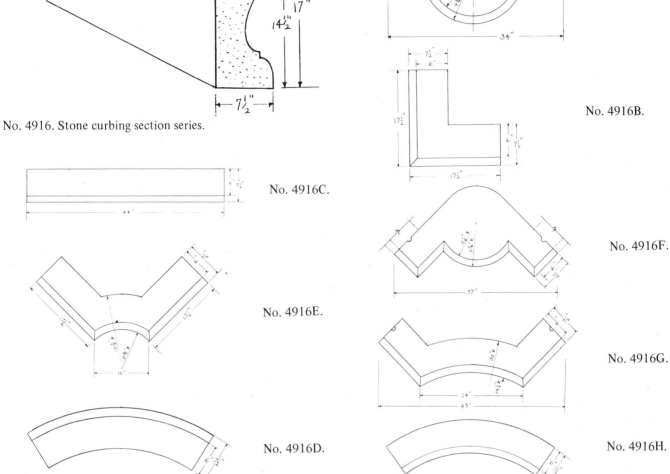

No. 4916A.

No. 4916B.

No. 4916C.

No. 4916F.

No. 4916E.

No. 4916G.

No. 4916D.

No. 4916H.

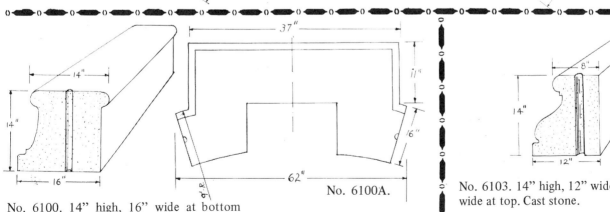

No. 6100A.

No. 6103. 14" high, 12" wide at bottom. 8" wide at top. Cast stone.

No. 6100. 14" high, 16" wide at bottom 14" wide at top. Cast stone.

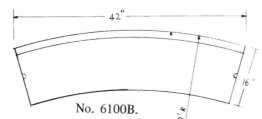

No. 6100B.

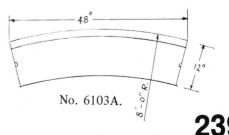

No. 6103A.

POOL CURBING

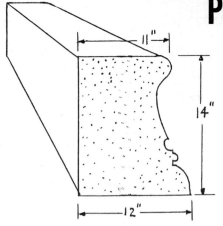

No. 5555. Stone curbing section series.

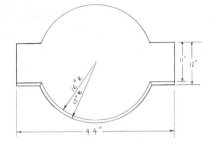

No. 5555A.

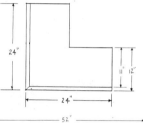

No. 5555B.

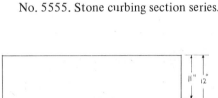

No. 5555C.

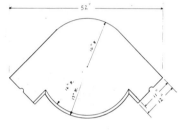

No. 5555F.

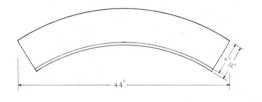

No. 5555D.

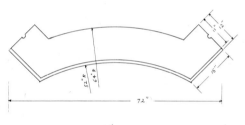

No. 5555G.

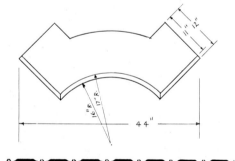

No. 5555E.

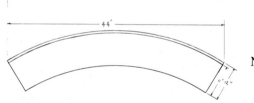

No. 5555H.

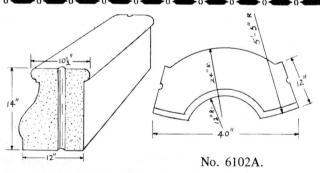

No. 6102A.

No. 6102. 14" high, 12" wide at bottom 10½" high at top. Cast stone.

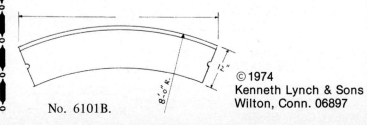

No. 6101. 6" high, 12" wide at bottom 11" wide at top. Cast stone.

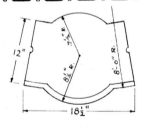

No. 6101A.

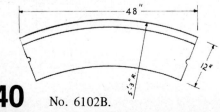

No. 6102B.

No. 6101B.

No. 5488. Elaborate fountain arrangement which can be made as large or small as you wish. We have the largest collection of shells and bowls ever assembled and we have special saucer-like pedestals to receive them. These can be moved around like chessmen to make any assembly you wish and water can spill from one level to another and be pumped up and around at will. Statuary of all kinds can be added as can trees, shrubs, etc. Lighting effects of all kinds can also be added.

All you need is a slab of concrete on which to start the pool, then add the curbing which creates a pool and install the various elements which you see here. It is all relatively simple and we would be delighted to help you.

No. 947A. Cast Stone Fountain . Very well engineered. 7' diameter x 11' high, not including the round base in pool. NOTE: Any finial of proportionate size may be used on the top.

On the 947 series bowls, as shown above, we now have added bowls up to 144" diameter.

947 SERIES

Shell-Bowl-Knode type stone fountain. The 947 series is the most rugged of all stone fountains. It has many features which make it particularly desirable.

It is very easily assembled in the field, it is very strong, and it is absolutely frost-proof. Freezing will not hurt this fountain. Just shut it off in the wintertime, drain it and let the ice and snow accumulate.

The bowls and other parts are available from stock from 18" diameter up to 7' diameter.

This fountain comes equipped with a metal armature which can take care of lights in the bowl, and it uses re-circulated water. It is definitely a one-time investment. It is safe to say that if vandals climb on it no harm is done. They would actually have to come equipped with destruction tools to hurt this fountain.

We could most likely give you delivery on a large fountain of this kind within four weeks of the date your order is cleared and accepted here at Wilton.

A telephone call will get you immediate answers to any questions involving this fountain.

No. 947-C.   Sectional view of the 947 series Stone Fountain.

© 1974
Kenneth Lynch & Sons
Wilton, Conn. 06897

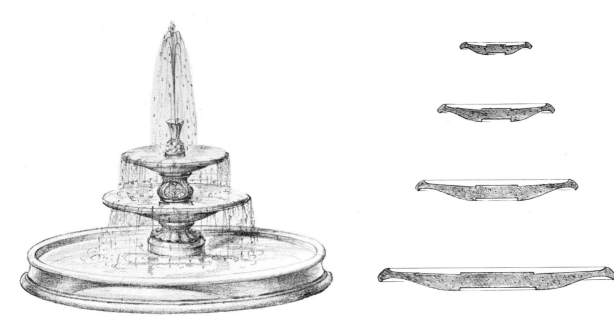

No. 947B. Stone Fountain from stock
parts can have one to five bowls.
Bottom pool of suitable size.

No. 947. Series Stone Fountain Bowls,
18" dia, 30" dia, 42" dia, 60" dia, 84"
dia. can be used all together to form
one large fountain or any part thereof.

Bowls are available
in 18" diameter up to
12' diameter.

Illustration of the installation of Fountain No. 947 at a Southern County seat. The lead pine cone on the top is very tastefully made from parts shown in another part of this catalog. The fountain was intalled directly in front of the court house
prior to the reconstruction of an old and important plaza. The architect and the County supervisors were highly pleased
with this excellent piece of work.

©1974
Kenneth Lynch & Sons
Wilton, Conn. 06897

No. 4845. Stone Fountain using No. 275 curbing numbers with center pedestal and one of the 947 series bowl with a special pedestal for the pineapple.

It is designed to be 12 feet long by 8 feet wide. Sizes, of course, may vary. Lights can be used as well as other jets.

©1974
Kenneth Lynch & Sons
Wilton, Conn. 06897

No. 4755. This is a special pool and fountain design for a very grand estate. It was never built. We are thinking about it. It was to be modeled specially and it was laid out to be 18 ft. in diameter. Your inquiry is invited. Cast Stone.

No. 4740. Elaborate Stone Fountain made for the restoration of large old estate. We show this by permission of the owners. The fountain comes in pieces ready to be set on existing masonry and is 18 ft. extreme dimensions and is approximately 40 in. high to the top of the coping. We believe the area between the scrolled arm rests was intended either for seating or is for replacing a floral arrangement. The ornament in the center is of bronze.

No. 1260. This is the world's largest fountain available from stock. The base pool should be at least 32' in diameter. The first bowl is 16' in diameter; the next bowl is approximately 8' in diameter; and the over-all height is approximately 14' high. However, it can be made higher by the installation of more base members at the bottom. This can be a completely self-contained fountain with pumps in the base member, night illumination, sequenced programming, Additional water effects can be had by introducing the spray ring which would shoot water toward the center bowls. The curbing should be 36'' high.

We believe that if you install a slab on which we can work, we could deliver this fountain to your premises and erect it withing 60 days from date of order

Fountain at Long Beach, California, made of a combination of stone and Armorstone. This beautiful installation at Bella Fontana Park is a great joy to all who behold it.

Kenneth Lynch & Sons made and delivered this fountain in very short time. This fountain is No. 1260 shown on the facing page. We could hardly write about this fountain and the great privilege it was to install it in this wonderful city without paying honor to the contractor who did the field work. His name will be furnished to anyone upon request and he is one of the most able craftsman we have ever encountered. Your inquiries are invited.

Fountain shown operating at night with lights playing on the water.

Fountain shown lighted at night in silhouette.

No. 946. Design D. Stone Fountain using No. 946 series bowl 6' diameter with No. 677, "Vintage," 60" high. NOTE: Other statues may be used in the center of this bowl.

No. 1345. Fountain using No. 946, 4' diameter bowl and No. 972 "Otter Girl," 41" high.

No. 946. Design E. Stone recirculating Fountain, 6' diameter at the largest bowl x 10' high. NOTE: The figure at the top could be substituted using a pineapple or some other ornament; a pump can be installed in the base. This large fountain must be used with a pool under it, and the pool should be at least 14' to 16' in diameter and using a 24" high curbing.

© 1974
Kenneth Lynch & Sons
Wilton, Conn. 06897

No.946. Design B. Fountain, 36" diameter x 72" high.

No.946. Design A. Stone Fountain, largest bowl 4' diameter; over-all height 7' 6".

No.946. Design C. Stone Fountain with two bowls. Can be the combination of the following:
6' bowl with either 4' or 3' bowl.
4' bowl with either 3' or 30"bowl.
3' bowl with either 30" or 21" bowl.
Note alternate finial using a Pineapple.

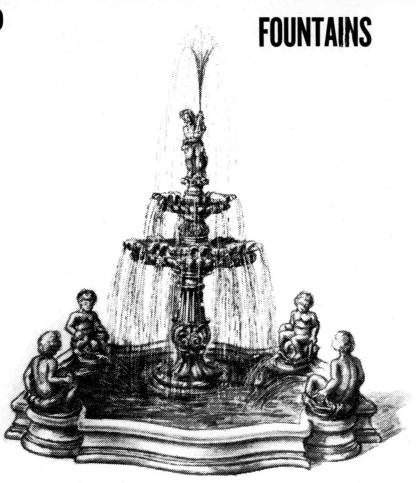

No. 4728 Very lively stone fountain using No. 946 fountain complete with a No. 1161 pool is 82 in. by 82 in. However, larger size should be considered.

No. 4724 Fountain arrangement using a No. 946 Bowl 4 ft. in diameter mounted by a Madonna No. 2893 30 in. high in lead. The pool is made of our 275 curbing 8 ft. in diameter.

©1974
Kenneth Lynch & Sons
Wilton, Conn. 06897

No. 4759. Stone fountain 7 ft. 6 in. high and can be made higher with no problem. The pool is made of No. 275 curbing and is 16 ft. square. The Figures are No. 2846, Boys Riding Dolphins, and the Shells are No. 247 series. This is an extremely lively and beautiful fountain operated with recirculating pumps.

No. 4757. Stone fountain arrangement using center fountain No. 1075 with pool curbing No. 275. Pool size ius 16 ft. by 12 ft.

© 1974.
Kenneth Lynch & Sons
Wilton, Conn. 06897

No. 1075. Stone Fountain, 76" high overall. Ready to receive any ornament on the top. The largest bowl is 66" dia. and the base on the ground is 34" dia. x 26" high.

© 1974
Kenneth Lynch & Sons
Wilton, Conn. 06897

No. 4757. Stone fountain arrangement using center fountain No. 1075 with pool curbing No. 275. Pool size is 16 ft. by 12 ft.

No. 4736. Stone pool 5 ft. 6 in. in diameter with No. 964 figure and a No. 12 pump case. Directly in the water a pump can be installed and jets fastened to the side of the pump case to give this fountain much life.

©1974
Kenneth Lynch & Sons
Wilton, Conn. 06897

No. 897. Stone fountain, 79" high
by 40" wide.

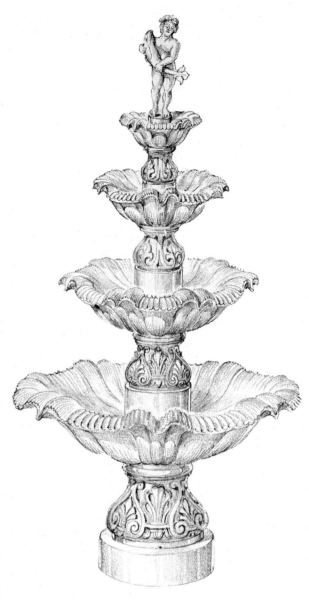

We show here Bowl Cascade Tiered Fountains. Nos. 897
and 897-A are basically the same, there being a slight difference in the knodes and in the base. The following possible
arrangements are recommended.

Single Bowl, 60" diameter. Single Bowl, 40" diameter.
Both of these can take figures up to 80% of their diameter.

Two-tiered fountains can be made using a 60" bottom bowl
and a 40" bowl directly above it. Of course, the 80% rule
about a figure or other ornamentation still applies. Another
two-tiered fountain could be a 40" bowl with a 27" bowl a-
bove it.

An illustration of a three-tiered fountain is shown. It can
be sized as indicated in the caption, or it could be made of
other bowls shown on this page as described above.

We also show the four-bowl version, which is No. 897-A.
In this design we have four bowl diameters: 20", 27", 40"
and 60".

No 897A. Stone Fountain. This is another version of our very famous
fountain. This one is 5' diameter at
the largest point and 8' high. All parts
may be purchased separately. Note adjoining photograph of similar fountain,
in the three shell version.

© 1974.
Kenneth Lynch & Sons
Wilton, Conn. 06897

FOUNTAINS

FRONT ELEVATION

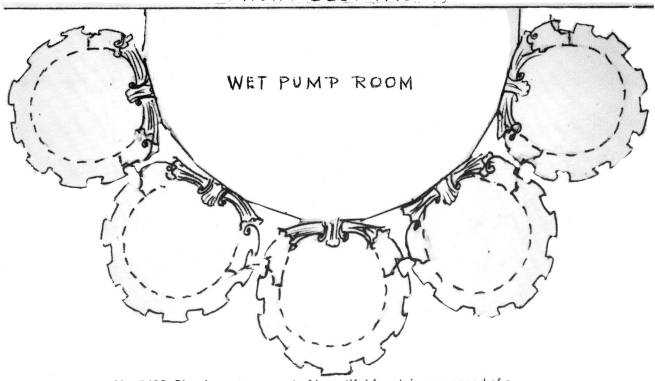

WET PUMP ROOM

No. 5489. Simple arrangement of beautiful fountain composed of a
dozen very large stone shells, a pedestal and a figure. A proper pool
must be arranged on a concrete slab; however it is all very easy, as the
pumps are submersible and hidden from view under the pedestal
which supports some of the shells and figures. Size is no problem.
Let us try to help you.

© 1974.
Kenneth Lynch & Sons
Wilton, Conn. 06897

FOUNTAINS

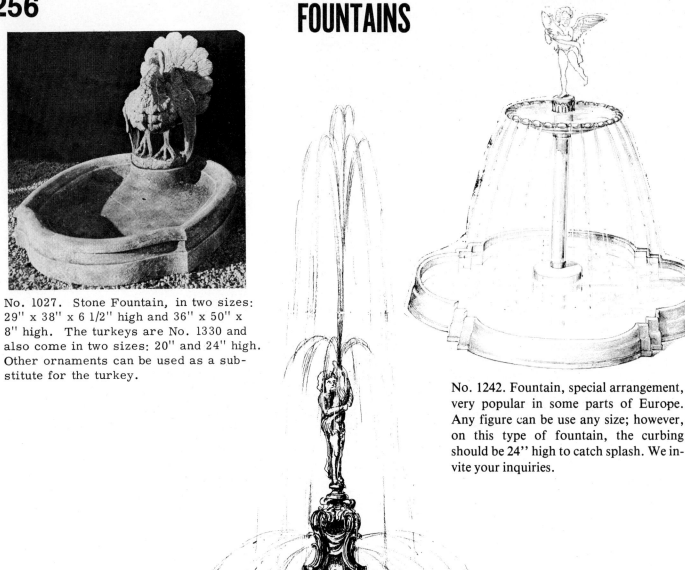

No. 1027. Stone Fountain, in two sizes: 29" x 38" x 6 1/2" high and 36" x 50" x 8" high. The turkeys are No. 1330 and also come in two sizes: 20" and 24" high. Other ornaments can be used as a substitute for the turkey.

No. 1242. Fountain, special arrangement, very popular in some parts of Europe. Any figure can be use any size; however, on this type of fountain, the curbing should be 24" high to catch splash. We invite your inquiries.

No. 1259. Stone Fountain. The bottom pool should be approximately 20' in diameter and the lower bowl is 12' in diameter. From the grade line to the top of the ornamental pedestal on which the figure sits, the height is approximately 10'. This is an adjustable measurement depending upon how many blocks we put under the pedestal and how many steps we introduce. It can even be made higher. The figure shown is merely a suggestion; any one of our many figures could be used. This can be a completely self-contained unit requiring only electricity. The curbing should be 24" deep for such a large pool.

No. 1160. Stone Fountain, 8' tall; pool is 72" x 120".

No. 9. Stone Fountain, 36" diameter x 68" high. Other figures may be used.

No. 997. Stone Fountain, 29" dia. x 31 1/2" high to top of basin. The figure is 18" high. Other figures may be substituted.

No. 1055. Stone Fountain, pool 73" diameter, 10" curbing height; block in center 10" high; fountain 64" high.

No. 944. Stone shell cascade fountain, 53'' from floor to top bowl. The bottom bowl is 36'' in diameter; middle 28'' in diameter, top 20'' in diameter.

No. 1328. Stone Shell Cascade Fountain, massively carved 64½'' high by 42'' wide with a 36'' projection. Note: There is a 14'' pump case projecting at the rear of this fountain. This serves to great advantage as it gives an area for plant decoration completely across the rear of the fountain and gives you absolute access to the pump. However, if this fountain is used with a bottom pool, this pump case can be eliminated.

No.1293. Stone Shell Fountain arrangement 42'' wide by 48'' high. can Have recirculating pump.

No. 1005 and 1006. Stone Fountain. The Shell, No. 1005, is 29'' wide; the overall composition is © 1974. 29'' high.

Kenneth Lynch & Sons
Wilton, Conn. 06897

No. 1089. Stone Fountain, 60" long, 32" projection. The bowl itself is 14" high; the figures are 28" high; and the pedestal is 34" high. All pieces can be purchased separately, if so desired.

No. 699A. Stone, shell with pedestal and dolphin. Pump receptacle under dolphin and self-contained recirculating fountain. 26" in diameter. Shell is No. 131 with base 14" high.

No. 1333. Stone Cascade Shell Fountain with recirculating pump in bottom shell. 64" high x 42" wide. Figure may be changed. Also looks well on low, carved, massive pedestal. Also used in pool.

© 1974
Kenneth Lynch & Sons
Wilton, Conn. 06897

No. 1146. Stone Fountain, 53" high, 32" wide, base 18" x 18". Completely self-contained. All parts may be purchased separately. Half round.

No. 2050. Complete fountain unit with pump included, furnished in stone. It is 34" high including base. 36" dia. more elevation can be gained by selecting any one of our many blocks or some similar arrangement.

FOUNTAINS

No. 1041. Stone Fountain. Pool is 53" x 33" x 10"; the figures are 35" high and they are 18" wide at the base. These two boys are playing with a jug of water, one spilling the water into the other ones shell which, in turn, makes the water fall into the pool. All can be purchased separately.

No. 1144. Stone Fountain, 36" high, 64" wide, 32" front to back. NOTE: Pool can be purchased separately from other parts.

No. 1143. Stone Fountain, 52" high x 62" wide. Any other figures can be substituted or the pool can be used separately.

No. 1028. Stone Fountain. Pool is 53" x 33" x 10" high; the pedestal is 21" high x 10" square; the figure is 24" high; the base on the figure is 12 1/2" square.

No. 999. Stone pool, 60" wide, 36" front to back, 10" high.

© 1974
Kenneth Lynch & Sons
Wilton, Conn. 06897

No. 1161. Stone Fountain, 82" x 82". Each Cherub is piped from the Dolphin he is riding. The curbing is 10" high and the figures are 22" high.

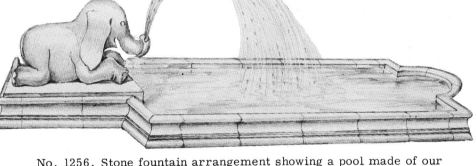

No. 1256. Stone fountain arrangement showing a pool made of our curbing No. 275 using Elephant No. 270 complete with recirculating pump, etc.

This entire arrangement should be at least 12 feet long to put it in proper scale. If you like elephants, this is a most elegant arrangement.

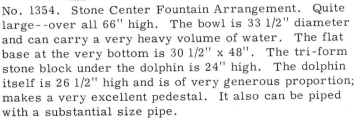

No. 1354. Stone Center Fountain Arrangement. Quite large--over all 66" high. The bowl is 33 1/2" diameter and can carry a very heavy volume of water. The flat base at the very bottom is 30 1/2" x 48". The tri-form stone block under the dolphin is 24" high. The dolphin itself is 26 1/2" high and is of very generous proportion; makes a very excellent pedestal. It also can be piped with a substantial size pipe.

No. 1164. Stone Fountain, for against wall 52 1/2" high, shell 27" diameter. Parts may be used separately.

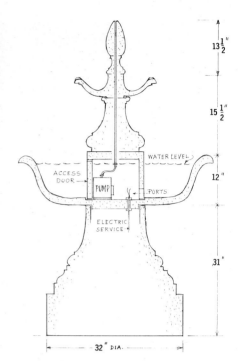

No. 4860
Stone Fountain. Self contained, see
sectional drawing. It is 6' high overall -
the top bowl is 20'' in diameter and the
bottom bowl is 48''. Diameter of the base
is 32''.

No. 0928. Stone fountain finial, 44'' high by
21'' largest diameter with 13'' square base.
Piped with bronze armature. Five jets. Pedestal and pool not included.

© 1974
Kenneth Lynch & Sons
Wilton, Conn. 06897

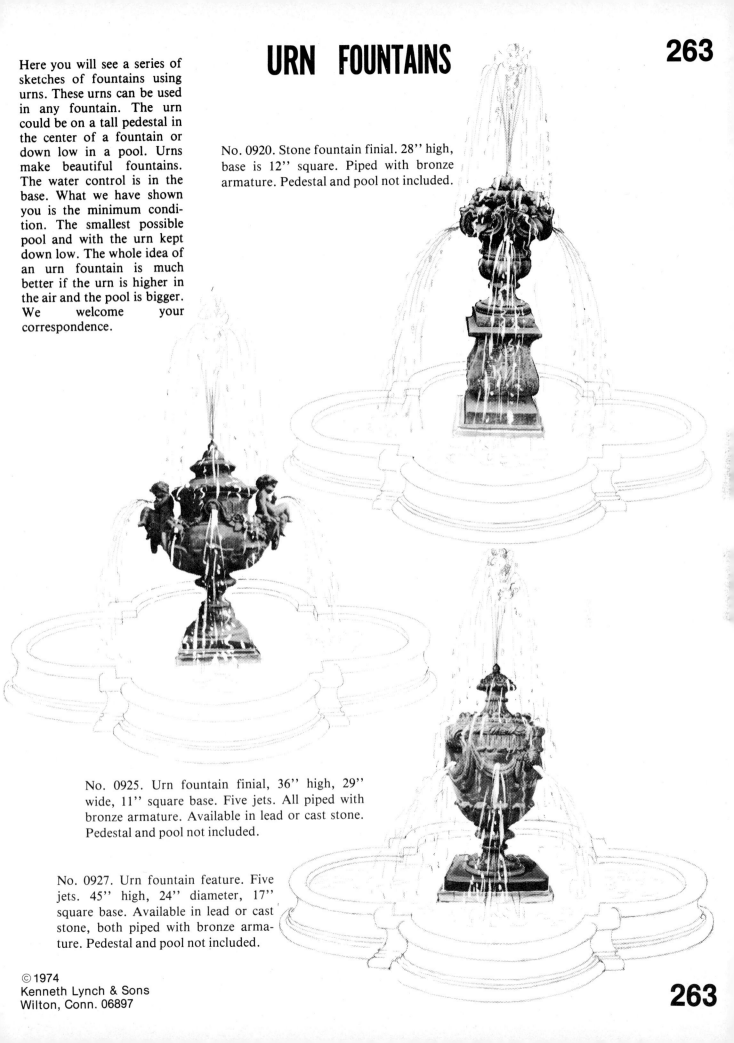

Here you will see a series of sketches of fountains using urns. These urns can be used in any fountain. The urn could be on a tall pedestal in the center of a fountain or down low in a pool. Urns make beautiful fountains. The water control is in the base. What we have shown you is the minimum condition. The smallest possible pool and with the urn kept down low. The whole idea of an urn fountain is much better if the urn is higher in the air and the pool is bigger. We welcome your correspondence.

No. 0920. Stone fountain finial. 28" high, base is 12" square. Piped with bronze armature. Pedestal and pool not included.

No. 0925. Urn fountain finial, 36" high, 29" wide, 11" square base. Five jets. All piped with bronze armature. Available in lead or cast stone. Pedestal and pool not included.

No. 0927. Urn fountain feature. Five jets. 45" high, 24" diameter, 17" square base. Available in lead or cast stone, both piped with bronze armature. Pedestal and pool not included.

Kenneth Lynch & Sons
Wilton, Conn. 06897

URN FOUNTAINS

Here you will see a series of sketches of fountains using urns. These urns can be used in any fountain. The urn could be on a tall pedestal in the center of a fountain or down low in a pool. Urns make beautiful fountains. The water control is in the base. What we have shown you is the minimum condition. The smallest possible pool and with the urn kept down low. The whole idea of an urn fountain is much better if the urn is higher in the air and the pool is bigger. We welcome your correspondence.

No. 0923. Stone fountain finial. 47" high, 23½" diameter, 18" round base. Piped with bronze armature.
Pedestal and pool not included.

No. 0930. Stone fountain finial. 48" high x 22" diameter. Piped with 5 bronze jets and bronze armature. Pedestal and pool not included.

No. 0922. Stone fountain finial. Piped with bronze armature. 47" high, 23" diameter, 13½" square base. Pedestal and pool not included.

© 1974.
Kenneth Lynch & Sons
Wilton, Conn. 06897

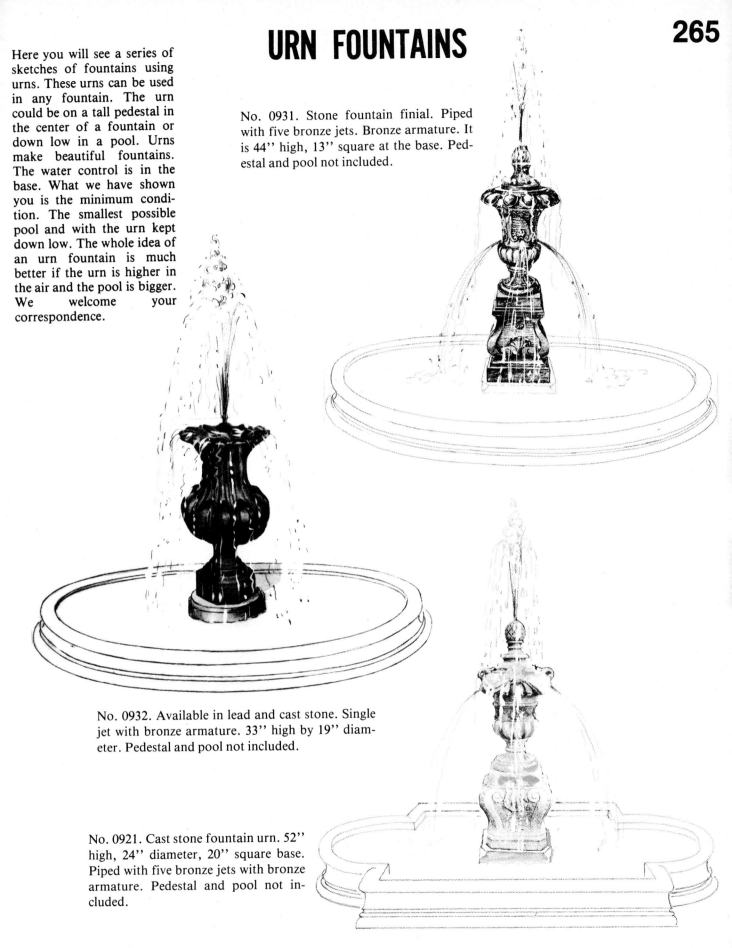

Here you will see a series of sketches of fountains using urns. These urns can be used in any fountain. The urn could be on a tall pedestal in the center of a fountain or down low in a pool. Urns make beautiful fountains. The water control is in the base. What we have shown you is the minimum condition. The smallest possible pool and with the urn kept down low. The whole idea of an urn fountain is much better if the urn is higher in the air and the pool is bigger. We welcome your correspondence.

No. 0931. Stone fountain finial. Piped with five bronze jets. Bronze armature. It is 44" high, 13" square at the base. Pedestal and pool not included.

No. 0932. Available in lead and cast stone. Single jet with bronze armature. 33" high by 19" diameter. Pedestal and pool not included.

No. 0921. Cast stone fountain urn. 52" high, 24" diameter, 20" square base. Piped with five bronze jets with bronze armature. Pedestal and pool not included.

URN FOUNTAINS

Here you will see a series of sketches of fountains using urns. These urns can be used in any fountain. The urn could be on a tall pedestal in the center of a fountain or down low in a pool. Urns make beautiful fountains. The water control is in the base. What we have shown you is the minimum condition. The smallest possible pool and with the urn kept down low. The whole idea of an urn fountain is much better if the urn is higher in the air and the pool is bigger. We welcome your correspondence.

No. 0924. Stone urn finial. 44" high, 12" square base. Five jets. Piped with bronze armature. Pedestal and pool not included.

No. 0929. Stone urn finial. 44" high by 21" diameter with a 13" square base. Piped with five bronze jets and bronze armature. Pedestal and pool not included.

No. 0926. Stone urn fountain finial. 48" high, 22" diameter, 17" square base. Piped with bronze armature, five jets. Pedestal and pool not included.

© 1974
Kenneth Lynch & Sons
Wilton, Conn. 06897

No. 4754. Stone pool using No. 275 curbing. The Urns are No. 113 and the Benches are No. 1100. As shown it is 10 ft. in diameter. The water play arrangement is specially designed for this pool as usual and it is made of bronze and contains recirculating pumps.

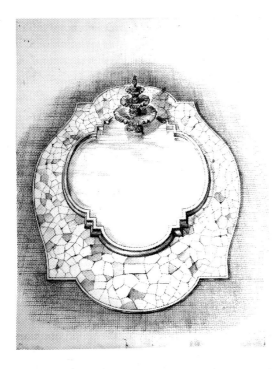

No. 1237. Stone Fountain arrangement perhaps inspired by one of the great fountains of Rome. This could be made to almost any size and entirely from stock parts which we have. The curbing would be No. 275 or one of the taller curbings depending upon the size fountain you were building. The stone shell cascade at the end could be any one of our cascade fountains. All completely self-contained.

© 1974.
Kenneth Lynch & Sons
Wilton, Conn. 06897

No. 4668. Large lead fountain composed of a group of dolphins around a central column supporting a large shell which in turn supports a boy with his dolphin squirting water. The supporting dolphins likewise all are involved with water play. This fountain can be made in a variety of sizes. The illustration shown is 7' 6" in diameter.

No. 4756. Lead and stone fountain using Figure No. 2407 which is 30½ in. high with stone bottom bowl No. 2106-A 25 in. in diameter. The cistern is 42 in. across the flat side and is 24 in. high. The overall height is 6 ft.

No. 1243. Stone Fountain. This can be used with an almost half-round pool or a fully-round pool. The pool is 8' wide and the fountain is 9' high. The shells are No. 2047, 60", 48", 26", and 20". They are fastened together with a bronze armature and a recirculating pump can be installed in the base.

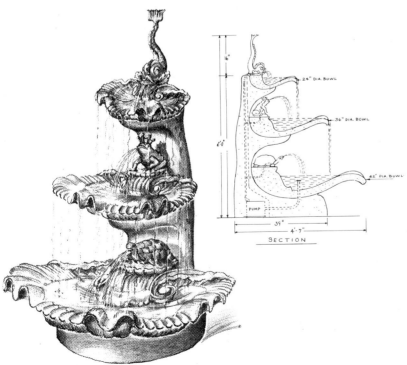

No. 5536. Stone Shell Fountain arrangement which can be used with or without the animals as shown on each level. It is 6 feet high to the top shell and whatever element is used above the top shell is an added height. As you can see in the sectional detail at the left, the cast stone column member supports the shells which are shipped separately and they are all piped in such a way so that the pump in the base recirculates the water. When used as shown it is intended to have a fine drip, not real active water because of the splash problem. If more water action is wanted then the entire device should be set in a larger pool at the base. Note shell sizes as shown on section drawings.

No. 4847 Sketch of fountain in Washington, D.C. The most interesting arrangement. The fountain is viewed from the top and being down below the walkway the wind does not get a chance to disturb the fountain. It is placed in the center of a turn-around for people coming to an apartment house and entering the garage. It is a most effective treatment. It is 22 ft. in diameter.

No. 4733 Pineapple fountain using lead pineapple with bronze leaves with base 46 in. high. The pool is 6 ft. in diameter and uses a No. 275 curbing.

© 1974.
Kenneth Lynch & Sons
Wilton, Conn. 06897

No. 4762. Beautiful stone fountain arrangement using Figure No. 1034 and Pool No. 1143. The base under the figure is No. 1092. The pool as shown is approximately 8 ft. wide by 6 ft. projection.

No. 4858. Fountain using No. 275 curbing and a No. 1092 Pedestal. The Figure is No. 1034 63 in. high. The pool is 8 ft. by 6 ft.   All Stone.

No. 4846 Fountain composed of No. 275 curbing 10 ft. in diameter. The lead jet device in the center is No. 524 and is 28 in. in diameter and it is all supported by a special pump case containing the recirculating pump.

No. 4849 Stone fountain arrangement composed of our No. 275 curbing 12 ft. in diameter with a 1076 pedestal and a special wrought lead leaf arrangement at the top. The pump case which is in the water is designed to receive the pump and activate the fountain.

No. 4851 Fountain stone composed of No. 275 pool curbing 8 ft. in diameter with 4076 floral spray arrangement mounted on a lead pump case it is 3 ft. high. Designed to go directly on the customers slab.

No. 4850 Stone and bronze fountain. The pool is 12 ft. in diameter and it is composed or our No. 275 curbing. There is a special lead pump case and the bronze her is our No. 4582. This part is 24 in. in diameter.

No. 4763. Pool 8 ft. in diameter with No. 275 curbing. The column is No. 327 and the bowls are No. 485 26 in. in diameter. The figure is No. 2889 the top. The other figures are No. 968 with Frog and No. 156.

No. 905. Triform fountain on antiqued cast stone lattice urn which acts as a water reservoir and contains recirculating pump. The figure in the top shell is available in either lead or bronze. The figure shown is Dancing Boy No. 2444 and the overall height is 43" The fountain diameter is 32". Other figures can be subsituted.

No. 4764. Special fountain composed of pool curbing No. 275 8 ft. in diameter. The column is No. 327 40 in. high. The Bowl is No. 695 26 in. in diameter. The figures shown are No. 968 with Frogs 14 in. high and No. 2890 22 in. high. This fountain requires a special cast base under the column. This also acts as the pump case for the recirculating pumps.

No. 1239. Stone Fountain with frog and lily pad arrangement. Under the frog is pump equipment. Lights can be added. The pool can be made from our No. 275 curbing sections and can be any shape.

© 1974.
Kenneth Lynch & Sons
Wilton, Conn. 06897

No. 4848 Stone fountain using Figure 963 and Bowl No. 2050 with No. 275 curbing. It is 72 in. wide by 42 in. projection.

No. 4742 - Fountain arrangement using eliments of No. 275 curbing 8' in diameter by 10" high. The inserted member is No. 1231 and the Pedestal is No. 148. It is all cast stone and can be piped for water.

No. 4760. Fountain composed of No. 275 curbing 16 ft. in diameter. The bowl is from our fountain No. 1075 and is 66 in. in diameter and the base likewise comes from that fountain. Directly under this base there is a cast in place pedestal for the fountain to sit on and contains the pumping arrangement.

No. 4731 Lead figure Judy with Flute 42½" high and a pool using No. 275 curbing 6'x3'.

© 1974.
Kenneth Lynch & Sons
Wilton, Conn. 06897

No. 1258. Stone and lead fountain. Over-all height is 11' and the suggested diameter is 16'; however, it could be greater. The stone bowl 897 Series is 5' diameter. The large lead bird #2892 at the top is a reproduction of a famous antique from the Nineteenth Century. It can be made completely self-contained with pump in the base.

No. 4741. An unusually beautiful stone fountain arrangement. The pool is 7' wide with a 3' 6" projection. However, a wider pool can be furnished. The figure is No. 1144 and the total height is 4' 6".

No. 4753 Beautiful lead fountain using a larger "Growing Things" No. 2911 in lead. The special pool is 6 ft. by 3 ft. 6. The curbing is No. 1503 by 8 in. high.

No. 4745. Special lead pool composed of No. 2360 lead border 6 in. high. It is 5 ft. x 3 ft. in size and is composed pedestal mounted with Figure No. 889 which is 36 in. high.

© 1974.
Kenneth Lynch & Sons
Wilton, Conn. 06897

No. 669. Recirculating Fountain, stone, 24 1/2" wide, 30" front to back, 30 1/2". high. NOTE: This is an exact duplicate of one we found in Italy where peasants cooled their feet and dogs had a drink.

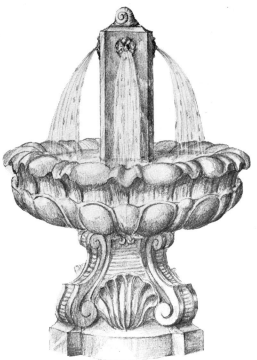

No. 1248. Stone Fountain, 40" diameter x 48" high. This is a completely self-contained fountain and can be used independently or in the center of another pool. All parts may be purchased separately.

No. 1246. Stone and lead Rain Tree Fountain, **40"** diameter x 63" high. The Rain Tree is composed of a bronze armature which not only carries the water but supports a tightly designed pattern of lead leaves over which the water falls. All parts may be purchased separately.

No. 1247. Stone and bronze Rain bush, 40" diameter x 63" high. NOTE: All parts may be purchased separately.

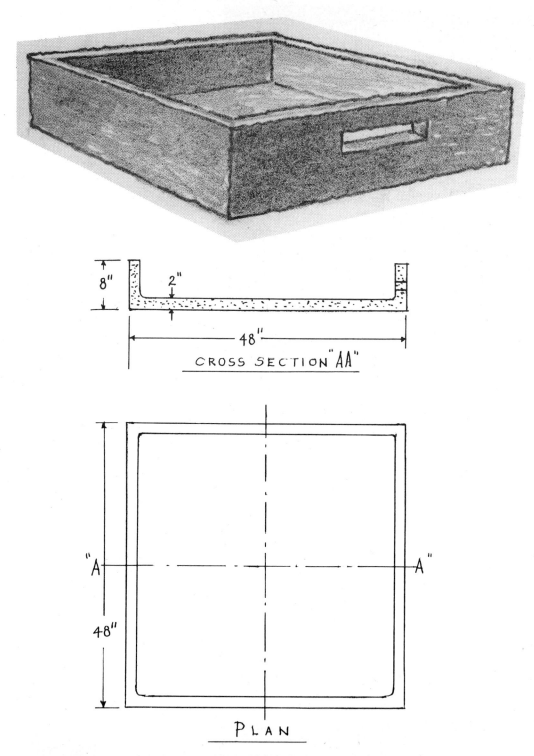

8"

2"

48"

CROSS SECTION "AA"

"A"   "A"

48"

PLAN

No. 5539. Cast Stone Caisson. These caissons which are 48" x 48" x 11" deep are furnished with any type of water opening the designer requests as the core for making the opening is inserted into the mold. By means of cleverly stacking and alternating these caissons, an infinite variety of fountain designs can be developed. The sketches which we offer are merely suggestions. Pumps of the proper capacity must be selected because with a design like this, vigorous flow of the water is very important, and without it all of the intent is lost. When we see your design, a system will be offered for tying these caissons together with stainless steel pins or hands.

© 1974.
Kenneth Lynch & Sons
Wilton, Conn. 06897

CAISSON FOUNTAINS

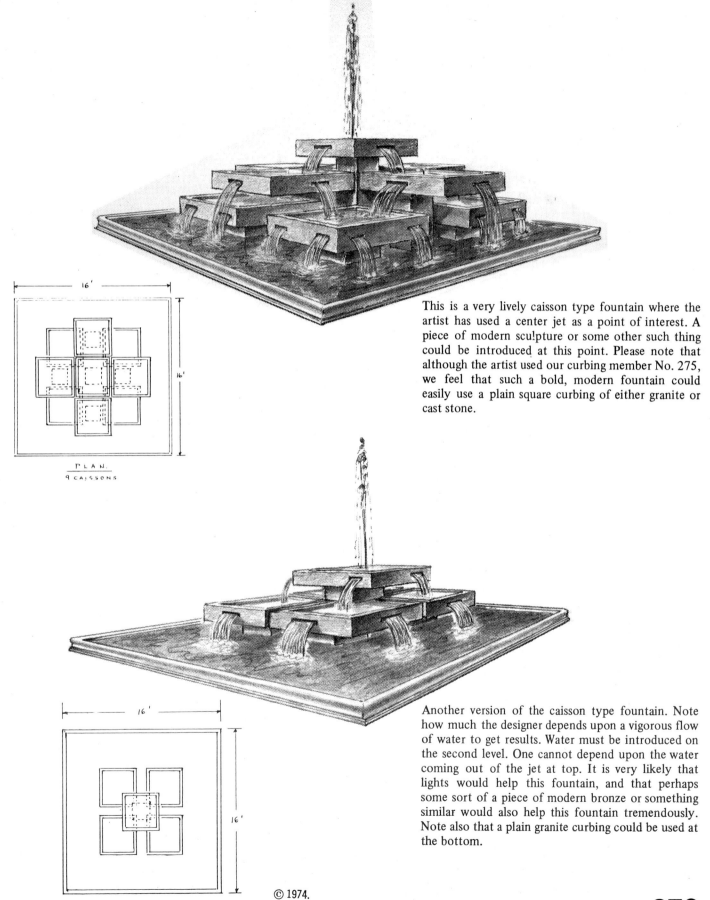

PLAN.
9 CAISSONS

This is a very lively caisson type fountain where the artist has used a center jet as a point of interest. A piece of modern sculpture or some other such thing could be introduced at this point. Please note that although the artist used our curbing member No. 275, we feel that such a bold, modern fountain could easily use a plain square curbing of either granite or cast stone.

PLAN
5 CAISSONS

Another version of the caisson type fountain. Note how much the designer depends upon a vigorous flow of water to get results. Water must be introduced on the second level. One cannot depend upon the water coming out of the jet at top. It is very likely that lights would help this fountain, and that perhaps some sort of a piece of modern bronze or something similar would also help this fountain tremendously. Note also that a plain granite curbing could be used at the bottom.

© 1974.
Kenneth Lynch & Sons
Wilton, Conn. 06897

No. 4746 Special fountain using No. 1143 Pool 62" wide with Figure No. 889 which is 36" high. The Pedestal is No. 1081 and is 15" high and 12" square at the top. Larger pools can also be used.

No. 1241. Stone Fountain. This fountain composition, using Geraldine Lewis's stone "OTTER GIRL" who has two shells in her hand which drip into the larger shell at the bottom, is indeed very beautiful. The whole composition is 64" high and 26" wide. NOTE: You will find the stone "OTTER GIRL" illustrated among the stone figures in this catalog and it comes in two separate sizes.

No. 93. Stone shell, 13 1/2" high, 28 1/2" dia.

Fountain assembly, composed of Column No. 130 - 30" high, Shell No. 131 - 24" x 26" with pump pocket and Figure No. 124 - 21" high - All cast stone.

© 1974

Kenneth Lynch & Sons Wilton, Conn. 06897

No. 605. Cascade Pool Fountain made in many sizes in both lead and Armorstone. Self-contained, with pump, etc. Usually furnished with iron armature which is movable horizontally many degrees to get the effects illustrated.

The lead bowls are 18'', 24'', 36'', or 48'' in diameter.

Armorstone bowls are 24'', 36'', 40'', 51'', and 66'' in diameter. Copper bowls are now available in all sizes.

NOTE: This arrangement has been with as few as three bowls and with as many as five bowls.

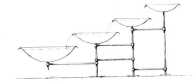

ALL JOINTS ADJUSTABLE 360. HORIZONTALLY

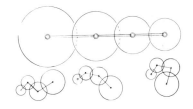

PLANS OF A FEW POSSIBLE ARRANGEMENTS.

No. 2925. Raintree and Pool, 5' diameter x 5' high. Pool is lead, tree is bronze. Recirculating pump in base.

No. 2915. Modern Cascade Fountain, 52'' diameter x 60'' high. Pool is all lead and the cascade is bronze. Recirculating pump in the base raises water to top whence it falls down from leaf to leaf.

No. 2923. Lead Pool with bronze cascade fountain, 52'' diameter x 66'' high. Recirculating pump in base.

No. 4888. Stone figure 21″ high seated on rock in pool approximately 4′ in diameter made of 1503 border with Deer No. 170.

No. 4895. "The Little Thinker." This delightful figure of a child in a pensive mood is the work of Geri Lewis-Amendola. It is 20″ high and is on a base 9″ x 11″. It is available in bronze, lead or stone.

No. 4882. Stone figure seated on shell watching water.

No. 4883. Stone figure 21″ high with Sundial arrangement.

No. 4887. Figure 21″ high with pool and Urn No. 4520-D. The Turtles are No. 2233.

No. 4889. Stone figure watching pool made of 605 bowls.

No. 4884. Composition showing figure No. 4895 with Frog in site in built pool.

No. 4890. Stone figure 21″ high watching Frog in rustic pool.

No. 4886. Stone figure 21″ high with pool 3′ in diameter made of No. 1503 border.

No. 4885. Figure in stone 21″ high with 36″ diameter pool made of No. 1503 lead border. The Duck is No. 2137.

© 1974.

Kenneth Lynch & Sons
Wilton, Conn. 06897

No. 4095. Hand wrought bronze cascade leaf form complete with pump in base; can be made to any size. Size shown here is 2'.

No. 4554. Copper Cattail Fountain Centerpiece. Pump can be located in base. 30" high over all, special sizes to order.

No. 4099. Bronze Fountain Ornament with stone base suitable for housing pump for recirculation of water; 18" diameter, but can be made in any other size.

No. 4868 Stone Japanese lantern seated on a simple block pedestal our No. 92 which is hollow and takes a recirculating pump as shown in accompanying cross sectional sketch. A gentle spray is produced out of the top of the lantern and is effective both ornamentally and as a bird bath. It can be wired for light and becomes a most attractive arrangement. The top is 17" diameter and the overall height of the lantern itself without the No. 92 base is approximately 18"

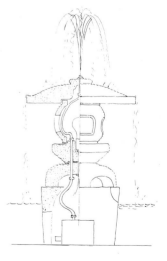

© 1974.
Kenneth Lynch & Sons
Wilton, Conn. 06897

No. 4749. Special composition using lead figure of Judy with Flute and King Frogs and a stone pump case. Overall height is 54 in.

No. 4729. Center fountain arrangement of lead. It is 54 in. high overall and the Piping Boy No. 2453 entertaining his friends the King Frogs. The pump case at the bottom is special and holds the pump necessary to operate the fountain. This would require at least 10 in. of water in the surrounding pool.

No. 4726. Fountain arrangement composed of the Otter Girl which can be had in either lead or stone. It is 5 ft. 6 in. high overall using the 41½ in. Otter Girl. The pump case is used to conceal the pumping mechanism.

© 1974.
Kenneth Lynch & Sons
Wilton, Conn. 06897

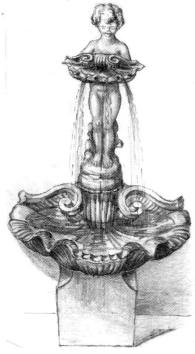

No. 4857. Stone fountain arrangement using
Pedestal No. 92 of stone Bowl No. 2050
36 in. The Figure No. 889 36 in. high.
This arrangement must go in a pool.

No. 4730. Beautiful fountain arrangement showing the Truesdale Fawn blowing water
into the shell which falls into another pool below. It is then recirculated. The pedestal
is stone No. 1092. The figure is No. 2644 and is 24 in. high. The shell is No. 2410-B
and is 21 in. in diameter. Note: It is not impossible that under very tight control conditions that this could be made recirculating, for it would have to necessarily restrict
the amount of water used.

No. 4750. Lead fountain using Figure No.
2103 22 in. high with a 2410-B bowl 21 in.
in diameter. The pump case at the bottom
is special and the whole device recirculates
from the cistern like pump case.

No. 4966. Frog Fountain made in lead. One of a
pair using King and Queen Frogs. The bowl is beautiful in its utter simplicity with a carefully detailed
molding at the top. These two attractive fountains
were 32'' in diameter.

© 1974.
Kenneth Lynch & Sons
Wilton, Conn. 06897

WALL FOUNTAINS

No. 4853. Special lead fountain using lead St. Francis Figure No. 118 30 in. tall. The bowls are No. 2414 30 in. and 16 in. size. The back is 64 in. x 48 in. The pool is 48 in. wide with a 24 in. projection. The border on the pool is No. 2364 which is 6½ in. high. It works with a recirculating pump.

No. 4758 Interesting stone corner fountain using our No. 275 curbing with St. Francis Figure No. 1261 36 in. high. The pool is 5 ft. x 3 ft.

No. 2062-B Lead wall bowl with Dolphins 23" wide x 28" high. The Bowl is No. 2414 30" wide with a pump case built in.

No. 4791 Lead wall fountain similar to our No. 2062-A. It is 32 in. wide by 36 in. high and has a 9 in. projection.

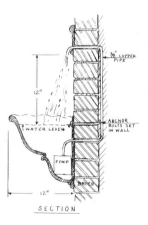

No. 4859 Lead wall bowl 27 in. wide using a shell as a jet. It can recirculate within itself as shown on the special sectional drawing accompanying it.

No. 4790 Wall fountain. This spill way is for water to go into a larger pool which can work from a recirculating pump at the bottom. The back is 28 in. wide. The overall height is 22 in. **All Lead.**

No. 4789 Delighful little wall fountain used as a recirculating and spill way to a larger pool below. It is similar to our No. 4548. It is 16 in. high and has a very shallow projection. **All Lead.**

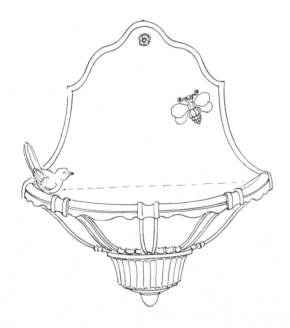

No. 4667. Lead Wall Fountain showing a variation of No. 4665. Note that the Sea Horses are removed and birds and bees are added. Other ornaments shown elsewhere in this catalog may be used on these fountains.

No. 4666. A variation of No. 4662, showing other ornament being used.

No. 1332. Stone Cascade Fountain
Assembly, 42" wide x 76" high. Completely self-contained. Urn is No. 1344;
Shells are No. 2047 series; Figure is
No. 2442.

No. 4520C. Two tiered Fountain.
Armorstone bowls that drip perfectly.
Large bowl 72" Dia. Small bowl 36" Dia.
All set into stone urns. This fountain is
completely self-contained with recirculating
pump. Can be used with top figure as
selected or a jet. Overall height without
pedestal 54". With pedestal you may add
about 20".

© 1974.
Kenneth Lynch & Sons
Wilton, Conn. 06897

No. 4520A. Stone Basketweave Urn with
Armorstone Fountain completely self-
contained and completely movable. 72"
diameter x 45" high. Other diameters
on special order.

No. 4520B. This is another view of this self-contained Fountain complete with recirculating pump and which comes in
two **sizes:** 36" diameter x 22" high plus the height of the figure selected and 72" diameter x 45" in height. This Fountain can have a spray ring squirting jets of water toward the
center, or it can have four jets squirting upward. Completely self-contained with pump in base.

No. 4748. Lead wall fountain using our extremely decorative Ram's Head No. 2071. The wass bowl is our No. 4584. It is 26'' high overall. The Ram's Head is, of course, 11'' x 16''. The Bowl itself is 27'' wide with a 12'' projection and it can carry a recirculating pump.

No. 291. Wall fountain using Plaque No. 291 and Bowl No. 4583. This is all lead and the pocket at the bottom takes a recirculating pump. It is 26'' high overall and is 19'' wide with an 8'' projection.

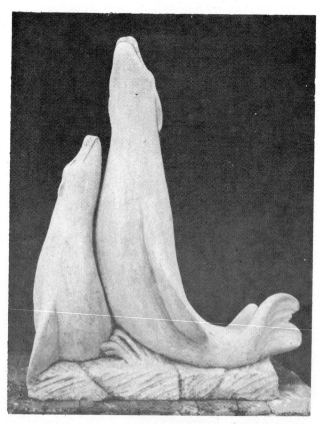

The above fountain was designed by Thomas Wood and Associates of Lexington, Kentucky. It shows imaginative use of our materials with old weathered boards as a background

No. 1029. Stone Seal fountain, 33'' high on 14'' x 21'' base, piped.

No. 4723. Special fountain using Fish No. 2470 and No. 507 Pedestal installed in brick pool built by others.

No. 4743 Lead fountain composed of No. 2025 Dolphin which is 15 in. high and a No. 1628 wall bowl 18 in. wide. The special lead bowl can either sit directly above a lower stone fountain on a special stone arrangement or brackets could be made. This is 3 ft. wide.

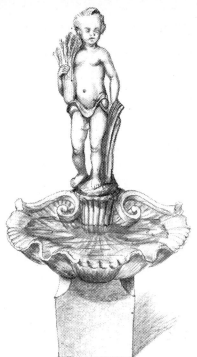

No. 4852. Fountain center device using No. 92 stone pedestal 12 in. x 12 in. with a No. 103 figure 35 in. high. The shell is No. 2050 36 in. in diameter. The recirculating pump can be arranged in the base.
All Stone.

No. 4821. Fountain arrangement using Shell No. 2050 and Dolphin No. 2025. It is 4′ high overall.
All Stone.

No. 4739. For sure a firm by the name of Lynch had to do a fountain with a Leprechaun involved. The informal pool is made of fiberglass and is quite shallow. The figures are No. 2005 furnished in lead. The Duck is No. 686 and the Turtle is No. 2459. The Frog is No. 2030. The Mushroom is 30 in. in diameter by 24 in. high. The whole device works with a recirculating pump and our little friend is sheltered from the water by staying under the mushroom.

© 1974.
Kenneth Lynch & Sons
Wilton, Conn. 06897

No. 4744. Stone fountain with lead wall plate and lead Lion Mask No. 2145. The back is 6 ft. wide and 6 ft. high. This is a very lively fountain indeed.

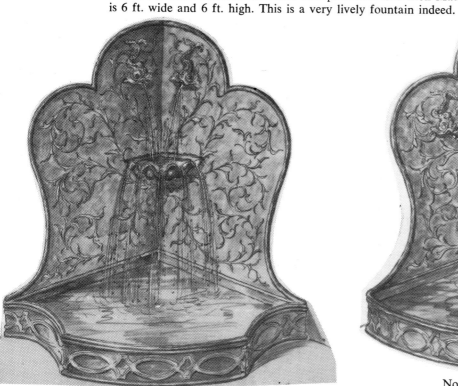

No. 4752. Lead fountain specially designed to fit in a corner. It uses No. 2360 border 6 in. high. The entire fountain is 4 ft. high and is 4 ft. across the front.

No. 4767. Special lead corner fountain 4 ft. high and 4 ft. across the front. The two highly decorative dolphins spouting water are from a special French collection and are reproduced by permission of the Craft Center Museum.

No. 4667. Lead Wall Fountain showing a variation of No. 4665. Note that the Sea Horses are removed and birds and bees are added. Other ornaments shown elsewhere in this catalog may be used on these fountains.

No. 4666. A variation of No. 4662, showing other ornament being used.

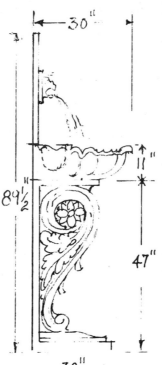

No. 6139. Stone fountain on bracket. A competely self-contained fountain 89½'' high overall. 30'' projection and 30'' width. The lion's head is in bronze and, of course, it can be replaced using any other mask or a figure can be placed directly at the back of the shell, a figure not to exceed 26'' in height. Total price in stone $1,400.00.

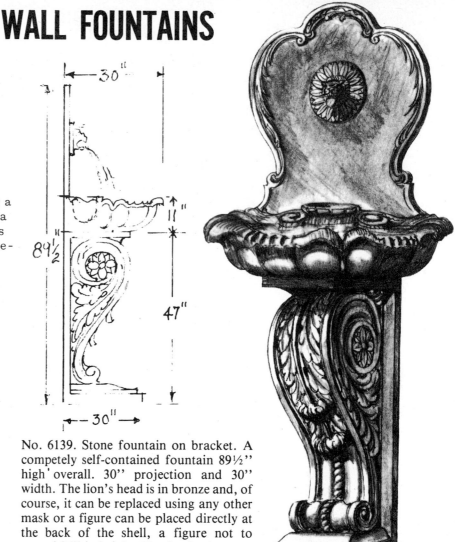

No. 2377. Wall basin bird bath, furnished in two sizes: 22'' wide and 28½'' wide, can also be furnished with rosette fill pipe centered near upper bird and spill over lips. Available in Lead or Bronze.

No. 291. Frog wall fountain, cast lead or cast stone, 14'' x 18'', by K. Sterling; a very beautiful piece, piped from flower.

© 1974.
Kenneth Lynch & Sons
Wilton, Conn. 06897

No. 895. Dancing Girl
Fountain Assembly, Lead
Figure, Stone Pool,
Wrought Iron Treillage.
Pool is 60'' wide, projection 36''. The Treillage is
7' high. Figure is piped,
water overflows from shell,
base of pedestal is a pump
case for recirculating
pump. Note: No. 889
Stone Figure at left may
also be used.

No. 894. Piping Boy
assembly. Piping Boy is
lead figure No. 2453 on a
30'' pedestal with pump
case at the bottom. Pool is
60'' wide with a 36'' projection. The wrought iron
treillage is seven feet tall.

No. 4854. Garden compo-
sition showing lead figure
No. 2206 43'' high using
Pedestal No. 507 18'' and
garden border edging No.
1503 with 6'' height. Is
laid out to be 6' wide by 3'
projection.

No. 2919. Lead Pool, 7' 3" wide, showing the double wall idea containing the water on the inside of the pool but giving a planting border all around the edge. The figure is, of course, "JUDY WITH FLUTE," 42" high.

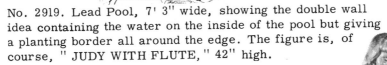

No. 2949. Lead Pineapple Fountain designed by Mr. William Maler of Richard Plumer, Inc., decorators. This is a very sophisticated use of forged bronze leaves with a verde antique finish on them. The pool is 42: wide and the pineapple with base is 46" high.

No. 2884. Lead Pool, 60" wide with recirculating pump and lead figure of "JUDY WITH FLUTE." Approximately 60" high overall.

© 1974.
Kenneth Lynch & Sons
Wilton, Conn. 06897

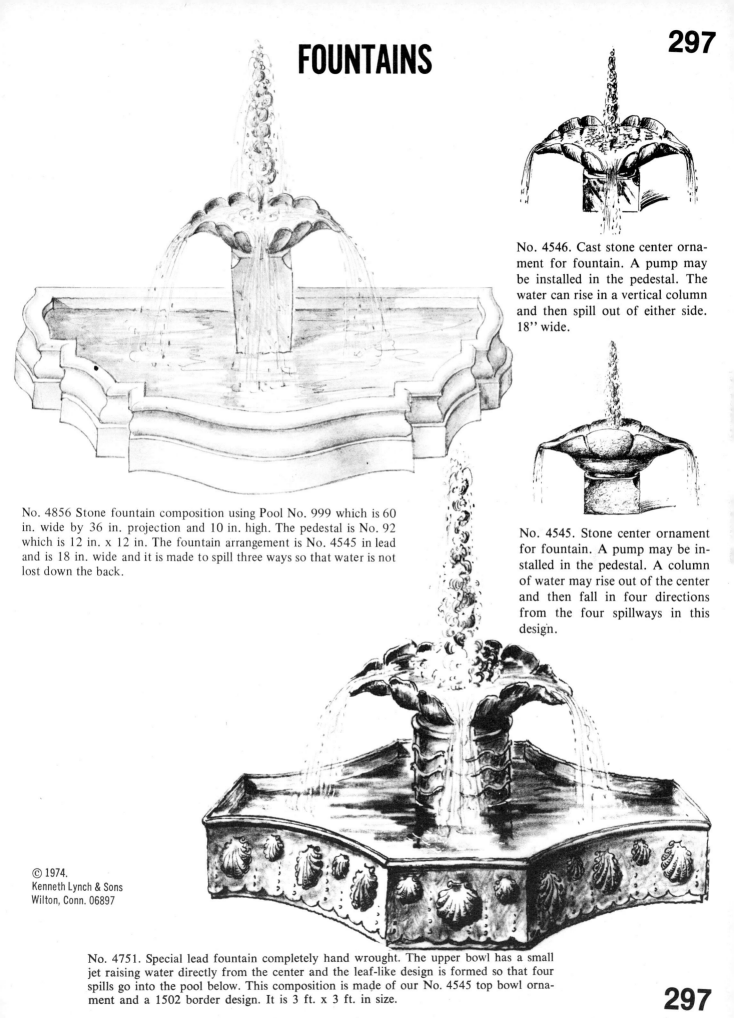

No. 4546. Cast stone center ornament for fountain. A pump may be installed in the pedestal. The water can rise in a vertical column and then spill out of either side. 18" wide.

No. 4545. Stone center ornament for fountain. A pump may be installed in the pedestal. A column of water may rise out of the center and then fall in four directions from the four spillways in this design.

No. 4856 Stone fountain composition using Pool No. 999 which is 60 in. wide by 36 in. projection and 10 in. high. The pedestal is No. 92 which is 12 in. x 12 in. The fountain arrangement is No. 4545 in lead and is 18 in. wide and it is made to spill three ways so that water is not lost down the back.

© 1974.
Kenneth Lynch & Sons
Wilton, Conn. 06897

No. 4751. Special lead fountain completely hand wrought. The upper bowl has a small jet raising water directly from the center and the leaf-like design is formed so that four spills go into the pool below. This composition is made of our No. 4545 top bowl ornament and a 1502 border design. It is 3 ft. x 3 ft. in size.

No. 4548. Lead Wall Fountain with small reeded edge. Furnished with spillways at front if so ordered. 16" wide x 16" high.

No. 2912. Hand wrought lead fountain bowl, 5' long. Gift of Mr. Keith Funston to Trinity College.

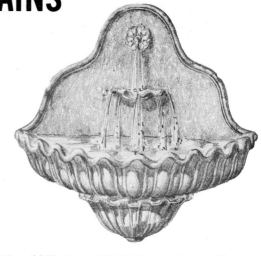

No. 4662. Lead Wall Fountain, self-contained recirculating, equipped with stainless steel A frame for ease of mounting, 27" wide.

No. 4664. Lead Wall Fountain, self-contained recirculating, equipped with stainless steel A frame for ease of mounting, 19" wide.

No. 4669. Lead Wall Fountain, self-contained recirculating, comes equipped with a stainless steel A frame on the back for ease of mounting, 31" wide.

No. 4663. Lead Wall Fountain, self-contained recirculating, equipped with stainless steel A frame for ease of mounting, 27" wide.

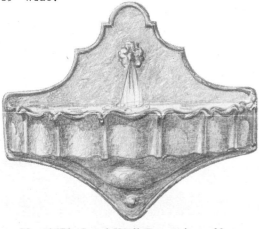

No. 4670. Lead Wall Fountain, self-contained recirculating, comes equipped with a stainless steel A frame on the back for ease of mounting. Available in two sizes, 22" wide and 28" wide.

No. 4665. A Lead Wall Fountain, self-contained recirculating, equipped with stainless steel A frame for ease of mounting, 19" wide.

No. 4549. Lead Fountain, 67" high x 64" wide at bottom, 27" projection

© 1974
Kenneth Lynch & Sons
Wilton, Conn. 06897

No. 660. Verde Antique Aluminum Wall Fountain, 24" wide x 36" high. Piping and pump incl'd.

No. 653. Verde Antique Aluminum Wall Fountain, 24" wide x 36" high. Piping and pump incl'd.

No. 2918. Lead Wall Fountain, 19" wide x 20" high. Recirculating pump is concealed in shell; water can come from jet near fiddle.

No. 2928. Lead and Wrought Iron Wall Fountain, 24" wide, 46" high. Recirculating pump is in lower shell, water spouts from upper shell.

No. 647. Wall Fountain, Verde Antique, Aluminum, 20" wide x 34" high. Pipe and pump incl.

No. 2373. Lead wall fountain, 25" high x 15" wide. Larger sizes available.

No. 2930. Lead Frog Wall Fountain, 18" wide x 36" high. Recirculating pump is in shell.

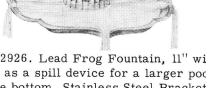

No. 2926. Lead Frog Fountain, 11" wide, used as a spill device for a larger pool at the bottom. Stainless Steel Bracket. Frog optional.

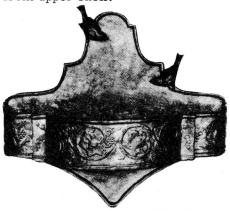

No. 2377. Lead, 22 or 28" wide.

© 1974
Kenneth Lynch & Sons
Wilton, Conn. 06897

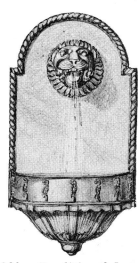

No. 2931. Traditional Lead Wall Fountain, 19" wide x 35 1/2" high. Recirculating pump is in shell.

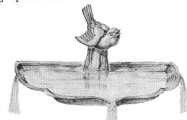

No. 2927. Lead Bird Fountain, 11" wide, used as a spill device for a larger pool at the bottom. Stainless Steel Bracket.

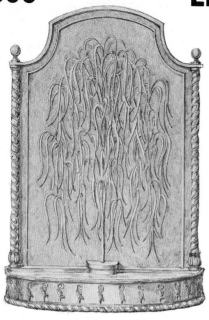

No. 2934. Lead Willow Tree Fountain, 6' 5" high x 4' 9" wide. The Willow tree is made of green bronze. Recirculating pump in pool.

No. 2935. Lead Raintree Fountain, 6' 6" high x 4' 6" wide. The Raintree is of bronze; pool and backplate is of lead reinforced with bronze. Recirculating pump in pool.

No. 2932. Lead Fountain, 4' 9" wide x 72" high, designed to sit on floor. Water is recirculated and spilled down over the vines into bottom pool. It is possible this could be furnished in Armorstone.

No. 2936. Lead Raintree Wall Fountain, 6'9" high x 4'8" wide. Tree is made of green bronze. Recirculating pump in pool.

No. 2933. Lead Floor Fountain, 5' 9" high x 3' 5" wide, suitable to receive any piece of statuary on its corbel. Recirculating pump in pool.

No. 2950. Lead Floor Fountain, 3' 7" wide x 5' 7" high. Recirculating pump in base.

No. 2929. Lead Wall Fountain, 4' 8" high, 31" wide. This can take a figure 24" to 30" high. Designed to receive a figure of your choice.

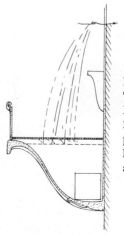

No. 2929. Section. Typical section through lead wall fountain No. 2929. This deep, one-piece, shell-like pool has an anti-splash screen and pump.

© 1974
Kenneth Lynch & Sons
Wilton, Conn. 06897

No. 4609. Fountain assembled from lead and Armorstone parts. The frog pool at bottom is 6' diameter. The crane pedestal is made of lead, as are the other parts of the fountain. completely self-contained with pump.

No. 2916. 30" diameter Lead Pool with 10" high figure, all lead. Pool is generally partly filled with stones for birds.

No. 2902.A. Lead Frog Fountain on swan base. Recirculating pump, 31" high x 30" dia.

No. 2922. Lead Fountain Figure with stone shell, 42" diameter, 32" high. The figure is 20" high and is a magniticent reproduction fo an English figure, late 19th century. See figure No. 1679. NOTE: The figure is beautifully modeled. There is a butterfly on the right arm; in the left hand there appears to be a torch. It is a helmeted figure and its real origin is unknown.

No. 2921. Fountain arrangement in lead with 30" diameter shell containing pump pocket. The figure is No. 1679 and is 20" high. Other figures may be substituted.

No. 4610. Lead Fountain with Armorstone pool, 6' diameter x 5' 10" high.

LEAD FOUNTAINS

No. 2917. Lead Column Fountain, 7' high; column 22" diameter; pool at bottom, 5' diameter. Recirculating pump is in base and water is pumped up to top whence it cascades from shell to shell.

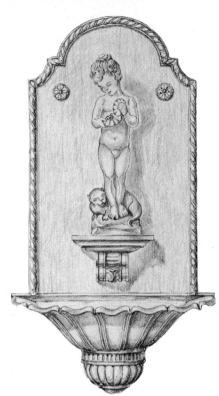

No. 1253. Armorstone wall fountain with very subtle greenish-brown patine similar to old bronze; however, it is not so heavy as lead or bronze, but looks very attractive. It is 23" wide by 40" high. The figure shown is the Otter Girl by G. Lewis, sculptress. However, this figure, which is No. 972 and which is shown in another part of the catalog, is only used to illustrate the use of this wall fountain and its built-in corbel. Any figure can be stood on this corbel. We invite you to select your own. Recirculating pump usuable.

No. 2843. Lead Frog Fountain with four frogs squirting toward the center, 16" high x 23" diameter.

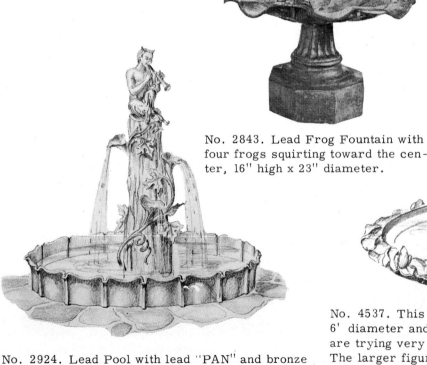

No. 2924. Lead Pool with lead "PAN" and bronze vine, 48" diameter x 48" high. Recirculating pump in base.

No. 4537. This is our famous lead "MUSICIANS" fountain, 6' diameter and 6' high. The little musicians at the top are trying very hard to outdo their brothers at the bottom. The larger figures are standing on a stone base which is used not only as a pedestal but also a s a pump case for the recirculating pump. Not only do all figures have water pipes, but the upper shells overflow as well.

No. 1250. Stone Fountain, using the famous "JUG BOY". This composition is 30" wide x 40" high and can be put up on a pedestal or just mounted on the wall. You will find a photograph of the "JUG BOY" in with our illustrations on stone figures.

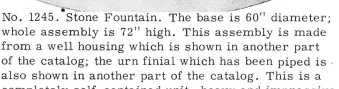

No. 1245. Stone Fountain. The base is 60" diameter; whole assembly is 72" high. This assembly is made from a well housing which is shown in another part of the catalog; the urn finial which has been piped is also shown in another part of the catalog. This is a completely self-contained unit, heavy and impressive.

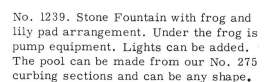

No. 1239. Stone Fountain with frog and lily pad arrangement. Under the frog is pump equipment. Lights can be added. The pool can be made from our No. 275 curbing sections and can be any shape.

No. 1251. Stone Tree Fountain 22 3/4"high with two birds, can be used with any pool. Made of #275 curbing. Lead birds may be selected from our Bird Section; pump can be installed in base of tree.

No. 695. Stone Fountain, 26" diameter x 30" high. Other figures may also be used.

© 1974.
Kenneth Lynch & Sons
Wilton, Conn. 06897

No. 4825. Special lead pool 4 ft. 6 in. in diameter made of lead border No. 1503. The Bird is No. 2248.

No. 4765. Lead Duck Fountain using our No. 2475 Duck with lead pool 6' in diameter made of 1503 border 8'' high.

©1974
Kenneth Lynch & Sons
Wilton, Conn. 06897

No. 1001. Stone Wall Bowl, 60'' wide x 30'' projection. NOTE: In the photograph to the right you see a beautiful assembly designed by Mr. Nelson Breed, A.I.A. At the very bottom is a basin made from our No. 275 curbing. Directly above this is a Wall Bowl No. 1001 which has a built-in counter balance into the wall. Directly above this is a lead Rosette which spills into the basin. Then directly above the Rosette is a cast stone wall capping with Pineapples No. 692 to the left and to the right.

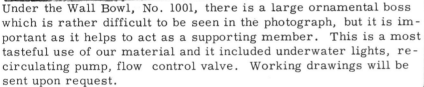

Under the Wall Bowl, No. 1001, there is a large ornamental boss which is rather difficult to be seen in the photograph, but it is important as it helps to act as a supporting member. This is a most tasteful use of our material and it included underwater lights, recirculating pump, flow control valve. Working drawings will be sent upon request.

No. 1006. Stone Shell, 29''wide, 24'' front to back, 13'' high.

No. 1110. Stone Shell on pedestal. 60'' diameter x 18'' high. NOTE: The base is 28'' square and 24'' high.

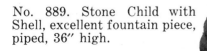

No. 889. Stone Child with Shell, excellent fountain piece, piped, 36'' high.

No. 1093. Stone shell fountain, 54'' wide.

© 1974.
Kenneth Lynch & Sons
Wilton, Conn. 06897

STONE SHELLS

The shells shown on this page are large and beautiful with good detail. This is the first time such shells have been offered. They come in two standard projections only: 6' or 8'; however, by assembling with sections, they can be made to almost any length in multiples of 2'. For horizontal use, they should always have a base as illustrated below. For vertical use, special arrangements are made depending upon job conditions.

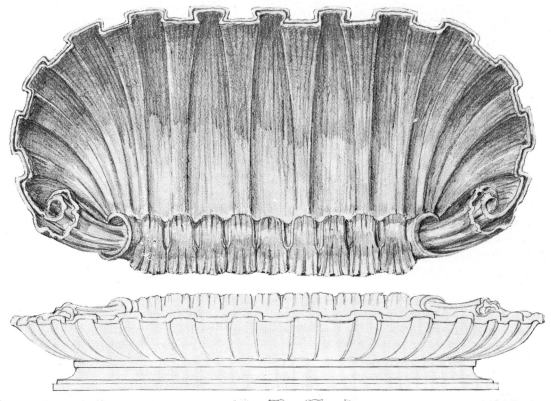

No. 1320. Armorstone shell, 6' projection x 14' wide. Made in segments as shown and can be given to you in any length. Very strong, indestructible stone finish. Can be used as main pool for fountain pump pocket can be added, etc.

No. 1207. Same as above except that it projects 8'.

NOTE: In all cases, the ends of the shell are 3' and the center sections, which are as many as you desire to use, are 2'. The only difference being that you can get an 8' projection; however, this makes an enormous difference.

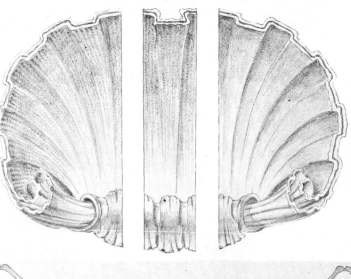

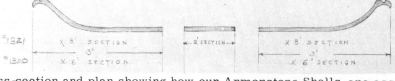

Cross-section and plan showing how our Armorstone Shells are assembled. For instance, the shell 1321 end segments are 8' projection x 4; wide. The center section is 2' wide x 8' projection. Of course, you can add as many center sections as you wish, thereby developing any length of shell you are able to assemble. We also show the dimensions of the cross-section of No. 1320. Each end would be 3' wide x 6' projection and the center member would be 2' wide x 6' projection. Combining assembly of any number of these units you can develop a very large shell.

© 1974.
Kenneth Lynch & Sons
Wilton, Conn. 06897

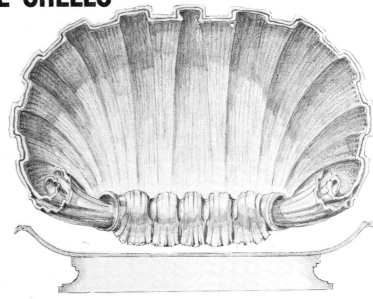

No. 1320. Armorstone development of the 6' diameter shell. This is a 6' projection x 10' wide. Drawn for scale illustration only.

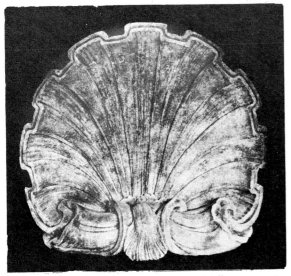

No. 1111. Stone Shell. 72" wide x 68" projection. (This is the only size furnished in stone). This is a most beautifully executed piece of work and is a fine addition to any fountain, pool or planting arrangement. Shown with this are other shells developed from this design which we offer in Armorstone, which is very strong but much lighter in weight. Can be used vertically or horizontally.

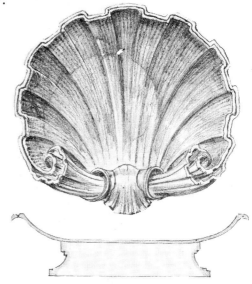

No. 1320. Armorstone Shell, with base 6' diameter.

No. 1321. Armorstone Shell, with base 8' diameter.

No. 2049. Cascade shell arrangement, furnished in either lead or stone. Size is 24" high x 36" wide.

No. 2048. Shell, furnished either in stone or lead. Size is 24" dia. x 8" high.

© 1974.
Kenneth Lynch & Sons
Wilton, Conn. 06897

SHELLS-BOWLS

No. 4958. Massive stone fountain bowl part of a circle as shown above and below. It is 77" wide x 50½" front to back x 22" high. Note: These are the bowl measurements only. The footed pedestal underneath is another piece and could be substituted for any similar piece to raise or lower the bowl. There are very few of these massive bowls available and this one comes with a drain and must be kept free of water in freezing winter weather. Made of cast stone.

© 1974.
Kenneth Lynch & Sons
Wilton, Conn. 06897

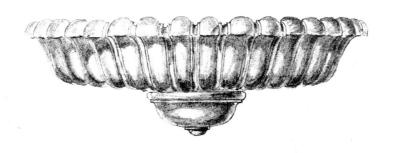

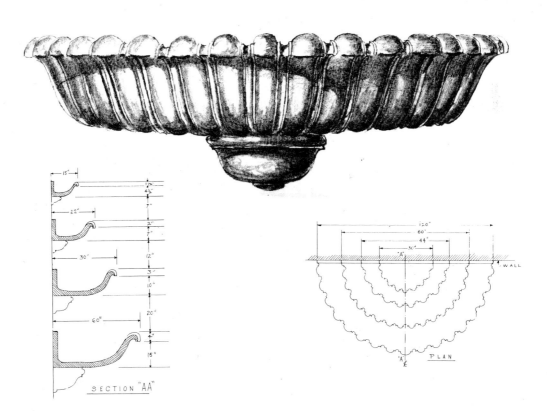

No. 4815.   These are special
armor stone bowls three sizes 120 in. wide, 60 in. wide, 44 in. wide and 30 in. wide.
Plan and section are shown and are used for cascade wall fountains.

No. 2133. Cascade shells, lead. Designed to be used singly or together. Made in many sizes. 9" wide x 5" projection, 12" wide x 7" projection, 15" wide x 8" projection and 24" wide x 13" projection.

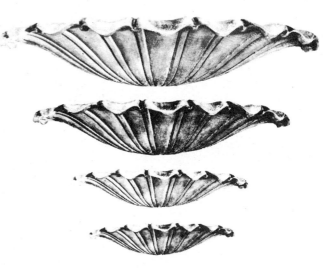

No. 2414. Wall Bowl, lead. 16" wide x 9½" projection. 20" wide x 13" projection. 24" wide x 15½" projection. 30" wide x 19" projection.

No. 2007. Unusually beautiful lead shell. 28" wide x 25" projection. 36" wide x 25" projection. 40" wide x 25" projection. NOTE: SEE NO. 2000-A IN BIRD BATH SECTION.

No. 2335A. Wall Bowl, 18" wide, 8" deep, 9" projection, will take re-circulating pump, cast lead.

No. 1628. Wall Bowl, Lead. 18" wide x 10" projection. 24" wide x 12" projection. 28" wide x 25" projection. 36" wide x 25" projection.

No. 2135. Wall Shell, cast lead or Armorstone ©, 27" wide, 10½" high, 12" projection. NOTE: ON SPECIAL ORDER AND IN LEAD ONLY THIS SHELL CAN BE MADE WIDER TO A MAXIMUM OF 36".

No. 2136. Wall Bowl, beautiful modeling, 31" wide, 8" high, 9" projection. NOTE: ON SPECIAL ORDER ALSO MADE 36" WIDE.

No. 2334A.Wall bowl, lead, 19" wide, 5½" high, 8" projection. NOTE: SMALL MEMBER CAN BE ADDED UNDERNEATH TO ACCOMODATE RE-CIRCULATING PUMP.

No. 4583. Lead Shell, 19" wide, 8" projection. Note pump pocket.

No. 2106A.Round lead basin. Two sizes: 15" dia., 25" in dia.

No. 2134. Round basin, 30" in dia. furnished full round, half round or quarter round. Lead only.

No. 2336. Lead overflow shell 13" wide by 9".

No. 2102. Lead shell. Three sizes: 15" dia. 21" dia. and 26" dia.

No. 4584. Lead Shell with pump pocket, 27" wide x 12" projection.

No. 2147. Lead shell. Three sizes: 9" x 7", 12" x 7", and 20½" x 13".

No. 370. Cast stone or cast lead (Lead number is 2021) Size: 20" wide, 15" projection, 5" high.

No. 2148. Furnished in lead, No. 2138 Bird, 5 1/2" high, lead.

STONE SHELLS

Shells can be stacked; they are stone; they have pump pockets (except the smaller sizes); they will drip; can have figures on them. They can be used as planters and are highly decorative.

No. 2047 series. Stone Shell, 26" wide.

Any of these shells, with a recirculating pump and decorative spouting figure make a fine simple fountain requiring no plumbing.

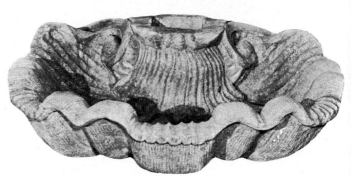

No. 2047 series. Stone Shell, 48" wide.

No. 2047 series. Stone Shell, 54" wide.

No. 2047 series. Stone Shell, 60" wide.

©1974
Kenneth Lynch & Sons
Wilton, Conn. 06897

STONE SHELLS

Note pump pocket for recirculating pump such as on pages 171, 172 & 173.

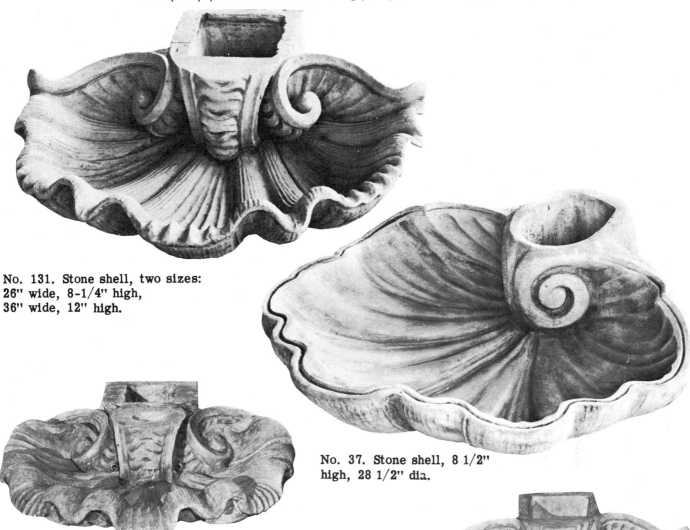

No. 131. Stone shell, two sizes:
26" wide, 8-1/4" high,
36" wide, 12" high.

No. 37. Stone shell, 8 1/2"
high, 28 1/2" dia.

No. 131 series. Stone Shell, 42" wide.

No. 131 series. Stone Shell, 26" wide.

No. 37. Stone shell, 8 1/2"
high, 28 1/2" dia.

© 1974
Kenneth Lynch & Sons
Wilton, Conn. 06897

MASKS
ALL PIPED
BRONZE, LEAD OR STONE

No. 2150. Lead Mask, 8'' x 10''.

No. 2169. Cat Tail Girl, 8½'' high, cast lead.

No. 2146. Roman Mask, cast lead, 10'' high.

No. 2145. Lion Mask, cast, stone or lead, 12-3/4'' dia. by J. Kuthmayer.

No. 4612. Lion Head, 11 1/2'' wide x 10 1/2'' high. Drilled for water. Lead or bronze.

No. 1202. Stone Lion Mask. Very impressive, 23'' wide x 33'' high, 6'' projection. Can be drilled for water.

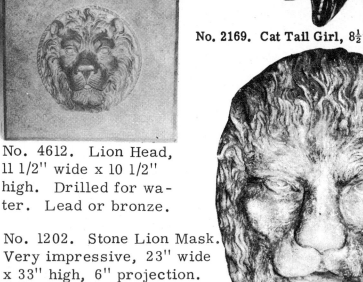

No. 2144. Lion Mask by Joseph Kuthmayer, furnished in bronze, lead, or stone. 6 1/2'' dia.

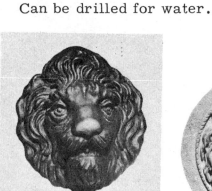

No. 2878. Lions Head, 10'' x 11'' x 5'' projection. Old Roman model.

No. 2105. Lion Mask, lead or stone, 8 1/2'' dia.

No. 4613. Lion Head in three sizes: 8'' x 7 1/4'', 6 1/2'' x 5 3/4'' and 4 3/4'' x 4''. Available in lead or bronze.

LIONS MASKS
ALL PIPED

Of all the masks the lion mask is the most popular. Many designers have masks which they want reproduced and we certainly do this with no trouble in bronze, lead or stone.

No. 4912 Forged Copper Lion Mask.

These forged copper lion masks are available in many sizes as listed below. Note that these sizes are approximate within the half inch and modelings vary from piece to piece. Send for book 7474 for more exact information.

| 6" x 6" | 6½" x 6½" | 7" x 7" | 8" x 9" | 9" x 10" |
| 10" x 12" | 13" x 14" | 17" x 22" | 9" x 11" | |

Note: The material is forged sheet copper.

No. 4968. Lion Mask. Bronze, Lead, or Cast Stone. 20" high overall, 14" wide, 11" projection. Piped. Modeled by architect for special project.

No. 462. Lion Head, cast stone, 13" x 14".

No. 5510. Stone Lion Mask. Drilled for water pipe. Made of extra thick stone for structural reasons. The Lion Mask without the stone around the outer edge is 16" high x 13½" wide x 6" thick. If we leave the stone around the outer edge, it is 19½" high x 16 3/4" wide x 6½" thick. This latter way is the way the old Roman's made their fountains, and, of course, it is stronger and better.

No. 4676. Lion's Head. Available in Cast Stone, Lead, or Bronze. Measures 13" wide by 16" high by 6½" projection. Available with mounting back (not shown). Other sizes available upon request.

24" wide x 36" high x 6" projection,
18" wide x 30" high x 5" projection,
6" wide x 10" high x 4" projection.

No. 5422. Lion's Head. 19" high, 14" wide and 9" projection. In bronze, lead or stone.

See price list for illustrations of additional lions heads.

MASKS
ALL PIPED
BRONZE, LEAD OR STONE

No. 6098. Hippo Head, F. Konopka, SC. cast stone, marvellously impressive detail. Good water flow. Size 18″ long, 14″ wide, 14″ high. Pipe size to suit.

No. 5563. This is the much revered "Father Thames Mask". The orifice on this mask gives you a broad jet and requires a slightly larger feedline than normally would go to a mask. One can see these masks on the banks of the Thames squirting water as they have done for so many years. Available in bronze, lead and stone. Size 12″ x 15″ with a 3″ projection.

No. 1426 Cast Stone 15″ long, 10″ wide

No. 1427 Cast stone 16″ high, 8½″ wide

No. 6007. Stone Mask, piped for water. Original found in back garden in Florence. Easily affixed to wall. Size 9½″ x 7½″. Projection 5″.

©1974
Kenneth Lynch & Sons
Wilton, Conn. 06897

No. 2071. Garlanded Rams Head Mask in cast lead, 11'' x 16''.

No. 1337. Rams Head, antique reproduction, 14'' wide x 8 1/2'' high, piped. Available in bronze, lead or stone.

No. 2157. Rams Head, cast lead, 11½'' x 11''. NOTE: This will be furnished in cast stone on special order.

No. 2739. Rams Head Mask, 9½'' in dia., cast lead.

No. 2858. Lead Rams Head, very good detail. 14'' high x 16½'' wide at horns. Piped.

No. 1598. Mask, Lead or Stone. When made in Stone, is on round plaque. Piped 6'' x 8''.

No. 806 Zodiac stone water spouts. Two sizes.
7'' x 7''
5'' x 5''

No. 3075 24'' x 25'' copper.

No. 3075A 19'' x 25'' copper.

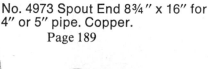

No. 4973 Spout End 8¾'' x 16'' for 4'' or 5'' pipe. Copper.
Page 189

No. 4972 Spout End 6'' x 7'' for 1'' or 1½'' pipe. Copper.

No. 806 Zodiacs available in bronze, lead and stone piped for water. maximum ¾'' tube. These strongly modeled Zodiacs set in a bold rope moulding make an ideal water spout.

© 1974.
Kenneth Lynch & Sons
Wilton, Conn. 06897

These pool fillers are actually pipe covers and seats combined. We have had many requests for these. Other designs can be made and we would welcome your ideas as always.

No. 4982. Stone pool filler cover with lead Zodiac as selected by you. Size is as shown on the accompanying section. If you wanted to have it cemented permanently in place it is easy enough to do this as there should be plenty of room for this seat type filler cover to fit around any existing pipe.

No. 1201. Stone Cherub riding wave. Piped up to 1" for filling pool or fountain effect. 2' high.

No. 4983. Cast stone pool filler cover which also acts as a seat. The sizes are shown in the sectional detail. The area away from the pool can be ornamented with a mask, a rosette or any similar ornament selected from our collection.

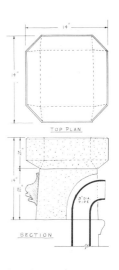

Kenneth Lynch & Sons
Wilton, Conn. 06897

No. 6097. Great Lobster pool filler. This remarkable piece of work is a welcome addition to our tremendous collection. The sizes are 34" long x 22" wide x 17" high. The base if 26" x 15". It can be piped for water.

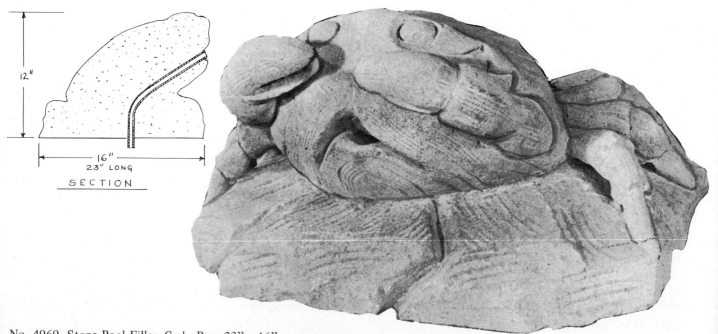

12"

16"
23" LONG
SECTION

No. 4969. Stone Pool Filler. Crab. Base 23" x 16" x 12" high. It will take a large pipe. The detail is exceptionally good and very carefully modeled.

© 1974
Kenneth Lynch & Sons
Wilton, Conn. 06897

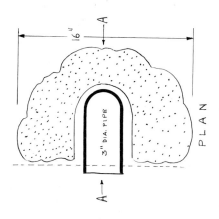

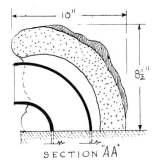

SECTION "AA"

No. 4985. Cast stone pool filler with large orifice. This was used to cover pipes which recirculate the water into the pool. They can be cemented around your pipes in any way you wish. This is a matter of judgment in the field. These are strong enough to be used for seats and the size is as shown in the sectional views. No piping is included. These are seat type covers.

No. 94. Cast Stone Goat. Very strong, wonderful modeling. 28" high on a base 30" long x 18" wide. This is an ideal pool filler and can be piped to order as large at ¾"

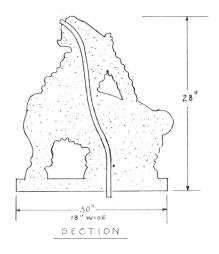

SECTION

No. 94. Sectional drawing showing how it is piped.

No. 6098. Hippo Head,   cast stone, marvellously impressive detail. Good water flow. Size 18″ long, 14″ wide, 14″ high. Pipe size to suit.

PUMP CASE PEDESTALS

No. 4959 - Pump case and fountain arrangement. This pump case acts as a pedestal for almost any statue or other ornamental piece. It is 17" in diameter and 16" high. It has four lead shells on the outside all which are controlled individually with small valves from the inside and the recirculating water is pumped directly to these shells. You can get as much water flow or as little as you wish and all of this adjusting is easily done. This is incredibly simple and you can get a real musical fountain effect from it or a very quiet fountain effect. Make up water for whatever pool you are using must be kept at a 10" depth at least so that the pump will not run hot as the pump being submerged depends upon the water to keep it cool. The top member is of cast stone. This closes off the access hole and gives you a firm place to seat a central ornament as shown in the accompanying sketch. Lights can be placed in the water and that would be an added feature. The whole pump case acts as a pedestal as well as a fountain.

No. 4811. Portable water reservoir for fountain. Any shell or figure can be installed on top of such a reservoir and this has the advantage of having a special tray around the bottom which is permanently mounted on a dolly so that it can be moved to a different location. The shell, or whatever arrangement one has on the top, can be made to be completely recirculating and likwise can be removable for transit. The fountain fits down inside the lead tank and is accessable from the rear. Sizes optional, but generally not over 24".

No. 4811. Lead water Reservoir for fountain showing method of filling in rear spout. This reservoir can be used with almost any arrangement above it and can have a dolly under it for easy removable. This is generally made about 18" in diameter to whatever height the customer orders and whatever arrangement is wanted on the top, such as a shell figure, etc. can be accomplished.

No. 4747. Special fountain using water reservoir No. 4811. It is all lead and operates as shown on the accompanying sectional drawing. Other designs can be worked up by the customer. The shell is No. 2410-B 21 in. in diameter. The Squirrel is No. 2140. It is 40 in. high overall. The study of the sectional drawing shown herewith showing exactly how it operates.

No. 3572. CAST STONE RECTANGULAR. 25½" x 21½" Base, 7½" High.

No. 3580. A BASIC STYLE. 10½" Diameter top, 16" Diameter bottom, 5¼" High.

No. 3563. CAST STONE RECTANGULAR. 18½" x 14½" Base, 4½" High.

No. 3557. SIMPLE, CLASSIC STYLE. 28" overall diameter, 6" Thick, 24" Diameter top, 18½" Bottom.

No. 3562. FUNCTIONAL CAST STONE ROUND ADAPTOR. 16½" Diameter top, 11" Diameter bottom, 8" High.

No. 3573. VERSATILE, GRACEFUL. 16¼" Diameter top, 19¾" Diameter bottom, 3¾" High.

No. 3564. CAST STONE SQUARE. 18½ x 18½" Base, 3" High.

No. 3560. CAST STONE RECTANGULAR. 29" x 16" Base, 4" High.

No. 3561. VERSATILE CAST STONE ADAPTOR. 17" Dia. top, 19" Dia. bottom, 5" High.

No. 3556. SOLID STYLE. 20" Overall diameter, 3" Thick, 17½" Diameter top, 16½" Diameter bottom.

© 1974.
Kenneth Lynch & Sons
Wilton, Conn. 06897

STONE ADAPTORS

These cast stone pedestal adaptors are designed to be used either side up, depending on pedestal and/or subject dimension. Measurements are for adaptors as pictured.

SQUARE PEDESTAL ADAPTORS

No. 1210. 17 3/4'' sq x 5'' thick.

No. 1211. 17'' sq x 7'' thick.

No. 1212. 15 3/4'' sq. x 4'' thick.

No. 1213. 13 1/2'' sq. x 3'' thick.

No. 1214. 13 1/2'' sq. x 2 1/4'' thick.

ROUND PEDESTAL ADAPTORS

No. 1215. 17'' dia. x 8'' high.

No. 1216. 17'' dia. x 5 1/2'' high.

No. 1217. 15 1/2'' dia. x 2 3/4 high.

No. 1218. 13'' dia. x 4'' high.

No. 1219. 10'' dia. x 2 1/2'' high.

No. 1220. 8'' dia. x 4'' high.

No. 500 All Sizes

No. 222.
4-1/2'' high, 9-1/2'' dia. or 6'' high, 10-1/2'' dia.

No. 178. 5½'' high, 11½'' long, 14'' wide.

No. 458. Stone, 10'' x 10'' x 6''.

No. 262. Heighth 5'', bottom dia. 9'', top dia. 8''.

© 1974.
Kenneth Lynch & Sons
Wilton, Conn. 06897

No. 3359. PRACTICAL, NON-OBTRUSIVE. 14" Top diameter, 10" Bottom diameter, 5" Thick.

No. 3571. RECTANGULAR STYLE. 25½" x 21½" Base, 4" Thick.

No. 3370. EXCELLENT PLATFORM ESPECIALLY WITH A SUNDIAL. 14" Overall diameter top, 13½" Platform diameter top, 17½" Overall diameter bottom.

No. 455. 13½" by 13½" by 8½".

No. 3558. STONE ADAPTOR. 10½" Diameter top, 14" Diameter bottom, 5" High. (Reversible).

No. 979. USEFUL AS AN ADAPTOR OR SIMPLY AS A BASE. 3" Diameter top, 9½" Diameter bottom, 5" Thick.

No. 152. 15½" sq. base by 7½" high.

No. 3555. CAST STONE CLASSIC. 17" x 17" Base, 16½" Diameter top, 16½" High overall.

No. 1002. Stone Block, 7" high x 11" diameter, top diameter 9".

© 1974.
Kenneth Lynch & Sons
Wilton, Conn. 06897

STONE PEDESTAL PARTS

No. 92. English Block Base. The most practical base of all. Furnished in several sizes as follows:
    10'' x 10'' x 10'' high,
    10'' x 10'' x 18'' high,
    12'' x 12'' x 12'' high,
    14'' x 14'' x 14'' high.
NOTE: Other sizes made on special order at very modest prices.

No. 498. Special Block, 14'' x 14'' with shells which can be piped.

No. 978. Stone, 8'' high x 15'' diameter at bottom and 10'' diameter at top.

No. 12. Pump case, stone, 9-3/4'' high, 14 1/4'' dia.

No. 249. Hollow pump case, 6 1/4'' high, bottom 13'' x 11''. Top 11'' x 9''.

No. 243. Cast stone, 7'' high, 9 1/4'' in dia.

No. 501.
All Sizes

No. 503.
All Sizes

No. 24. Octagonal Base, 9'' high, 12'' dia.

No. 1278. Plain Stone Pedestals, furnished in almost any size. These two shown are 15 1/2'' high and 27 1/2'' high.

No. 1284. Stone Stump, 30'' high x 24'' diameter.

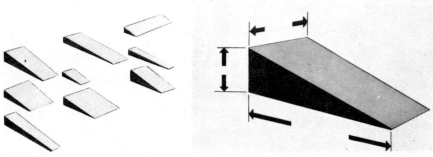

No. 499. Lead wedges. We furnish lead wedges in any size. Excellent for blocking statuary and elements. May be purchased assorted. Sizes: 1/4'' to 0'', 3/8'' to 1/8'', 1/2'' to 1/4'', 5/8'' to 3/8'', 3/4'' to 1/2''.

© 1974
Kenneth Lynch & Sons
Wilton, Conn. 06897

PEDESTALS

No. 3549. Cast stone Leaf Form Knode-type base. It is 13½" high with an 8" diameter top and 11" diameter bottom. Suitable for use as a pedestal or a knode member.

No. 3577. CLASSIC STYLE PEDESTAL. 11¼" Dia. top, 18" Dia. bottom, 28½" Height.

No. 587. LEAF QUADRI-FORM SCROLL PEDESTAL. Cast stone, 14¼" High, 17" Across base, 9" across top.

No. 3578. Cast stone pedestal member, linenfold design at the neck. It is 17½" high with a 24" square base. It is 14½" in diameter at the top and the small fitter member shown at the top can be removed.

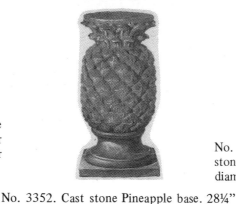

No. 3352. Cast stone Pineapple base. 28¼" high with a 12" diameter top. The actual base is 13½" x 13½" square. The modeling is extra strong in detail. This base can be used to support a figure, a table top or for any other use.

No. 3582. Pedestal of cast stone with inset panels. 34" high, 18" square at the top, 23" square at the bottom. It is decorative and very appropriate for use under a sundial or a piece of statuary. It can be further elevated by a block under the base.

No. 3550. CAST STONE DECORATIVE PEDESTAL. 10½" Diameter top, 15" Diameter bottom, 15½" High.

No. 3567. Elegant leaf design base made of cast stone, 26" high, 14" top diameter, 27" bottom diameter. Very stable.

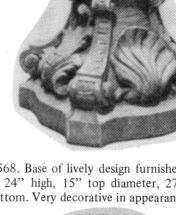

No. 3568. Base of lively design furnished in cast stone, 24" high, 15" top diameter, 27" across the bottom. Very decorative in appearance.

No. 3566. Turned and carved pedestal of generous proportions. It is furnished in cast stone. 30" high, 16" diameter at the top and 26" diameter at the bottom.

No. 3551. GRACEFULLY STYLED CAST STONE PEDESTAL. Seven sizes available.

Hgt.	Top Dia.	Bottom Dia.
11½"	4½"	5½"
13¾"	5¾"	6"
15 5/8"	5½"	6¼"
17¾"	6½"	7 1/8"
19 5/8"	7"	7 1/8"
21½"	7¾"	8¾"
23½"	8 3/8"	9 3/8"

PEDESTALS

No. 1011. Stone Pedestal, 20" high x 12" square top.

No. 767. Florentine Base. 34" high, 14" wide, 14½" deep.

No. 193. 36 inches high with 13 inch top.

No. 583. Wall pedestal, cast stone, 36" high, 14" sq. top.

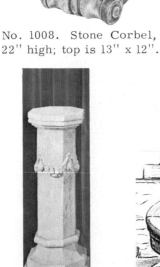

No. 1008. Stone Corbel, 22" high; top is 13" x 12".

No. 395. Stone Pedestal 43" high.

No. 1083. Stone pedestal, 20" high, 12" square at bottom, 9 1/2" square at top.

No. 4672. Stone Pedestal on raised platform. Very good design to mount sundial in public parks, etc. Bottom step is 60" diameter. Overall height, including pedestal, is 48". The top diameter of the pedestal is 12".

© 1974.
Kenneth Lynch & Sons
Wilton, Conn. 06897

PEDESTALS

No. 577. Pedestal, very rich, your choice. 39" high, Cast Stone.

**No. 73.
Height -
34 1/2
inches
Top 11 1/2".**

No. 362.
Stone Pedestal, 30 1/2"
high x 17"
wide.

**No. 327.
Height -
40 inches
Top 14" sq.**

No. 1317. Special Stone Pedestal with lead overlay. Stone and lead look very well together. This is 24" high x 16" sq.

**No. 373.
Height -
30 inches
Top 11 1/2".**

**No. 91.
Two sizes
24 1/2" high
14 1/2" top;
35" high
16" top.**

No. 194.
Height -
41 inches
Top 8 1/2".

No. 232.
Stone pedestal, 24 1/2"
high x 12"
diameter top.

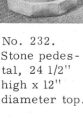

**No. 260.
Stone Pedestal, 35" high
x 12" top.**

No. 119.
Stone Pedestal, 24" high
x 10 1/2" top.
NOTE: The
sundial is No.
1505, bronze.

**No. 253.
27 inches
high with
18 inches
wide.**

No. 126.
Stone Pedestal, 30 1/2"
high, 10" dia.
Top. NOTE:
Dial is No.
1505.

PEDESTALS

No. 261. Pedestal, cast stone. Top 9" x 9", base 12" x 12", 26" high.

No. 960. Stone, 30" high x 12" square top also 20" high x21" square top. 20" high x 18" square top.

No. 1020. Stone Pedestal, 24" high x 13" square, top and bottom.

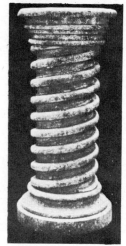

No. 1102. Stone pedestal furnished in four sizes; 24" high x 12" dia. 30" high x 14" dia. 36" high x 16" dia. 36" high x 18" dia.

No. 1091. Stone pedestal, 18" diameter at bottom, 11" diameter at top, 8" high.

No. 506. Stone Pedestal with garland, 24" high x 14 1/2" square at the top x 17" square at the bottom.

No. 506 — A. Stone pedestal, 24" high x 20" square.

No. 507. Reproduction cast stone base, 18" high.

© 1974
Kenneth Lynch & Sons
Wilton, Conn. 06897

330

No. 1347. Stone Pedestal, 16" high, 13 1/2" x 22" top.

No. 1092. Stone pedestal, 18" high, 26" square base, 19" square at top.

© 1974.
Kenneth Lynch & Sons
Wilton, Conn. 06897

No. 1021. Stone pedestal by Walter Schwartz, Miami. 25'' high, 11'' top diameter, 12'' bottom diameter.

No. 1076. Stone pedestal, 25 1/2'' high, 18'' diameter at bottom, 8 1/2'' diameter at top.

No. 1064. Stone pedestal, 34'' high, 22'' square at base, 18'' square at top.

No. 1077. Stone pedestal available in three sizes:
24'' high x 16'' dia.
28'' high x 18'' dia.
38'' high x 18'' dia.

No. 1099. Stone pedestal, 30'' long, 24'' high 16'' wide.

No. 1013. Stone Pedestal, 18'' high x 12'' square top.

No. 1069. Stone pedestal, 30'' high, 14'' diameter at top, 14'' diameter at bottom.

No. 1012. Stone Pedestal, 15'' high x 12'' square top.

No. 1326. Stone, 36'' high 11'' diameter.

No. 1096. Stone Pedestal, 30'' long, 16'' high, 24'' front to back.

© 1974
Kenneth Lynch & Sons
Wilton, Conn. 06897

No. 1019. Stone pedestal, 32 1/2" high, 13" square base, 6" diameter at top.

No. 983. Stone pedestal, 31" high, 13" square base.

No. 988. Stone pedestal, 30" high, 11" wide, bottom 16" wide.

No. 984. Stone pedestal, 24" high, 11" diameter at base.

No. 1018. Stone Pedestal, also used as pump case. 24" x 30" x 12" high.

No. 1014. Stone Pedestal, 22" high x 12" square top.

No. 1103. Stone pedestal, 24" high, 24" diameter at top, 30" diameter at bottom

No. 1080. Stone pedestal, 19 1/2" high, 13" square at top, 16" square at bottom.

No. 1081. Stone pedestal, 20" high, 18" x 18" square.

No. 507—A. Stone pedestal 24" high x 20" x 20".

© 1974

Kenneth Lynch & Sons
Wilton, Conn. 06897

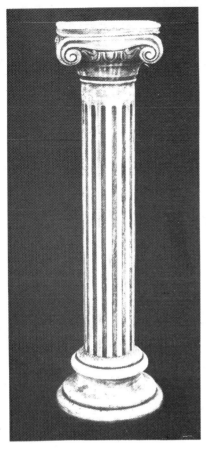

No. 1706. Stone pedestal. 42'' high with top 9''. Square base 12'' diameter.

No. 1713. Stone Bracket. 12'' high x 9'' wide x 6'' projection.

No. 2430. Stone. 20'' high. Top is 16''. Square bottom is 20'' square.

No. 1734. Stone. 20'' high. Top is 25'' x 18''. Base is 28'' x 21''.

the world's greatest collection of

SUNDIALS

For those who want to see pictures of hundreds of sundials send for book SUNDIALS & SPHERES. Soft Cover $4.00, Hard Cover $6.50, which includes separate price book.

No. 2500. Bronze Sundial. Generally furnished with green marble base. The main ring is 6' diameter. Drawings of this piece can be sent upon request.

No. 2500. Installation at Bloomfield, New Jersey.

No. 2500. Detail of bronze sundial. Very beautiful and monumental piece; green marble base.

The above group of photographs show No. 2500 installed at Bloomfield, New Jersey, and at Miami University, Oxford, Ohio.

© 1974.
Kenneth Lynch & Sons
Wilton, Conn. 06897

No. 2537.
Green-patinated
Bronze. 18'' high x
16½'' dia.

*Antique Reproduction

No. 2543.
Green-patinated
Bronze. A very
beautiful, highly or-
namental, im-
pressive sundial -
22'' high - 18½'' wide.

*Antique Reproduction

No. 2539.
Green-patinated
Bronze. 19½'' high x
17½'' dia.

*Antique Reproduction

No. 2540.
Green-patinated
Bronze. 21'' high x
18½'' dia.

*Antique Reproduction

No. 2546.
Green-patinated Bronze
- 20'' in dia.

No. 2541.
Green-patinated
Bronze. 25'' high x
20'' dia.

*Antique Reproduction

No. 2599.
Bronze Sundial. Very
special design 27'' tall,
21½'' diameter, 7'' Base
block.

*Antique Reproduction

No. 2538.
Green-patinated
Bronze. 22'' high x
18'' dia.

*Antique Reproduction

*NOTE: Re ''Antique Reproductions.'' The buyer must expect to receive the reproduction of
an antique with all the signs of the good life it has had including its wear and imperfections.

No. 1505. Bronze Armillary Sphere. Green patine antique finish with many symbols and signs of zodiac. Furnished in three sizes: 15" high x 12" dia.; 25" high x 20" dia.; 30" high x 24" dia.

No. 4236. Wrought Iron Sundial, 36" dia.

No. 4200. Bronze or Iron Sundial, 48" dia.

No. 2598. Armillary Sundial, wrought iron with lead ornament. Painted Antique green finish, highlighted with gold and natural lead color pieces. Made in three sizes: 36" dia., 48" dia. and 60" dia. It is furnished with a suitable stone base all ready to be mounted on a pedestal of selected height.

© 1974.
Kenneth Lynch & Sons
Wilton, Conn. 06897

No. 4564. Armillary sundial made of wrought iron of really monumental proportions. Garnished with bronze furniture in the form of zodiacs, lettering, etc. We can furnish these from stock materials up to 16' size from arrow feather to arrow head.

No. 4657. Armillary with zodiacs. Made in bronze or iron, 16" diameter and 20" diameter.

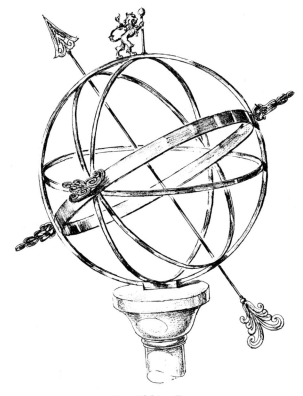

No. 4201. Bronze Sundial, English design, 30" dia.

No. 2313. Wrought Iron Sundial with lead zodiac. Intended to be used partly as a topiary frame. 36" and 48" dia.

© 1974.
Kenneth Lynch & Sons
Wilton, Conn. 06897

No. 2085.
Lead Atlas with stone sphere sundial - lead garnished - 32'' overall. Also 48''.

No. 2597.
Lead Atlas with Bronze Armillary 36'' to highest point, also 54''.

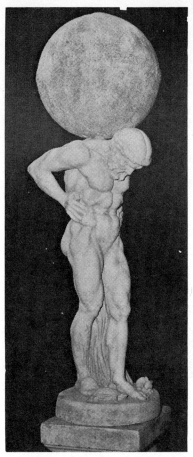

No. 2085-A. Stone "ATLAS", 51'' high overall. NOTE: The figure is 36'' high.

No. 4563. Armillary Sundial made in bronze. Two sizes: 18'' dia. and 36'' diameter.

No. 4561. Armillary Sundial made in bronze. 30'' over all, arrow feather to arrow head.

No. 4562. Armillary Sundial. 30'' long, arrow feather to arrow head.

© 1974.
Kenneth Lynch & Sons
Wilton, Conn. 06897

HEMISPHERICAL SUNDIALS

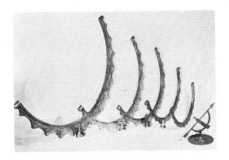

These illustrations show Hemispherical Dials being prepared. As you can see, we make them in many sizes. The design shown here if offered in 10", 20", 30", 36", 48", 60", 72", 96", 120", 144", 168', 192" sizes. This is measured from end to end of arrow.

We have made such Sundials as large as 28' in diameter, so actually we make any size on special order. Mostly, we furnish the 10" thru the 48" sizes. There is nothing so impressive!

In the sizes 10" thru 48", we furnish them in bronze, aluminum (antiqued green) and cast iron. In sizes over 48", they are furnished in wrought iron.

The equatorial band on sizes over 30" is generally garnished in lead and is illuminated with Roman numerals, signs of the zodiac, wind symbols, names of astronomers, explorers, symbols of astronomy, heraldic devices related to explorers and other symbols, all of which are very interesting to look at and study.

This band is inlaid with 23-karat gold, Royal red, Cavalry yellow, Field green, plus the natural color of the lead and other appropriate, tastefully chosen illumination and gives you a very lively equatorial band to view. This is indeed a most beautiful creation.

The foregoing description applies only to Sundials (Hemispherical) over 30". Hemispherical Sundials under 30" have an equatorial band with much ornament but of the same parent material as the Sundial itself as there is not room on these smaller equatorial bands for the elaborate illumination described in the foregoing.

No. 2601. Large Bronze Hemispherical Dial with zodiac symbols. 30" and 36" long arrow end to end. It would be difficult to tell you the importance of this piece of work.

No. 2601-A. Large bronze Hemispherical Dial with zodiac symbols, 30" and 36" long arrow, end to end. Mounted on special base of bronze directly under the sundial. The stone pedestal is No. 253.

No. 4558. Special Hemispherical Dial, bronze or iron, 48" over all.

No. 1506. Bronze hemispherical Sundial with signs of zodiac. Beautiful green patine. Furnished in three sizes: 10", 20" and 30" high. Antique in appearance.

No. 4559. Double Hemispherical Dial, 48" long, furnished in bronze or iron. Will tell time in two different locations.

BOOK

Book available "SUNDIALS AND SPHERES"

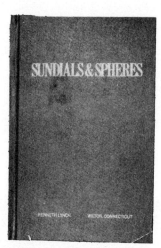

This is the real Architect's and Decorator's book, the whole story, size 9 x 14". Over 350 photographs and drawings showing the prior and available art of sundials, spheres, and direction markers — including nine full color photographs of famous historical sundials. The rich historical and scientific background of sundials is reflected in this picture presentation. A wide variety of sundials and related items are shown, including Atlas sundials, armillary sundials, hemispherical sundials, stone sundials, constellation figures, terrestial spheres, globes and globe harnesses, Zodiac figures, direction markers and pedestals. Information on the historical and scientific background of sundials, design, installation and readings is also provided. As part of the presentation of prior sundial art, a collection of drawings of ancient sundials. And there are 8 pages of full-color photographs of famous, museum-piece sundials and spheres.

Written and compiled by Kenneth Lynch

Published by The Canterbury Publishing Company
Box 488, Wilton, CT 06897

(Printed by Rand McNally)

It is available as: title #7374,
            Hardcover . . . . $ 6.50
            Softcover . . . . $ 4.50
This price includes postage & handling.

Illustration #3416
Once again you will see how a beautiful arrangement can be made by perfect use of stone work to support this sundial. It is #4557, the base is #1317, and the urn shaped pedestal is #1150.

No. 5450. Stone Sundial with bronze gnomon. Base at front for small dedication plate. 18" Dia. x 3" thick.

No. 4692. Bronze Hemispherical Sun Dial on special stone pedestal. Made in 30" and 36" sizes only. All bronze. Pedestal is 36" high and is massively in proportion to the Sundial.

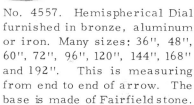

No. 4557. Hemispherical Dial furnished in bronze, aluminum or iron. Many sizes: 36", 48", 60", 72", 96", 120", 144", 168" and 192". This is measuring from end to end of arrow. The base is made of Fairfield stone.

No. 4550. Armillary Sundial Base Plate. A very decorative addition to any sundial installation. Bronze or Eternity lead reinforced with stainless steel. 21" diameter. A must!

No. 4560. Quadruple Hemispherical Dial furnished in bronze or iron, 48" over all from arrow tip to arrow tip. Will tell time in four different locations

No. 4693. Elaborate Hemispherical Dial, furnished in both bronze and iron in many sizes. On heavy stone base with bold rope mould around edge. The illustration shows an acanthus leaf pedestal; however, any of the suitable pedestals in the Pedestal Section of the catalog could be used. Sizes begin at 36" and go thru to 192".

© 1974.
Kenneth Lynch & Sons
Wilton, Conn. 06897

Illustration No. 3434.
Bronze hemispherical sundial on elegant stone pedestal of Palladio design. The pedestal measures 42" overall. The sundial is similar to Illustration No. 4557 and is 36" from arrow tip to arrow tip. It is approximately 64" overall. Hardly enough could be said about the impressiveness of this sundial.

Illustration No. 3425
Stone sundial with bronze gnomon on stone pedestal, No. 1077. The sundial is 31" wide. The seated figure is No. 964 and is 15½" high; the standing figure is No. 2890 and is 22" high. Both of these figures are made of lead. There is a leaden sculptured background for the two figures which serves as a connecting piece. The overall height is approximately 66" and, of course, it could be increased in height by adding suitable blocks under the pedestal or setting it on high ground.

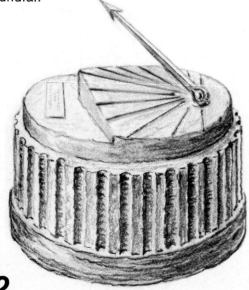

No. 5449. Stone Sundial 18" Dia. x 8" high. Craggy Texture, Smooth Top. Excellent place for dedication plate.

© 1974
Kenneth Lynch & Sons
Wilton, Conn. 06897

Illustration #3454

Vertical sundial of considerable merit. Adjustable bronze gnomon mounted on stone face with decorative stone pedestal. The sundial itself is 18'' wide; the pedestal is 22'' high. It is approximately 34'' high over all.

Illustration No. 3471

Stone sundial with bronze gnomon. The numerals are of lead. Any pedestal could be used. The one shown is No. 1077 which is available in several sizes. The sundial is 31'' wide, and the model is cut from a solid block of stone.

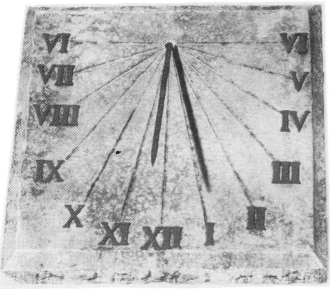

Illustration #3537

Wall sundial, antique reproduction, stone with lead numerals and bronze gnomon. Size: 16'' x 16'' x 2'' thick.

Illustration #3536

Spanish wall sundial made of stone with lead numerals and bronze gnomon. Size: 23'' x 23'' x 2½'' thick. Fine antique appearance.

© 1974.
Kenneth Lynch & Sons
Wilton, Conn. 06897

Illustration #3463

There are three smaller sizes of hemispherical sundials of great merit with zodiac bases which go on top of the stone. They are 10'', 20'', and 30'' high.

Shown above, on Pedestal #1102, it comes in three different heights — 24'', 30'', and 36''. See pedestal page for more information.

Illustration #3430

A melon-urn shaped pedestal of bold design using urn #813 which is 33½'' high. The step-like arrangement under the urn is available from stock supplies. Each step is 6'' in height.

For those who want to see pictures of hundreds of sundials send for book SUNDIALS & SPHERES. Soft Cover $4.00, Hard Cover $6.50, which includes separate price book.

©1974
Kenneth Lynch & Sons
Wilton, Conn. 06897

SUNDIALS

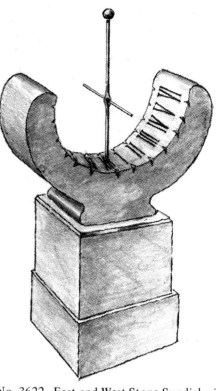

No. 3620. East and West Stone Sundial with Eternity lead tablature, framed in reeded molding. The gnomon is composed of a bronze sun and moon on the north-south line and by raising and lowering the gnomon, the sundial will tell time in corresponding locality. The bronze is furnished in verde green antique with golden highlights and the lead is Eternity lead which is a natural blue/gray lead. The stone is, of course, antiqued. This comes in two sizes 48" wide at $350.00 and 36" wide at $300.00, the base is 12" in diameter. It requires a stone pedestal at least 24" high and illustrated is our No. 1020 which is 24" high x 13" square. This unusual sundial is much admired by all who have seen it.

No. 3622. East and West Stone Sundial with bronze gnomon. This handsome rugged garden piece is available in two sizes. 36" wide and 48" wide. In 48" wide it is $300.00. In 36" wide it is $250.00. It requires a pedestal approximately 16" square and it is shown on a very simple pedestal in this illustration. However, you may choose a pedestal from the pedestal section but it is not included in the price.

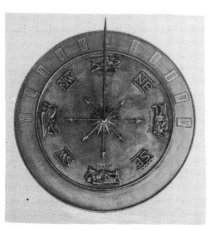

Illustration #3507
Bronze horizontal sundial with points of the compass in Greek. The figures are inspired by those on the cave of the winds at Athens. The sculptor was Joseph Kuthmayer. The numerals are gold inlaid lead. It is 16" in diameter. Use this sundial with a stone bezel.

©1974.
Kenneth Lynch & Sons
Wilton, Conn. 06897

Illustration #3506
Bronze horizontal sundial of great artistic merit. The numerals are of lead inlaid with gold. The figures on the perimeter are those of the twelve zodiacs. The inner figures are those of the winds taken from the Temple of the Winds in Athens, Greece and modeled by Joseph Kuthmayer. There is a convenient space for the inlay of a dedication plaque or a motto. Size: 25" in diameter over all.   Bronze
Use this sundial with a stone bezel.

No. 3565. The Kopernicus Calendar. This permanent calendar was designed by Dr. Nicholas Kopernicus, 15th century scientist and astronomer. Dr. Kopernicus was a Polish scientist whose discoveries in astronomy were the most important in their time. This great man led the way for people like Galileo and other greats who succeeded him. This calendar measures 4½" x 5½" it is highly ornamental, it is made of a hard pewter and comes complete with a stand to make it stand erect. Mr. Lynch originally produced these to honor his Polish friends who are much pleased to receive this permanent calendar work of art.

Illustration #3543
Unusual wrought-iron armillary sundial, extremely strong. It is garnished with the signs of the zodiac including their dates and names. These are done in Eternity Lead and have been highlighted in gold. The orb on the northern most point is made of bronze which is verde antique green. This is available in three sizes: 48", 60", and 72" in diameter.

Illustration #3524
Very ornamental, baroque sundial. It can be used either vertically on a wall or horizontally merely by changing the numerals. It is 2½" thick x 17½" in diameter. The numerals are of gilded lead and the gnomon is of bronze. It is rich and antique in appearance.

Note: The photographer laid the lead numerals on incorrectly and we are aware of this.

No. 2312.
Reproduction of Primative Bird Sundial - all bronze. Very unique - 15" from head to tail. Diameter of round base is 6".

No. 2310.
Stone pillar dial with English Lead figure seated at top. Bronze Gnomon. Pillar is garnished with lines of delineations and signs of the zodiac. This is a rich and handsome piece of work. The lead figure is 15" high. The column is 12" in diameter and 36" tall.

No. 2939. Lead Sundial, Peacock design. Actual lead sundial is 14 1/2" diameter x 6" high. Very rare item, original found in auction sale.

No. 2314.
Lead pillar dial with lead satyr playing flutes. Satyr is $6\frac{1}{2}$" tall. Pillar is 12" tall. Total height is $18\frac{1}{2}$". Star gnomon is bronze gilded. Very rich. Pillar dial also sold separately.

No. 2307.
The Andrew Whyte Sundial (Contemporary). The base is stone with a bronze duck head and bronze cat tail - 14" in diameter at largest point.

SUNDIALS

No. 2549.
Wall Sundial all bronze or lead with bronze gnomon, 15-5/8" x 12".

No. 2326.
Massive lead wall sundial with bronze gnomon. 48" x 24".

No. 2325. Wall Dial. 42" x 24" - bronze gnomon. Furnished in either lead also special sizes to suit.

No. 2104.
Bronze or lead - 3½" dia.

No. 2596.
Horizontal sundial of English origin with signs of the zodiac, enriched with cupids, crown and leaf, furnished in bronze, lead.

No. 2327. Bronze and stone Sundial, 15 1/4" diameter.

No. 2324.
Lead sundial of Tortoise & Hare - very beautifully executed with bronze gnomon. 11½" diameter.

No. 1508. Bronze, lead - all with bronze gnomon. 7" in dia.

No. 2550. Bronze, lead - all with bronze gnomon 10 1/2" dia.

No. 2321.
Bronze or Lead with bronze Gnomon 10" Diameter, 6".

No. 2548. Lead, bronze all with bronze gnomon. Most beautifully modeled. Ikaros and Daidalos with their wings of wax, flew too close to the sun. 16 1/2" diameter.

© 1974.
Kenneth Lynch & Sons
Wilton, Conn. 06897

No. 1507. Bronze, lead - all with bronze gnomon. 10 1/4" in dia.

SUNDIALS

No. 4237. Bronze,
11" diameter.

No. 2554. Bronze,
lead - all with bronze
gnomon. 11 1/2" dia.

No. 4620. Lead Sundial Bezel or
seating ring, made to fit all horizontal sundials of any diameter
over 8". It is 1 1/2" wide; therefore, will add 3" to the diameter
of any sundial. It gives the sundial tremendously added importance and is considered a "must."

No. 2555. Bronze or
lead all with bronze
gnomon. 11" dia.

No. 2545. Bronze,
lead: all with bronze
gnomon. 10" in dia.
This is an extra fine
quality piece.

No. 2553. Bronze,
lead - all with bronze
gnomon. 14" in dia.

No. 2556. Bronze or
lead - all with bronze
gnomon. 7 1/2" dia.

No. 4691. Stone Sundial with
bronze gnomon. Bold detail.
18" diameter, 2 1/2" thick.
Very impressive.

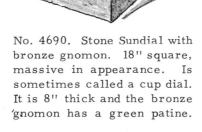

No. 4690. Stone Sundial with
bronze gnomon. 18" square,
massive in appearance. Is
sometimes called a cup dial.
It is 8" thick and the bronze
gnomon has a green patine.

No. 1510. Bronze, lead
-all with bronze gnomon.
10 1/4" in diameter.

Temple of the Winds at Athens. On the upper facia of each side, you will see identical figures which Mr. Kuthmoyer used as his inspiration when he modeled #2429 bronze directional marker.

No. 2429. Solid bronze Directional Marker of exceptional merit modeled by Joseph Kuthmeyer 13 3/4" diameter. The traditional Greek figures of the four winds are chiseled in sharp detail. Furnished in verde antique of statuary bronze.

No. 4502. Bronze Directional Marker with outer Zodiac Ring, 25" diameter.

No. 2703. Bronze Compass of unusual design. Engraved rising sun. Satin finish or verde antique. Two sizes: 14" diameter and 22" diameter.

No. 1310. Stone Directional Marker with signs of the zodiac and complete compass in center, 36" square. NOTE: This piece can be furnished in bronze on special order.

No. 2107. Directional Marker. Solid bronze 4" in diameter closed pattern. Verde antique or statuary bronze.

No. 2605. Directional Marker. Solid bronze 11½" in diameter, open pattern. Verde antique or statuary bronze.

SPHERES

Celestial sphere made for the New York World's Fair. The great Paul Manship was the sculptor. We made the sphere and its parts.

No. 951. Terrestrial sphere, furnished in Armorstone ©. Antiqued, & decorated in 23K. gold leaf and is the companion to celestial sphere on opposite side of page. The sphere is 24" in diameter.

No. 950. Celestial sphere, furnished in Armorstone ©. The sphere is 24" in diameter.

©1974
Kenneth Lynch & Sons
Wilton, Conn. 06897

SPHERES

TERRESTRIAL   CELESTIAL

GLOBES

ARMILLARY   GAZING

For complete information send for Book 7374

"Sundials and Spheres"   soft cover $4.00
hard cover library edition $6.50

(Book 7374)
This subject is elaborately treated with more than one thousand illustrations. Beginning with simple Gazing Globes through Giant Armillaries, the subjects are fully covered. Send for Book 7374 and be sure to specify Hard or Soft Covered Edition.

WeatherVanes

KENNETH LYNCH & SONS, INC.

Send for free book

BOX 488
78 DANBURY ROAD
WILTON, CONNECTICUT 06897-0488

Telephone: 203-762-8363

BOOK OF WEATHERVANES AND CUPOLAS

Over 1,000 weathervanes. The prior and available art of the weathervane and cupola is presented in pictorial detail. The emphasis is on traditional American weathervanes and cupolas. Only architectural quality weathervanes are offered, not retail store items. This volume also includes a short history of weathervanes, and information on specifying and installing weathervanes. Traditional and modern cupola designs are shown.

Published by the Canterbury Publishing Company, P.O. Box 488, Wilton, Ct. 06897. (Printed by Rand McNally)

Title# 7274 — Case bound hand Linen Cover, Library Edition, $6.50, including mailing. Softcover, $4.00.

No. 1538
Bull, 19th Century, 28" long, copper or gold

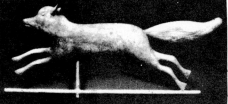

No. 2420
Running fox available painted or gilded, made of solid aluminum.
Length, 28".

No. 1541
Cow, 19th Century, 28" long, copper or gold leaf.

No. 2635
Rooster Weather Vane. Antique reproduction. 18", 24" and 30" high. Furnished in copper, gold leafed or verdi antique. Some sizes are available in wrought aluminum.

Note: This is without arrow

No. 3811
Pig, 19th Century reproduction, copper or gold leaf, 36" long.

No. 3855
Rooster Weather Vane attributed to Shem Drowne. 36" overall. Available in wrought copper, gilded or wrought aluminum painted.

© 1974.
Kenneth Lynch & Sons
Wilton, Conn. 06897

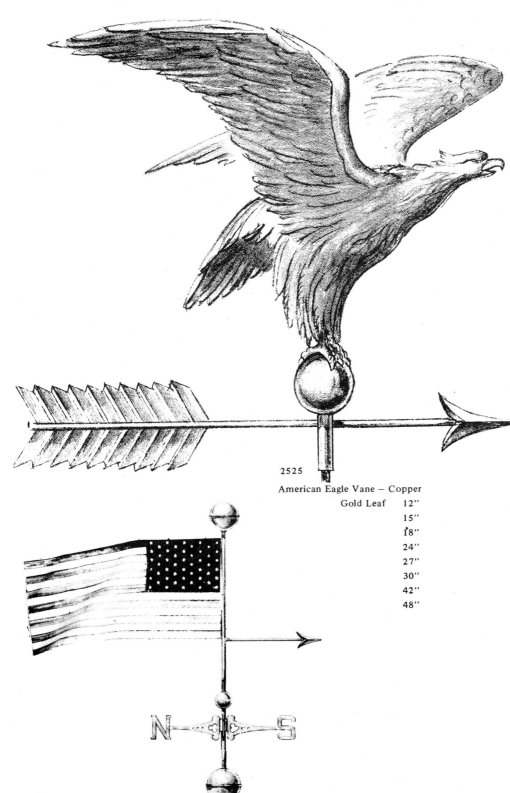

2525

American Eagle Vane — Copper

Gold Leaf	12"
	15"
	18"
	24"
	27"
	30"
	42"
	48"

No. 3889.
Flag Weather Vane, regular pattern. Wrought aluminum reproduction. Furnished in two sizes: 18" flag only, 30" flag only.

62" FLAG NOW AVAILABLE

No. 2525.
American Eagle Weather Vane. Furnished in gold leaf or in verde antique copper. This is the world's most important weather vane and has been made by this firm long before any records were kept. It is made in many sizes, 12", 15", 18", 21", 24", 27", 30", 36", 42", 48".

These weather vanes are always measured from one end of the arrow to the other. The wing spread and length of the arrow are always the same. The proper size cardinal points are furnished.

The weather vane shaft should go down into the building far enough to make it a good, strong installation. Sometimes in the case of church steeples we have made shafts as long as 30' to accommodate a special condition. Antique dealers have brought these vanes into us and by the markings we can generally tell if they were ours.

We have encountered dealers with weather vanes that were made before the turn of the century.

In purchasing a weather vane of this type it is always best to tell us what sort of covering there is on the roof, cupola or steeple. The reason for this is that we can furnish a shaft which will eliminate any possibility of electrolytic action. If we are not forewarned we will ship with an iron shaft. However, you must not mix an iron shaft with a copper roof. Therefore, this bit of information is very important to the owner.

The most popular sizes in this eagle weather vane are 24" through 36" and, of course, it is easy enough for any architect to draw this eagle in scale to see how it looks.

It is always better to purchase one slightly larger than slightly smaller as weather vanes which are too small tend to look very diminutive.

BASIC UNIVERSAL HARNESS FOR WEATHER VANES

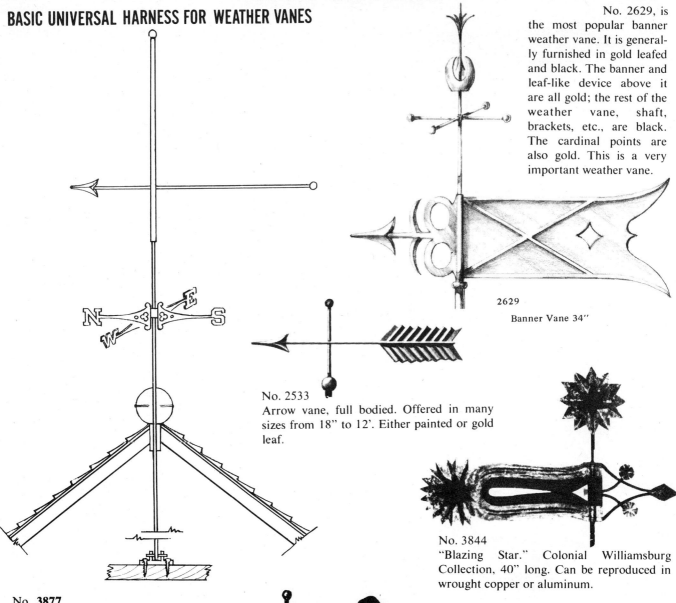

No. 2629, is the most popular banner weather vane. It is generally furnished in gold leafed and black. The banner and leaf-like device above it are all gold; the rest of the weather vane, shaft, brackets, etc., are black. The cardinal points are also gold. This is a very important weather vane.

2629
Banner Vane 34″

No. 2533
Arrow vane, full bodied. Offered in many sizes from 18″ to 12'. Either painted or gold leaf.

No. 3844
"Blazing Star." Colonial Williamsburg Collection, 40″ long. Can be reproduced in wrought copper or aluminum.

No. 3877
Basic weather vane harness. This is a complete unit ready to receive any silhouette-type motif the owner elects. The silhouette must work as a silhouette and it must be weldable to the frame shown above. It should make contact at the bottom bar and at least at one or two points along the vertical spire. Note Illustration #3876. The carpenter's feet are resting at the bottom bar and the plane and scroll shaving rest on another member coming out from the spire. This, likewise, is acceptable. Poor practice would be to have an illustration such as a dog with his nose touching the spire as this would tend to deform the figure. Good judgment must be used.

Vane Harness — Aluminum 40″

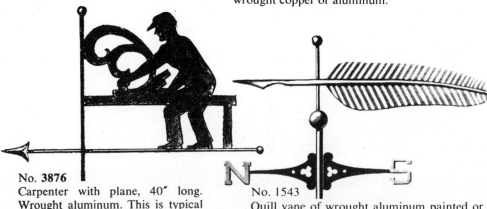

No. 3876
Carpenter with plane, 40″ long. Wrought aluminum. This is typical of the vanes which can be installed in unit No. 3877.

Alum 40″

No. 1543
Quill vane of wrought aluminum painted or gold leaf. Furnished in two sizes: 24″ and 36″ long.

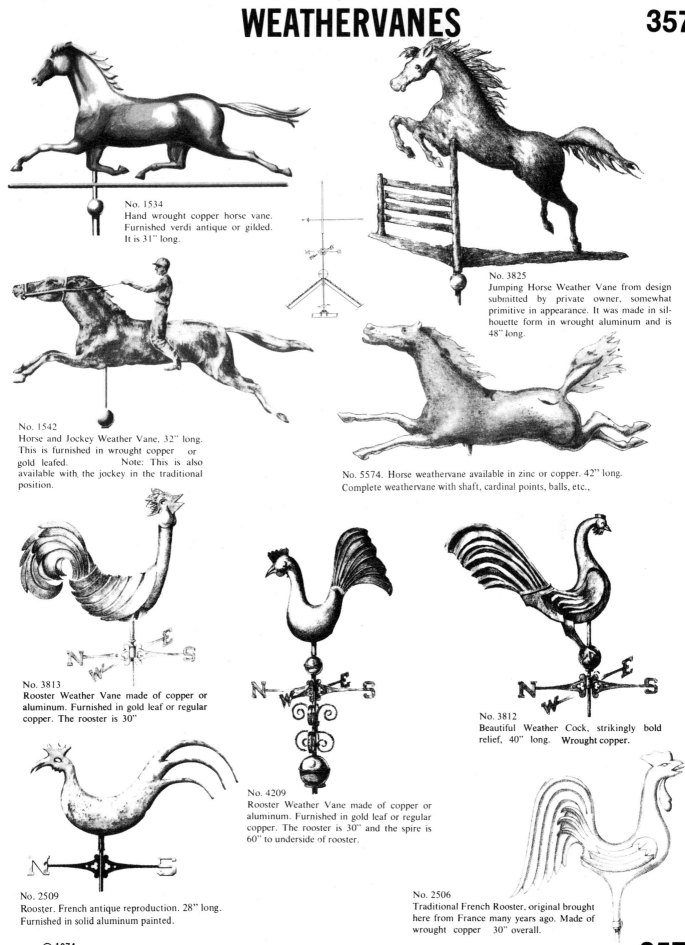

No. 1534
Hand wrought copper horse vane. Furnished verdi antique or gilded. It is 31" long.

No. 3825
Jumping Horse Weather Vane from design submitted by private owner, somewhat primitive in appearance. It was made in silhouette form in wrought aluminum and is 48" long.

No. 1542
Horse and Jockey Weather Vane, 32" long. This is furnished in wrought copper or gold leafed. Note: This is also available with the jockey in the traditional position.

No. 5574. Horse weathervane available in zinc or copper. 42" long. Complete weathervane with shaft, cardinal points, balls, etc.,

No. 3813
Rooster Weather Vane made of copper or aluminum. Furnished in gold leaf or regular copper. The rooster is 30"

No. 4209
Rooster Weather Vane made of copper or aluminum. Furnished in gold leaf or regular copper. The rooster is 30" and the spire is 60" to underside of rooster.

No. 3812
Beautiful Weather Cock, strikingly bold relief, 40" long. **Wrought copper.**

No. 2509
Rooster. French antique reproduction. 28" long. Furnished in solid aluminum painted.

No. 2506
Traditional French Rooster, original brought here from France many years ago. Made of wrought copper 30" overall.

© 1974.
Kenneth Lynch & Sons
Wilton, Conn. 06897

No. 3912 Sea Captain 36" High
Wrought naval aluminum,
polychromed, very decorative.

No. 2653
"Peg Leg." Wrought aluminum. 36" long.
Also known as Seaman Vane.

No. 2515
Sou'wester. Wrought aluminum. 26" long.

No. 2511
Sloop Hand wrought copper, 36" long.

No. 1537
All hand made copper schooner, 36" long.

No. 4118
Gaff rigged schooner, wrought aluminum,
36" long.

No. 2625
Swordfish weather vane, solid aluminum,
36" long.

© 1974.
Kenneth Lynch & Sons
Wilton, Conn. 06897

No. 3865

Wrought copper grasshopper modeled by Joseph Boulton, American Sculptor, for a special collection of Mrs. Stanford Brainard who is delighted to share this with others. This is not like any other grasshopper weather vane ever made. It differs in detail from those done by Shem Drowne in New England who made the famous grasshopper for Faneuil Hall in Boston.

The grasshopper shown above is correct anatomically and we are proud to be the conservators of these valuable molds. Available in green copper or gold leaf. The length is 32".

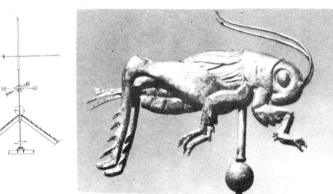

Illustration #3906 Cricket vane, hand wrought copper, 32" long, full relief. Complete with all non-ferrous parts.

No. 2632

Angel and Horn. Antique reproduction. 40" long. Solid aluminum. Painted body with gold leafed horn and white wings.

No. 2640

Weather vane like famous Kittery eagle. Solid aluminum. 30" long. Furnished painted or gilded.

No. 2639

Dolphin weather vane similar to London Fishmongers Guild Hall. 30" long, solid aluminum.

No. 2638

Mermaid.
Solid aluminum. Painted or gilded. 40" long.

No. 2514

Antique reproduction Whale weather vane, 30" long, solid aluminum.

No. 3838

Copper reproduction of primitive original in the Smithsonian Institution. Many makers have reproduced this weather vane during the last 100 years. Ours is 36" long.

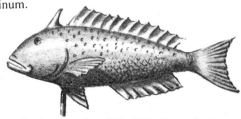

No. 3907 Fish vane. Design based on Tile Fish Cape Cod, 36" long. Wood body, metal fins and tail. Will last indefinatly. Painted, furnished complete. **This is now available in all metal.**

© 1974.
Kenneth Lynch & Sons
Wilton, Conn. 06897

BENCHES

New book of benches available. Book title No. 9074. Everyone in the building profession should have this BIG 80 page Book of Benches, more than 500 benches shown! Comes complete with estimate cost, price list for contractors. Write Kenneth Lynch & Sons (Book Department) and ask for Book No. 9074 with contractors cost data. (Soft bound $4.00, desk copy. Hard bound $6.50, library edition), or write Canterbury Publishing Company.

Note! Many floral, patriotic and symbolic back designs available in the big Bench Book.

No. 6737. Bench with back — 8' long. This is the bench we furnished for the New York World's Fair and is standard with the New York Park Department. This bench has heavy cast iron frame with wood seats.

No. 2724. A truly handsome Hand Wrought Iron Bench. Furnished 4', 5' and 6' long.

Send for the bench book No. 9074. Hundreds more designs.

© 1974.
Kenneth Lynch & Sons
Wilton, Conn. 06897

BENCHES

We offer more sizes, more design alternatives as well as more accessory alternatives in our teakwood benches than anyone else.

SEND FOR SPECIAL LITERATURE SHOWING DESIGNS, PRICES, ETC.
TO KENNETH LYNCH & SONS, BOX 488, WILTON, CONNECTICUT 06897

3280 Mendip Teak Bench
The 6 ft. length is the most popular

Available lengths	Approx. Cartoned Weight
4' - 0"	98 lbs.
5' - 0"	105 lbs.
6' - 0"	**115 lbs.**
8' - 0"	129 lbs.
8' - 0" with center leg	133 lbs.
matching chair	66 lbs.

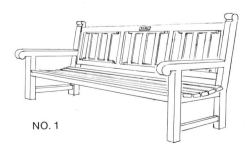

NO. 1

An attractive brass plate
engraved as you wish.

NO. 2

Lead ball terminals as
in the Rockefeller garden.

TEAKWOOD BENCHES

These great, carefully made Teakwood Benches have been popular in Europe for more than 100 years and never has one rotted or worn out! Even though not requiring paint they seem to last indefinitely.

At Canterbury, England, one may see more than a hundred Teak benches placed along the great stone wall facing the historic cathedral (John Lynch was dean in 1534!) placed there so the pilgrims may rest while visiting those great buildings.

Most of these benches have brass memorial plates to indicate the name of a grateful pilgrim donor. The giving of these teakwood benches has long been a custom at churches, gardens, libraries and resorts. How grateful are the users!

This is the basic Teakwood Bench. It is always available from stock. One size only, 6 feet long.
While this basic bench is very desirable in itself, we offer many variations in the form of a choice of back designs, memorial plaques and two lead finial ornaments.

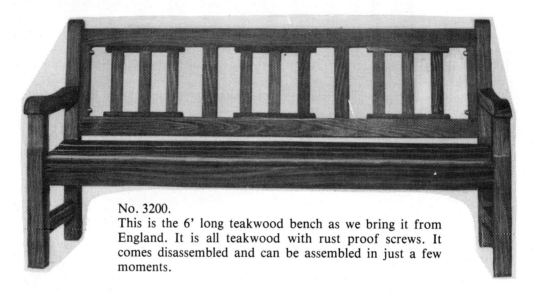

No. 3200.
This is the 6' long teakwood bench as we bring it from England. It is all teakwood with rust proof screws. It comes disassembled and can be assembled in just a few moments.

The making of a teakwood bench has become a special art. Our maker is certainly the leader in this field. We are very proud of the fact that we have an exclusive stock of these benches on hand in our warehouse at all times. A telephone call will get you immediate delivery.

This is a master architect's teakwood bench. It is made in England and brought to this country in complete container shipments. Wherever you go in England these benches are easily seen in parks, gardens, churchyards, etc. The English have been making them for years. They require no maintenance and they are only made in the 6' length.

#3265 Fox Hunting
Teakwood bench — 6' long only.
Shipped disassembled.

#3264 Horseshoe
Teakwood bench — 6' long only
Shipped disassembled.

TEAKWOOD BENCHES WITH A DECORATIVE BACK

These meaningful and artistic bench backs were designed to meet special requirements. They are beautifully molded and cast in all weather aluminum, painted white or Brewster green. They do much to add to the elegance of the Basic Teak Bench.

Memorial work is invited. Conservatism in lettering and size is recommended.

#3209 Eagle-American
Teakwood bench — 6' long only.
Shipped disassembled.

#3211 Music
Teakwood bench — 6' long only.
Shipped disassembled.

#3210 Morning Glory
Teakwood bench — 6' long only.
Shipped disassembled.

#3201 Trumpet Flower
Teakwood bench – 6' long only.
Shipped disassembled

#3207 Music
Teakwood bench — 6' long only.
Shipped disassembled.

#3204 Bamboo Design
Teakwood bench — 6' long only.
Shipped disassembled.

#3208 Laurel Wreath
Teakwood bench — 6' long only.
Shipped disassembled.

#3203 Regency Design
Teakwood bench — 6' long only.
Shipped disassembled.

#3212 Renaissance Design
Teakwood bench — 6' long only.
Shipped disassembled.

#3205 Pelicans
Teakwood bench — 6' long only.
Shipped disassembled.

#3206 Horse
Teakwood bench — 6' long only.
Shipped disassembled.

#3202 Harp
Teakwood bench – 6' long only.
Shipped disassembled

© 1974.
Kenneth Lynch & Sons
Wilton, Conn. 06897

No. 3278 The above illustration shows a beautiful teakwood bench designed as a memorial. There are still some excellent wood carvers available, although such work is costly. An alternative for such memorials is to apply a suitable plaque and we can make these to any size or description.

Illustration #4517
Chinoiserie Design
Teakwood bench
Six feet long only
Shipped disassembled

© 1974.
Kenneth Lynch & Sons
Wilton, Conn. 06897

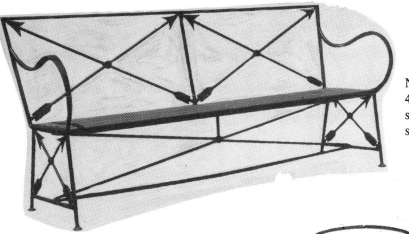

No. 2093. All Wrought Iron Bench, funished in 4'' and 6' lengths. This is a very beautiful and very strong bench, furnished with either iron or wood seats. Painted black or white.

No. 3783A. Wrought Iron Bench with all-brass decoration. Most beautifully modeled. 60'' long.

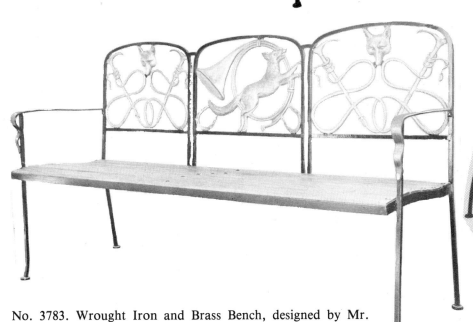

No. 3783. Wrought Iron and Brass Bench, designed by Mr. Teddy Tiffin about 1910, Wood seat, brass parts are polished and lacquered, iron is painted black or dark green. 60'' long.

No. 3795. Wrought Iron Arm Chair, brass ornament. ⁻

No. 1165. Stone Bench, very substantial, 65'' long. NOTE: This bench comes in six pieces and must be assembled with epoxy mortar.

No. 990. Stone Bench of an old, desirable design, 67'' long; back is 40'' high. NOTE: This bench comes in six pieces and must be assembled with epoxy mortar.

No. 1162. Stone Bench, 72'' long; back is 35'' high. NOTE: This bench comes in six pieces and must be assembled with epoxy mortar.

No. 1304. Stone Bench, 47½'' long.

© 1974.
Kenneth Lynch & Sons
Wilton, Conn. 06897

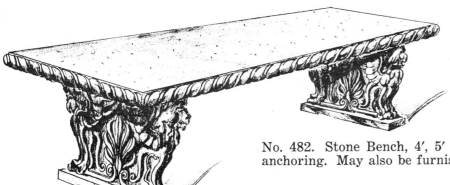

No. 482. Stone Bench, 4', 5' and 6' long. Use epoxy mortar for anchoring. May also be furnished curved.

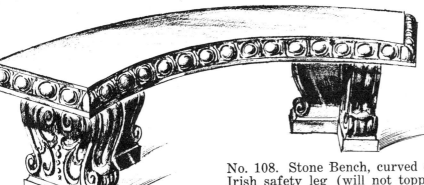

No. 108. Stone Bench, curved or straight. NOTE: "Tee" shaped Irish safety leg (will not topple). 48" and 60" long. Our bench of this design is far superior to those offered by any other maker.

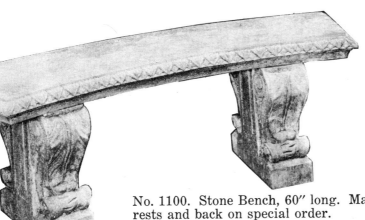

No. 1100. Stone Bench, 60" long. May also be furnished with arm rests and back on special order.

No. 1101. Stone Bench, 60" long. Use epoxy mortar to anchor. May also be furnished curved.

BENCHES

Illustration No. **3410**

Oak seats, carbon steel frame. Note contour seats extremely comfortable. Shipped disassembled in cartons as follows:

72" long bench with 3 legs

60" long bench with only 2 legs

Illustration No **3411**

Oak seated wrought steel bench furnished disassembled and packed in cartons.
Made in three important sizes, as follows:

48" wide with 2 legs

57" wide with 2 legs

72" long with 3 legs

Illustration No. **3412**

This is an oak seated bench with wrought iron supports. It is excellent for waiting areas, locker rooms, fine for parcel resting, etc. Available disassembled in four sizes as follows:

15" wide

48" wide

57" wide

72" wide with 3 legs

© 1974.
Kenneth Lynch & Sons
Wilton, Conn. 06897

Illustration #3245

This bench is cast solid in one piece and has an interior reinforcing frame of stainless steel. This is a very strong, heavy, and beautiful bench. It is shipped with a drum protecting each pedestal and a wood cover on the seat. Sand finish only. This bench is 6' long, 30" wide and 15" high.

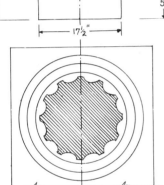

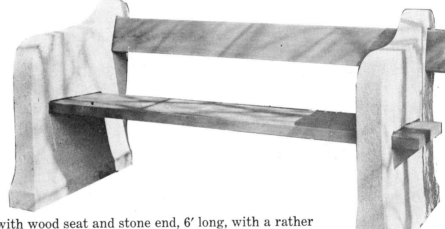

No. 469. Bench with wood seat and stone end, 6' long, with a rather high back, very desirable for older people. Can use epoxy mortar or angle iron brackets for anchoring.

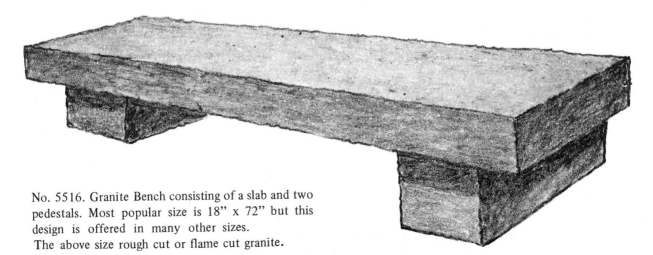

No. 5516. Granite Bench consisting of a slab and two pedestals. Most popular size is 18" x 72" but this design is offered in many other sizes.
The above size rough cut or flame cut granite.

©1974
Kenneth Lynch & Sons
Wilton, Conn. 06897

No. 1557. Wrought Iron Bench with brass garnishment, 48″ long. NOTE: We do not furnish cushions.

No. 1560. Iron Bench with wood seat, 48″ long. This is a great favorite among Interior Decorators.

No. 2725. Wrought Iron Bench to go around tree. The seat part is 17″ front to back. Generally, the opening for the tree is never less than 2′, so a minimum bench would be 5′ in diameter. Furnished in all diameters up to and including 12′. Shipped in sections.

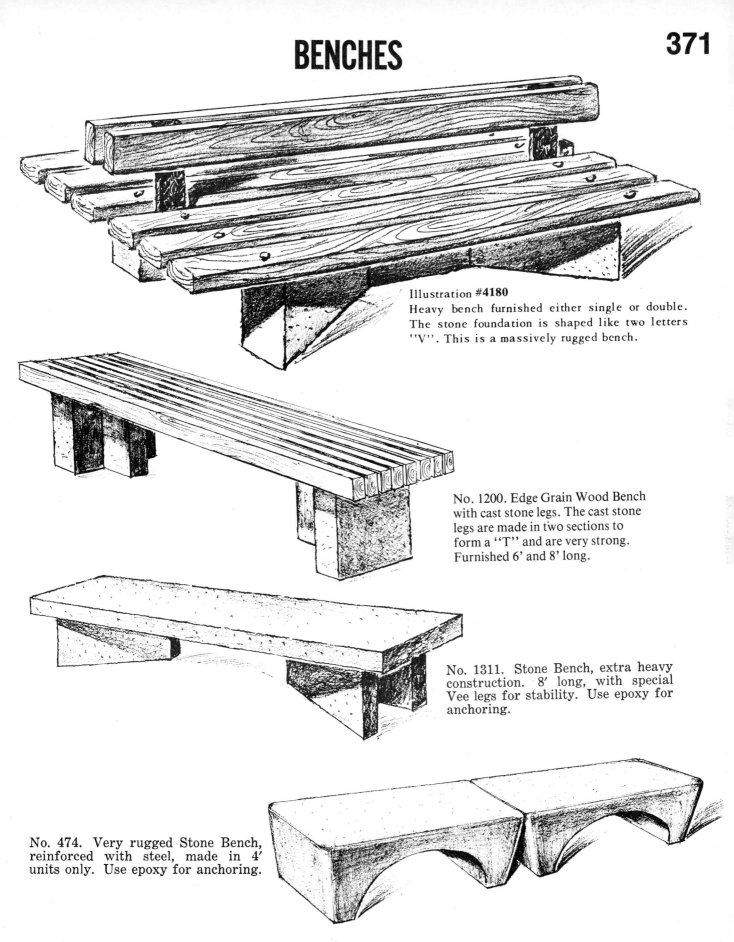

Illustration #4180
Heavy bench furnished either single or double.
The stone foundation is shaped like two letters
"V". This is a massively rugged bench.

No. 1200. Edge Grain Wood Bench
with cast stone legs. The cast stone
legs are made in two sections to
form a "T" and are very strong.
Furnished 6' and 8' long.

No. 1311. Stone Bench, extra heavy
construction. 8' long, with special
Vee legs for stability. Use epoxy for
anchoring.

No. 474. Very rugged Stone Bench,
reinforced with steel, made in 4'
units only. Use epoxy for anchoring.

© 1974.
Kenneth Lynch & Sons
Wilton, Conn. 06897

BENCHES

No. 2722. This is the least expensive of benches purchased by the Federal Government and Municipalities. It is a light weight bench but when ordered with three legs and compound cross braces as shown at the very bottom of this page, it becomes extremely strong. It can be furnished galvanized at no extra cost. The slats come painted green. See additional specification material on this page.

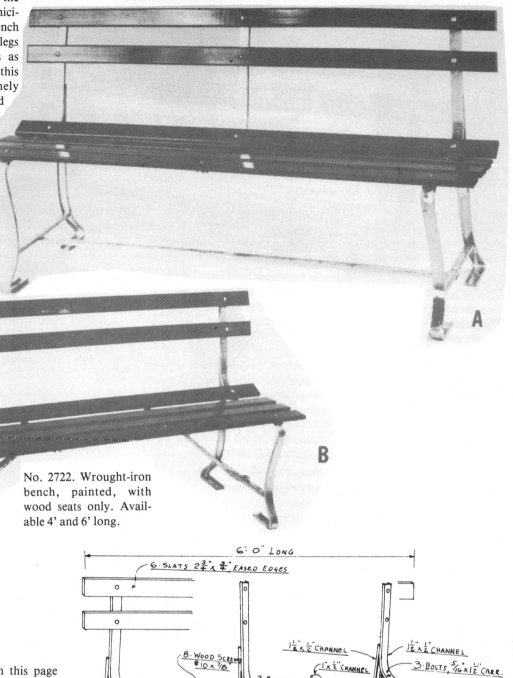

A

B

No. 2722. Wrought-iron bench, painted, with wood seats only. Available 4' and 6' long.

The benches shown on this page come disassembled only and are shipped one per flat carton. Note there are three distinct styles, A, B, and C. Exact price is controlled by quantity.

6' 0" LONG

6-SLATS 2¾" x ¾" EASED EDGES

8-WOOD SCREWS #10 x ⅞"

2-BOLTS, STOVE ¼" x 1"

1½" x ½ CHANNEL

1" x ½" CHANNEL

1½" x ½ CHANNEL

3-BOLTS, 5/16 x 1½ CARR.

15-BOLTS 5/16 x 1¼ CARR.

1" x ½" CHANNEL

3-BOLTS STOVE ¼" x 1½"

1" x ¼" CHANNEL

C

NOTE THAT MAJORITY OF BOLTS FOR ATTACHING SLATS ARE 1¼" LONG, BUT BECAUSE ONE SLAT IS ATTACHED AT THE CURVE IN THE CHANNEL, THERE ARE 3 BOLTS 1½" LONG.

© 1974.
Kenneth Lynch & Sons
Wilton, Conn. 06897

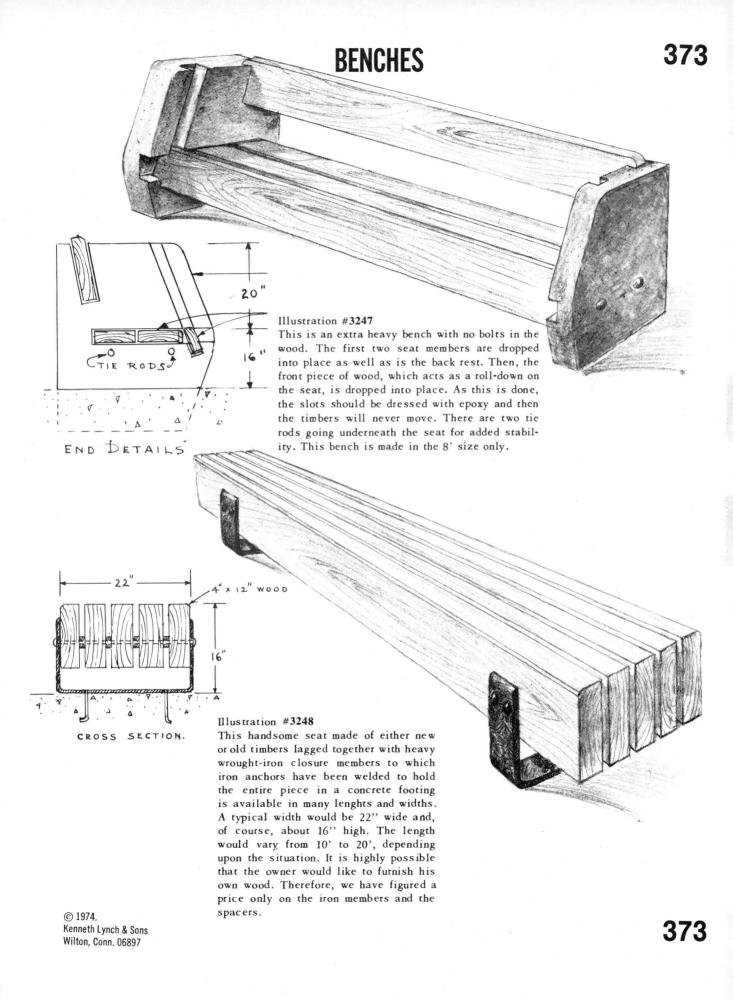

END DETAILS

20"

16"

TIE RODS

Illustration #3247

This is an extra heavy bench with no bolts in the wood. The first two seat members are dropped into place as well as is the back rest. Then, the front piece of wood, which acts as a roll-down on the seat, is dropped into place. As this is done, the slots should be dressed with epoxy and then the timbers will never move. There are two tie rods going underneath the seat for added stability. This bench is made in the 8' size only.

22"

4" X 12" WOOD

16"

CROSS SECTION.

Illustration #3248

This handsome seat made of either new or old timbers lagged together with heavy wrought-iron closure members to which iron anchors have been welded to hold the entire piece in a concrete footing is available in many lenghts and widths. A typical width would be 22" wide and, of course, about 16" high. The length would vary from 10' to 20', depending upon the situation. It is highly possible that the owner would like to furnish his own wood. Therefore, we have figured a price only on the iron members and the spacers.

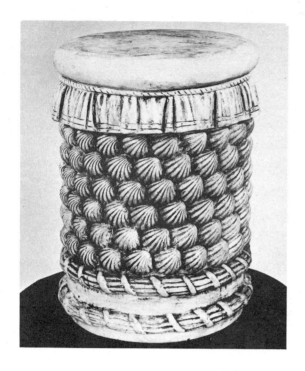

No. 586. Scallop shell hassock, 18 1/4" high by 14½" dia.

No. 584. Bamboo design, stone, 13-3/4" high, 14 1/4" dia.

No. 4809. Stone garden stool designed for children. Two pieces fit into one drum and they are shipped in pairs. They are 18" in diameter.

No. 4698. Garden seat of stone, 13" x 14" x 17½" high.

© 1974.
Kenneth Lynch & Sons
Wilton, Conn.- 06897

The designs shown on the Wrought Iron pages are greatly reduced in scale for reasons of economy in this publication. Any architect wishing to blow these up on his Camera Lucida may do so. However, we have in our files the original drawings from which these pieces were produced and they are all to scale. For a minimal charge, probably in the neighborhood of $100.00 we can give you a rather accurate scale reproduction of these illustrations.

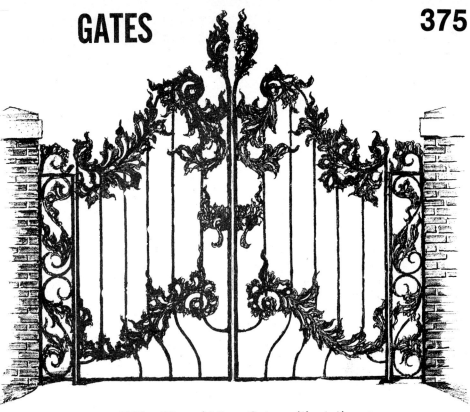

4384. Wrought Iron Gates with stationary side panels, 12' wide overall.

No. 4379. Elaborate wrought iron panel, 14' wide x 20' high.

Note! Regarding Wrought Iron Work, Gates, Fences, Railings, etc. — a new book is being prepared, properly illustrated. Order now.

No. 4391. Wrought Iron Walk Gate, 3'6" wide with wrought iron jamb members with scrolls on top.

No. 4385. Wrought Iron Gates with stationary side panels and overhead pediment for holding old-fashioned lighting fixture; 12' wide overall.

No. 4374. Wrought Iron Gates with very decorative pediment, 10' wide overall.

New Book

Note! New book on Wrought Iron by Kenneth Lynch will be ready late 1980. You may order now.

© 1974.
Kenneth Lynch & Sons
Wilton, Conn. 06897

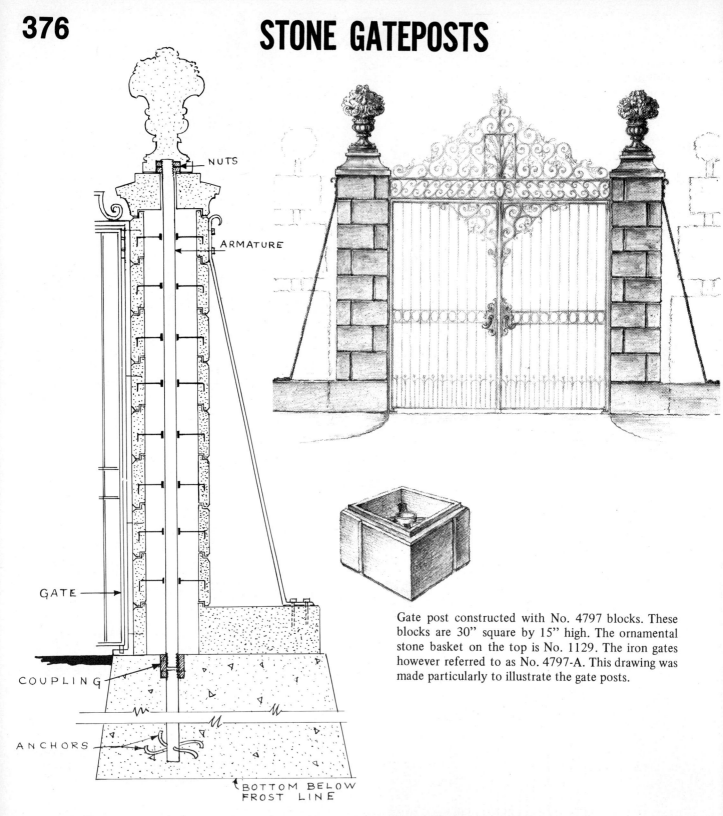

NUTS

ARMATURE

GATE

COUPLING

ANCHORS

BOTTOM BELOW
FROST LINE

Gate post constructed with No. 4797 blocks. These blocks are 30" square by 15" high. The ornamental stone basket on the top is No. 1129. The iron gates however referred to as No. 4797-A. This drawing was made particularly to illustrate the gate posts.

Typical construction assembly for stone gate post 4795, 4796 and 4797. By casting a concrete footing and anchor in the ground complete with iron as shown furnished by maker of the posts and gate, the entire stone post can be set up like a string of beads and all tightened together by the use of the steel armature which goes from top to bottom and is all tightened together with a giant nut. With the heel of the gate resting on the concrete and the top of the gate exerting its full force against the brace and the whole device steady by the heavy iron member down through the center, we then have a gate post which would be much stronger than anything which could be built by a mason. If there was never any possibility of wanting to move this post to another location, one could then fill the interior with concrete after it was all set up merely by pouring it in from the top. All gate post sections are 30" square by 15" high per piece.

© 1974.
Kenneth Lynch & Sons
Wilton, Conn. 06897

No. 4796 Gate posts. These cast stone members are 30" square by 15" high. These are main entrance gates and are not scaled for truck use. They would have to be made taller and wider for trucks. The Lion is No. 1085.

No. 4795. Gate posts constructed with No. 4795 sections. They are 30" square by 15" high. The Obelisks are also made of stone and are 58" high and the gate itself should be referred to as No. 4795-A. This size is excellent for passenger vehicle gates but where trucks are involved, they should be at least another 2 sections higher.

STANCHIONS

PORTABLE POSTS — ROPES — RAILS — BOOTHS — DISPLAY PANELS — SIGNS

WHOLESALE CATALOG FOR THE PROFESSION NUMBER 1776

Send for free Stanchion book

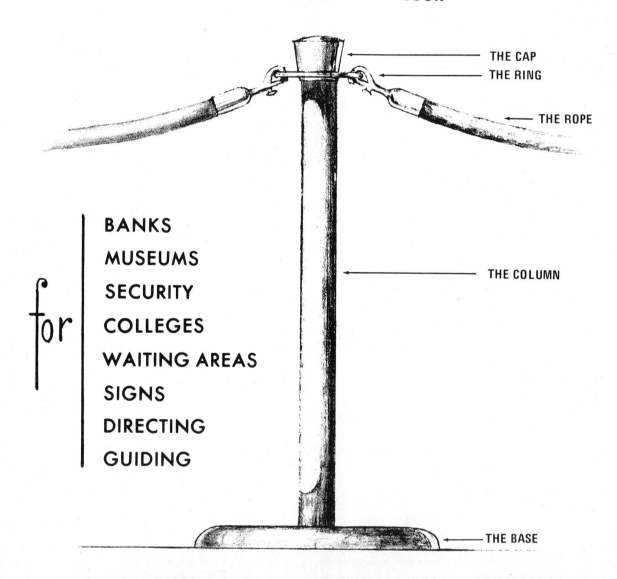

THE CAP

THE RING

THE ROPE

THE COLUMN

THE BASE

for
- BANKS
- MUSEUMS
- SECURITY
- COLLEGES
- WAITING AREAS
- SIGNS
- DIRECTING
- GUIDING

KENNETH LYNCH and SONS
WILTON, CONNECTICUT
06897

© 1974.
Kenneth Lynch & Sons
Wilton, Conn. 06897

Send for free Stanchion book No. 1776.

Notice! This book on stanchions is one of many done by the team of Mr. Andrew D. Crowell, Sr., and Mr. Kenneth Lynch, Sr., with more than 100 years of joint experience designing. Other books produced by this team are listed in the back pages and they cover such subjects as Benches, Weathervanes, Lighting Fixtures, Sundials, Garden Ornaments, Architectural Sheet Metal Ornaments, Art Gallery & Museum Equipment, Wrought Ironwork, Liturgical Art and years ago even included a study on horse stable fittings! Your inquiries are invited.

With both of the columns being round and being either an 1″, 1½″ or 2″ in diameter and being either chrome, natural metal, painted, etc., we find that the two basic differences in stanchions is the base design and the top design. We have converted the top into a tool. Regardless of which top you select it will still work as a tool.

The top is the finishing member for the stanchion. Basically there is the bollard top or we have the flat top.

Many buyers already own bollard tops and want to match them and generally they are in chrome. However, they are also available in brass, stainless steel, painted hammertone, etc., and it is purely a matter of taste.

Recently a new bollard top has been developed. It is made of a tough pleasant feeling plastic. It is clean looking and, of course, does not chip or scratch and it is less expensive.

The flat top illustrated here is preferred by many for three simple reasons. reasons.

1) It does not catch on coat sleeves and upset the stanchion.
2) People are less inclined to hang things on the top of the stanchion.
3) It is less expensive.

The bollard top is purely cosmetic.

The Base. We show many bases in this book ranging from 12″ in diameter to 24″ in diameter and made of every material.

The illustration at the right, our no. 101, has now become the most popular stanchion base and top combination. We believe the reason for this is the low profile of the base. It presents less area to kick or stumble on and they can be easily stacked and stored.

**BOLLARD TYPE
PROFILED BASE**

ropes

hook rope end

hook-type rope end

snap-type rope end

plastic rope

¾″ to 1½″ —all colors

velour or naughahyde rope
¾″ to 1½″—any color

**FLAT TOP
FLAT BASE
The Famous
"101"**

WALL PLATE

chain hook

twisted satin rope
1¼″—any color

Our ropes are 1/3 the weight of any other make.

DOUBLE LINE

For a double line of rope or chain, an additional loop can be provided at any point on the posts. See price list-**Additional Loop.**

STANCHIONS

Send for free Stanchion book No. 1776.

Deluxe Portable Post — 317 Series

The ultimate in design and materials, this post has found acceptance by leading cultural and civic centers.

With 12" diameter base.

317-12-1P	Polished chrome plated brass.
317-12-1S	Satin chrome plated brass.
317-12-2P	All brass post. Polished finish.
317-12-2S	All brass post. Satin finish.
317-12-6	English Antique finish all brass post.
317-12-8	Statuary Bronze finish all brass post.

With 15" diameter base.

317-15-1P	Polished chrome plated brass.
317-15-1S	Satin chrome plated brass.
317-15-2P	All brass post. Polished finish.
317-15-2S	All brass post. Satin finish.
317-15-6	English Antique finish all brass post.
317-15-8	Statuary Bronze finish all brass post.

Contemporary Portable Post — 318 Series

Lighter weight and lower cost distinguish this post. Suitable for normal traffic use.

318-1P	Polished chrome plated steel. Indoor use.
318-1S	Satin chrome plated steel. Indoor use.
318-2P	All brass post, polished finish. Indoor use.
318-2S	All brass post, satin finished and lacquered. Indoor use.
318-3	Stainless steel, satin finish. Indoor and outdoor use.
318-4A	Clear anodized aluminum. Indoor and outdoor use.
318-4B	Bronze anodized aluminum. Indoor use.
318-4G	Gold anodized aluminum. Indoor use.
318-5	Enameled steel post. Available in standard colors.
318-6	English Antique Brass finish. Indoor use.
318-8	Statuary Bronze finish on brass. Indoor use.

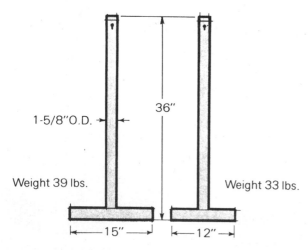

1-5/8"O.D. — 36"

Weight 39 lbs. Weight 33 lbs.

15" 12"

Recommended post spacing — 12" base — 5 to 9 feet
15" base — 6 to 10 feet

317 Series Posts are supplied with either keyholes or snap slots. Specify when ordering.

Keyhole
For use with Ball Type Rope Ends

Snap Slot
For use with Snap Type Rope Ends

Keyholes or Snap Slots are normally supplied in "3-way" position. "End," "corner" or "center" positions on request.

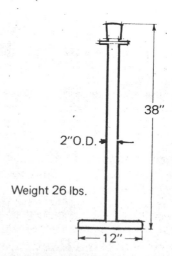

2"O.D. — 38"

Weight 26 lbs.

12"

Recommended post spacing — 4 to 7 feet.

Loop Arrangements
Unless otherwise specified, posts are furnished with universal loop.

Universal

© 1974.
Kenneth Lynch & Sons
Wilton, Conn. 06897

No. 66 Rubber Floor Protector
Permanently attached to underside of base. Optional, see price list.

TWO NEW STANCHIONS

**Send for free Stanchion
book No. 1776.**

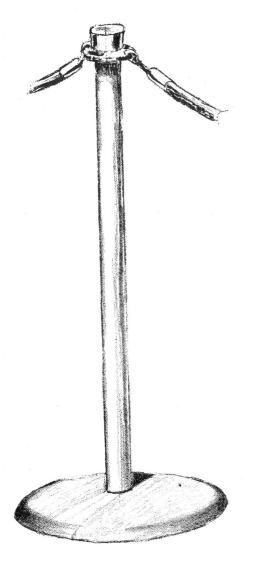

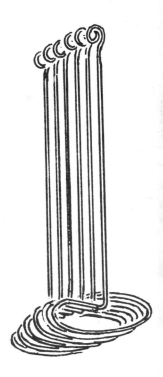

No. 199. All steel chrome plate
or painted finish stanchion. 16''
diameter base. This is the same
as the famous No. 101 except that
it has the bollard top. The bollard
top is available in either chrome
metal or plastic.

No. 663
Wrought iron stanchion, French opera house
design. This is a great stanchion made completely of wrought iron. It is light in weight
yet very stable. Rope can be quickly engaged
with top without the use of extra fittings. It
is designed for use with a sash cord or similar
material. Furnished in wrought iron only,
painted black. 40'' high.

Send for free Stanchion book No. 1776.

FORMED STANCHION BASES
SPECIAL ARCHITECTURAL DESIGNS

Standard Portable Post

310 Series

The most popular post for guiding traffic. A proven design, sturdily built for years of dependable service.

310-1P	Polished chrome plated steel. Indoor use.
310-1S	Satin chrome plated steel. Indoor use.
310-2P	All brass post, polished finish. Indoor use.
310-2S	All brass post, satin finished and lacquered. Indoor use.
310-3	Stainless steel, satin finish. Indoor and outdoor use.
310-4A	Clear anodized aluminum. Indoor and outdoor use.
310-4B	Bronze anodized aluminum. Indoor use.
310-4G	Gold anodized aluminum. Indoor use.
310-5	Enameled steel post. Available in standard colors.
310-6	English Antique Brass finish. Indoor use.
310-8	Statuary Bronze finish on brass. Indoor use.

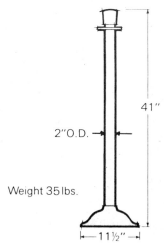

41"

2" O.D.

Weight 35 lbs.

11½"

Recommended post spacing — 5 to 9 feet.

Loop Arrangements
Unless otherwise specified, posts are furnished with universal loop.

Universal

No. 65 Rubber Floor Protector.
Permanently attached to underside of base. Optional, see price list

No. 332. Stone stanchion base. Decorative antique finish. 16" and 18" diameter. Accepts the three column sizes.

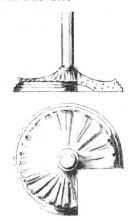

No. 334. Stone stanchion base for outside corner. 18" diameter. Accepts the three column sizes.

No. 333. Half round stone stanchion base. 18" diameter only. Accepts the three column sizes.

No. 336. Stone stanchion base for inside corner. 18" diameter.

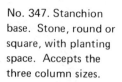

No. 347. Stanchion base. Stone, round or square, with planting space. Accepts the three column sizes.

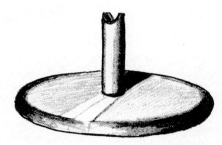

No. 303. Steel base. Available in chrome or hammertone finishes. In 12", 14", 16", 18" and 24".

ROPE & ROPE ENDS

Lynch Ropes are the accepted standard of leading architects, designers, and decorators. The finest in materials, construction, and workmanship insure lasting beauty through a long life of rough service. The velour is the finest quality, providing a look of elegance to all interior settings. Naugahyde, with its rich, smooth finish, provides an alternate look especially suitable under heavy duty conditions where cleaning of the rope may be required.

Our newest product, twisted plastic rope, has been primarily developed for outdoor use. A wide range of colors and the twisted texture also suggest many striking indoor applications.

Send for free Stanchion book No. 1776.

VELOUR OR NAUGAHYDE COVERED ROPE

No. 540

No. 550

STANDARD 1½″ DIAMETER COVERED ROPE
No. 541 Velour Covered   **No. 542** Naugahyde Covered
These are the standard ropes recommended for most uses. The cotton center is held secure by a closely woven braid insuring maintained uniformity of shape throughout a long life of flexing.
Colors: Velour—maroon, royal blue, hunter green, gold, pearl grey, brown, black or bright red.
Naugahyde— wine red, blue, white, green, brown or black. Swatch card on request.

These ropes are used with either No. 540 Hook Type Rope End or No. 550 Snap Type Rope End.

No. 440

No. 450

1″ DIAMETER COVERED ROPE
No. 441 Velour Covered   **No. 442** Naugahyde Covered
These ropes are recommended for use in lighter duty locations where a smaller diameter fits into the decor. These ropes are identical in construction to No. 541 and 542 except 1″ diameter.
Colors: Velour—maroon, royal blue, hunter green, gold, pearl grey, brown, black or bright red.
Naugahyde— wine red, blue, white, green, brown or black. Swatch card on request.

These ropes are used with either No. 440 Hook Type Rope End or No. 450 Snap Type Rope End.

NO. 695

Our unbreakable rope fitted out with a snap-type rope end. Snaps are chrome plated only. Rope must be cut to fit predetermined lengths and bent back on itself to be finished here at the factory before shipping.

No. 740

No. 750

COVERED CHAIN CORE ROPE
No. 741 Velour Covered   **No. 742** Naugahyde Covered
These ropes are recommended where great strength is required. The 1½″ rope has a welded chain core within the cotton center and braid.
Colors: Velour—maroon, royal blue, hunter green, gold, pearl grey, brown, black or bright red.
Naugahyde—wine red, or blue, white, green, brown or black. Swatch card on request.

These ropes are used with either No. 740 Hook Type Rope End or No. 750 Snap Type Rope End.

TWISTED ROPE

No. 440

No. 450

TWISTED PLASTIC ROPE
No. 443—1″ Diameter—Ideal for outdoor use. White, black, yellow, blue, red or gold.

Used with No. 440 hook or No. 450 snap type rope ends.

No. 240

Used with No. 240 hook type rope end only.

TWISTED PLASTIC ROPE
No. 243—¾″ Diameter—Ideal for outdoor use. White, black, yellow, blue, red or gold.

NO SNAP ENDS FOR ¾″ ROPE

No. 240

Used with No. 240 hook type rope end only.

TWISTED RAYON ROPE
No. 241—¾″ Diameter—Recommended where a small rope may be desired such as for church use at pews. Stocked in maroon, blue, green, white, gold or black.

© 1974.
Kenneth Lynch & Sons
Wilton, Conn. 06897

GAZEBOES

No. 4125. Garden House or Poolside House with sheltered benches. Made of marine grade plywood battened with an Armorstone roof and shippable in pieces ready for assembly. Size 12' x 16' and it is 12' high to the highest point. Sizes may be varied.

No. 5546. Gazebo, wrought iron with stone column bases and stone seats. 10' diameter, 8' to top of columns, 16' high overall. Size may be varied.

No. 4126. Gazebo-Dressing Room. Size 12' x 15' x 14' high overall. Note interesting plan with 2 showers and separate dressing rooms. Sizes are, of course, variable.

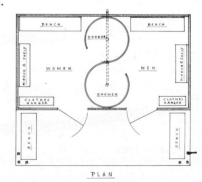

No. 2419. Garden house of wrought iron with Armorstone © roof. Benches are an integral part of the construction and are similar to bench #2093. They are made in several sizes from stock segments and are very easily assembled. Ten feet in diameter would be a good size as a minimum.

© 1974
Kenneth Lynch & Sons
Wilton, Conn. 06897

GAZEBOES

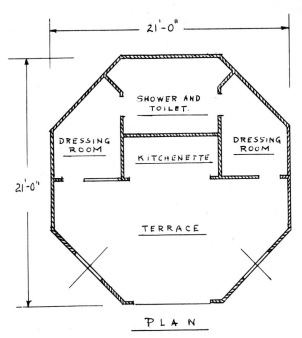

P L A N

No. 5554. This very beautiful Gazebo with an oyster white Armorstone roof which, of course, could be painted a different color, is all in stock ready for shipment. It is 21' x 21' octagonal and it was designed to have the plan as shown on left. It has also been developed so that it could be closed in completely as a house, insulated, heated, etc. This, of course, would be up to the buyer. It is intended to be put on a concrete slab of the proper dimension and could easily be erected very quickly. Considering the fact that in 1968 this building was offered for under $10,000.00 it is a tremendously good investment. We realize, of course, that to show such a thing in a permanent book of this nature is rather risky. However, it is so attractive that we could not resist the temptation. Contact either the publisher or the author for further information.

No. 4121. Gazebo with wrought iron rails and Armorstone roof. 12' x 16'. Size may be varied.

SNOW GUARD
Send for free book

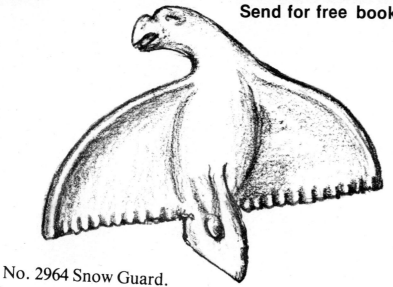

No. 2974 In copper in stainless steel
An integral engagement of the Snow-Guard hooks over head edge of slate and asbestos shingles without nailing. Snow-Guards on asphalt and wood shingles require nailing.

No. 2964 Snow Guard.

This is the most famous snow guard eagle in America. It is known as the Philadelphia Eagle and you will find it on buildings there 200 years old. Originally this eagle was made of cast iron and fastened to the slates with wrought iron straps. Over the years these rusted and became loose and fell into the streets. We are indebted to a fine antique collector for having preserved all of these for our use.

We have this exact eagle available in cast brass, cast bronze and cast lead and stamped copper all with copper or stainless steel straps.

The brackets for this famous eagle are made in all of the bracket designs shown in this booklet. Choose the correct bracket design for your type of roof or just tell us what roofing material you are using.

Please consult the chart in this book showing how these are to be spaced for these eagles, in order to be effective, must be properly distributed over the roof. Too few will result in no effect at all other than a cosmetic effect and the more you put on the more effective they are. However, use the enclosed chart as a guide.

Many people purchase these Philagelphia eagle as ornaments and, of course, they are available to you depending upon what quantity you want to purchase. We invite you to consult with us.

Prices. See price list. Quantity counts!

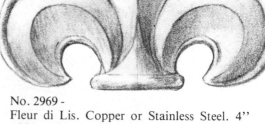

No. 2969 -
Fleur di Lis. Copper or Stainless Steel. 4'' wide x 2½'' high. All fastening systems apply.

No. 1983.
Eagle, original antique pattern in Lynch collection more than 100 years. It is 5'' high and 6'' wide. See cover for roof done with this bird. Available in cast Brass, Bronze, Lead or Iron and also in Stamped Copper. The Iron is bought mostly by collectors for display and not for roofs.

© 1974.
Kenneth Lynch & Sons
Wilton, Conn. 06897

No. 1777. Horse head bollard with bit rings of steel to connect the chains. In this case the height can vary and it can have a center chain to prevent pedestrian traffic as well as a chain connecting the head. This is entirely reinforced with steel and is taken from an old hitching post design. Blocks of curbing can be added underneath but the pipe must go through to a small fountain plug below grade. Your inquiry invited.

No. 1982. Cast stone bollard.

No. 3411. Horse head hitching post which is used to top the No. 1777 bollard.

No. 1975. Bollard. Cast iron and concrete. Heavy duty. Designed to hold largest ships. Very impressive looking. The iron alone weighs 600 pounds. The concrete is poured in place in a height to suit requirements.

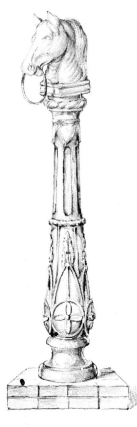

No. 1204. Stone Post, 56 1/2'' high x 7 1/2'' dia-mater. Reinforced with pipe. Anchors can extend into ground. Threaded inserts can be included to bolt on fence members (rails).

No. 4586. Bollard design taken from old hydrant. 42'' high. Very stable.

No. 4544. Cast Stone Hitching Post, 47'' high. Furnished with long ground anchor.

ARCHITECTURAL & DECORATIVE SHEET METAL ORNAMENTS

CATALOG #7474

ARCHITECTURAL SHEET METAL

This book contains 2,000 illustrations of available: Architectural Sheet Metal Ornaments, Sheet Metal Ceilings, Balusters, Urns, Capitals, Lantern Parts, Cartouches, Carytids, Brackets, Mouldings, Corbels, Crestings, Crockets, Dentils, Eagles, Festoons, Finials, Scrolls, Leaves, Weather Vane parts and Pineapples.

Building Ornaments of every description plus a 100 year old collection of Architectural Repousee Tooling.
#7474
Soft cover only . $3.50

SEND FOR BOOK NO. 7474.

© 1974.
Kenneth Lynch & Sons
Wilton, Conn. 06897

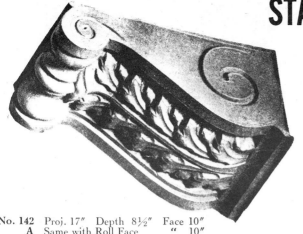

No. 142   Proj. 17″   Depth 8½″   Face 10″
A   Same with Roll Face   "   10″

No. 2902   12½″ x 21½″
A   9″ x 18″

No. 5409   9″ x 12″
A   9″ x 14″

No. 1464   5″

No. 535   11″

No. 1110

	¾″	**E**	2″	**J**	5″
A	⅞″	**F**	2½″	**K**	5½″
B	1″	**G**	3″	**L**	6″
C	1¼″	**H**	3½″	**M**	7″
D	1½″	**I**	4″	**N**	8″

No. 3290   9″ x 24″   **B**   9″ x 36″
A   9″ x 30″   **C**   9″ x 42″

No. 5000   12″
A   8″   Mitre 9″

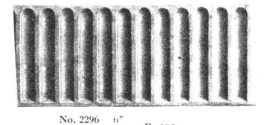

No. 2296   6″
A   7″   **F**   12″
B   8″   **G**   14″
C   9″   **H**   16″
D   10″

NO.	NECK	HEIGHT	ABACUS
4589	10″	8½″	21″
A	14″	8½″	23″
B	15½″	13½″	26½″
C	17″	13″	27″
D	18″	8½″	26″
E	20″	9″	28″
F	21″	13″	31″

NO.	NECK	HEIGHT	ABACUS
4542	7″	13″	12″
A	10″	12½″	17½″
B	11″	12″	17½″
E	14″	12½″	22″
F	15″	12″	22″

No. 5047   5½″   Mitre 7½″

SEND FOR BOOK NO. 7474.

© 1974.
Kenneth Lynch & Sons
Wilton, Conn. 06897

Art Gallery Supplies
Picture Rods, Picture Carts, Traffic Stanchions
SEND FOR BOOK 1070. PICTURE HANGING DEVICES

When ordering, send an accurate outline of the shape of your mouldings - bend a paper clip around it, for instance, or make a good sketch or send a piece of the moulding.

Up to 6' Long.

Up to 6' Long.

NEW ALUMINUM SECURITY MOLDING NO. 570 USING OLD ROD.

3/16" SQUARE STAINLESS STEEL C.D. FINISH

CADMIUM PLATED SPRING

ALUMINUM CAMS

"RUBBER-LIKE" PLASTIC ANTI CHAFING TIP

STANDARD ROD

No. 576
Wood O.G. moulding can be purchased from any lumber yard. Available in 12' lengths.

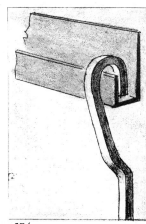

No. 574
Surface applied aluminum moulding can be painted out. This is a very excellent, simple moulding. Available in 12' lengths.

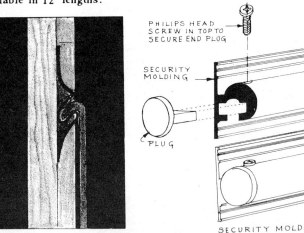

No. 575
Milcor moulding – to be installed prior to a room being plastered and should be ordered through your architect. Available in 12' lengths.

Wood Shipping Boxes at cost. They also act as storage boxes.
*FOB Wilton, Conn.

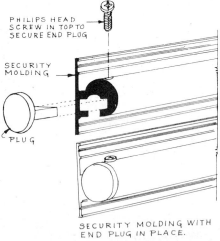

PHILIPS HEAD SCREW IN TOP TO SECURE END PLUG

SECURITY MOLDING

PLUG

SECURITY MOLDING WITH END PLUG IN PLACE.

No. 570
New security moulding made of aluminum. See preceeding page for complete story on this moulding. Available in 12' lengths.
Rods Complete up to six feet long

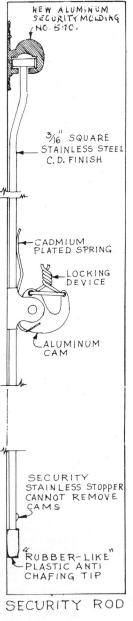

NEW ALUMINUM SECURITY MOLDING NO. 570.

3/16" SQUARE STAINLESS STEEL C.D. FINISH

CADMIUM PLATED SPRING

LOCKING DEVICE

ALUMINUM CAM

SECURITY STAINLESS STOPPER CANNOT REMOVE CAMS

"RUBBER-LIKE" PLASTIC ANTI CHAFING TIP

SECURITY ROD

ANGLE TACKS

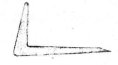

Angle Tack No. 121 — drive the long leg into the wall, the short end holds the glass and print. Box of 1,000 only $39.60 including air postage.

© 1974.
Kenneth Lynch & Sons
Wilton, Conn. 06897

Art Gallery Supplies
Picture Rods, Picture Carts, Traffic Stanchions
SEND FOR BOOK 1070. **ART STORAGE ROOMS**

Ideal for storing the finest art pieces without damage

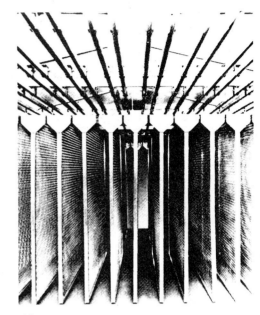

The illustrations on this page show a very elaborate installation made completely of aluminum for the storage of many paintings.

Artists who lend paintings for repeat exhibits are very greatful for the careful attention you give their work. Owners of fine work generally insist upon a first class storage room being provided when exhibits are being changed.

These photographs show one of the best installations we have ever seen. We can quote you on this work giving you a price per square foot of storage area on the panels.

If you have the funds to do such a good piece of work you will not regret having made this installation. These panels are rust free, require no maintenance at all, and should please every curator and exhibitor.

Your correspondence is invited.

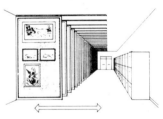

No. 680 View of Storage Rooms with Racks.

No. 679 View of Storage Room with Racks

PORTABLE STORAGE RACKS
THE ONLY TOOL YOU WILL NEED IS A WRENCH
SHIPPED READY FOR ASSEMBLY

NORMAL FLOOR SPACE REQUIREMENTS PER UNIT

	Panel Size	Floor Space
STYLE 683 - Back & Forth	4' x 8'	8' x 8'
STYLE 684 - Side Moved	8' x 8'	8' x 12'
8 panels per unit.		

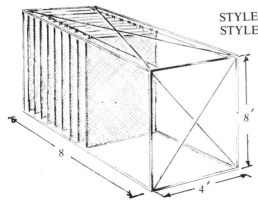

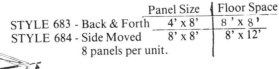

No. 683 Slides back and forth. Requires 8' x 8' floor space, including walkway (4'). Not the best choice. You must move all racks to get at the last one.

No. 684 Storage Rack requires 8' x 12' floor space which includes a 4' passage. This is the better system. Each 4' x 8' panel has it's own ball bearing track. Made of furniture steel. Readily available.

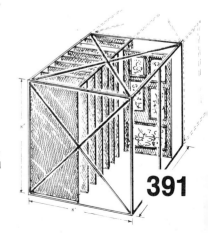

ABOUT LARGE CLOCKS READ THIS!

Everybody wants to know what time it is. While post clocks attract the most attention, there is likewise considerable interest in clocks which project from buildings, which are applied to the face of buildings. Normally these clock faces are in 24'' to 48'' diameters, however large clocks are made which will take up the entire side of a building. They have hands 10 and 12 feet long. All of this can be made available.

Electrically operated post clocks like the illustration to the left, are by far the most popular for they are practically indestructible and the electrical timing mechanism, operated through high quality gears is practically eliminating repairs.

It is always difficult to talk about costs when conditions are so unsettled. However, in the year 1976, post clocks, depending upon size vary between $10,000.00 and $30,000.00 each.

There are many varieties in clocks. For instance, just the case itself can be made to almost any design, or any shape. Of course, round is the traditional shape because the hands follow the line of a circle. However, we now have the new digital clocks which show numbers that change every second. This of course, can be rectangular.

Likewise, signs can be added or weather information.

One of the most interesting clocks has a weathervane on the top of it.

As you can see, the ideas are endless and we as clock craftsmen, can do almost anything with your ideas.

KENNETH LYNCH & SONS have been involved with Howard Clocks now for more than a century. While we are definitely not movement makers, we are the case makers, the post makers and even the installers. We deliver these clocks all over the United States and Canada.

All of these clocks can be used either indoors or outdoors. They are available with many innovations. We include illustrations of various bases, columns and cases.

Plexiglass is used as the protective covering for the hands and when we illuminate the clocks, we use transparent plexiglass.

Considering what these clocks will do for you, it is really a small investment. Just compare it with the cost of other types of notice, newspapers, signs, etcetera. No one ever gets mad at a clock. Clocks are loved by everyone.

In conclusion, you can have clocks with drinking fountains, seats, weathervanes, bulletin boards, lighting fixtures, etcetera. These clocks can become the focal point of any area. Remember, "Meet me at the clock at 5 o'clock".

Clocks are easily set with a switch timing device which can either speed up a clock or stop it until real time catches up with it. This is sometimes necessary when the electrical power has been off for a while. It is all very simple.

We invite your inquiry.

#4926
Reproduction of Howard Clock. This clock with a 4' diameter face is 19'' high. It is extremely heavy, full of nostalgia, and we always keep one available for shipment.

"We buy and sell old clocks either complete or in part. Contact us."

SEND FOR CLOCK BULLETIN.

© 1974.
Kenneth Lynch & Sons
Wilton, Conn. 06897

CLOCKS WITH BENCH

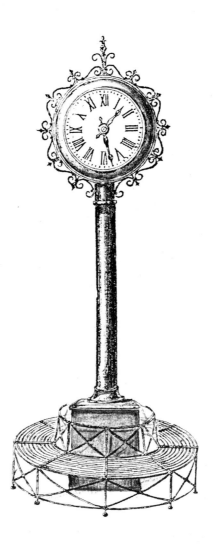

Clock with square bench taken from our regular bench catalog, it is #3361. It is 5' 2" square. It can be painted any color, and it is made to fit the clock. Bench adds about $900.00 to cost. "MEET ME AT THE CLOCK".

Clock with bench #3360. This round bench adds $1,100.00 to the cost of the clock. It is 62" in diameter. It is made completely of wrought iron, in any color. "MEET ME AT THE CLOCK".

Clock with bench #3362. This wrought iron bench 5' 6" in diameter will add approximately $1,100.00 to the cost. "MEET ME AT THE CLOCK".

© 1974.
Kenneth Lynch & Sons
Wilton, Conn. 06897

SEND FOR CLOCK BULLETIN.

"We buy and sell old clocks either complete or in part. Contact us."

STONE WALLS.

The Lynch family have certainly been building stone walls for a few hundred years both in Ireland and in America.

The famous expression of Mr. John M. Lynch to the effect that "there were two stones for every dirt". The stone, of course, became a product and a useable product.

Our old shops in Ireland were built entirely of stone for in Connemara you used what you had.

At Wilton most of the buildings are stone and about 55 years ago we began using the stones for decoration in the walls and it has been most successful. We have made these walls in one piece to be raised by a crane as big as 16 feet x 16 feet, but, of course, they could not be transported over the roads.

This building is standing in Wilton and it is beautiful.

We have many others where we cast pieces 8 feet x 16 feet. However, the most easily managed pieces were those that were 4 feet x 8 feet and 2 feet x 8 feet.

We show below a drawing of how we made these walls so many times and so successfully. As you can see we show a wood form but many times we cast these on a sand bed. Just make sure to rake it level.

A frame around the area you are going to cast is absolutely essential and generally this should be not less than 8" thick.

When using a form put down about 1" of sand and rub each stone in the sand until it is in contact with the bottom of the form. This will make sand come up between the joints which is good.

After you have all the stone laid in as neatly as you can get it, and do not worry about openings as they will not show after you raise the wall, then wash off the back side of the stones with a garden hose, place your wire, road mesh and reinforcing rods and your lifting eyes which are nothing more than pieces of iron bent like hairpins, and then pour redi-mix concrete on the back of this. Then level it off with the top of the form boards. Let it sit for about 7 days and then take away the form boards and lift this piece with a tractor or a crane. Wash off the face and you will see that the sand will wash away and you will have beautiful open joints in the stone.

Later you may tool these with cement if you wish. However, we find that just planting ivy does wonders.

We are sharing this with you as we have enjoyed making walls this way for so long. Just remember that every stone has at least one good face which can be exposed and the ugly, unuseable part of a stone can go up into the concrete and it acts as a good gripping surface so you always put the best surface of the stone down so that when you raise it you are looking at the best.

See adjoining page for one long wall which Mr. Lynch, Sr. did a few years ago and he purposely left it unfinished for this story. This wall is 2 feet high and 400 feet long and it was laid entirely by school boys as a summer project.

New Book

Write for new book on fences and walls. "To keep in — to keep out" by Kenneth Lynch ready late 1980.

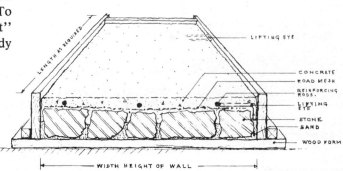

STONE WALLS.

View of completed wall. Note that although wall was cast in 8 foot sections, it still follows the terrain.

See curve of wall how well these 8 foot sections follow.

Note three stones left out for drainage pipes. Easy to do.

The white stones are actually styroform blocks placed in the mold to make a space for a connecting keystone.

The building of these stone walls is so simple and if you need help or instruction we have one person here who will, for a modest sum, help you get started.

Sections in 8 feet lengths can be trucked over the road from our quarry and we do offer this service. Your inquiry is invited.

Excellent view of white styroform insert which is easily removed and replaced with a keystone. This breaks up the straight line at the joint.

STEEL CEILINGS

No. 3332. **24" Multiple Plate**
24"x 96"

No. 3324. **6" Multiple Plate**
24"x 96"

The unit of measure of steel ceilings is 100 square feet called a "square". To measure the amount of material required for a room measure the length by the width and simply multiply. Do not deduct anything for skylights and other openings.

If the finish is to come down 12" on the side wall, of course this area must be added. Appropriate moldings are shown in the catalog and must likewise be added. By the use of brackets, modillions, rosettes, etc., the designer can go as far as he wishes with the finishing of a room using this material.

It is modest in price, it has never waned in popularity and it is still used by many leading chain stores. It is also fire-proof. It is easy to install and to paint. It comes unfinished ready for installation. When figuring the areas be sure to include beams that protrude down to the ceiling and any other areas which must be covered.

"Steel ceilings, also known as tin ceilings or zinc ceilings, have been manufactured now for more than 100 years.

In this little brochure, we show what designs are readily available from stock.

This material is shipped unpainted ready for installation with the special nails. See illustration.

We must call your attention to a book of sheet metal ornament which would be very helpful to anyone doing this work. It sells for $3.50. Please attach your check to your professional letterhead when ordering it as this book will not be sold to anyone not in the trade. Likewise note the special nail which is available."

No. 3335. **12" Multiple Plate**
24"x 96"

No. 3331. **24"x 96"**

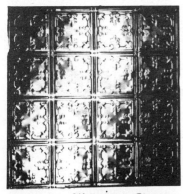

No. 3323. **6" Multiple Plate**
24"x 96"

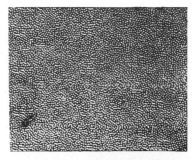

No. 3312. **Filler 24"x 96"**

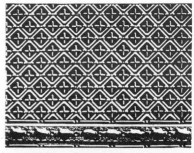

No. 3334. **Molded Filler 24"x 48"**

No. 3329. **12" Multiple Plate**
24"x 96"

No. 3330. **12" Multiple Plate**
24"x 96"

No. 3333.
Molded Filler 24x48"

No. 3300 Flush Back Panel
24" Multiple
24" x 48" or 24" x 96"

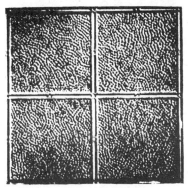

No. 3304.   12" Multiple
24" x 48" or 24" x 96"

No. 3308.   6" Multiple
24" x 48" or 24" x 96"

No. 3301 Flush Back Panel
24" Multiple 24" x 48" or 24" x 96"

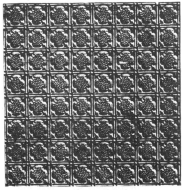

No. 3305.   3" Multiple
Suitable for use in homes
24" x 48" or 24" x 96"

No. 3309.   6" Multiple
24" x 48" or 24" x 96"

No. 3302.   24" Multiple
24" x 48" or 24" x 96"

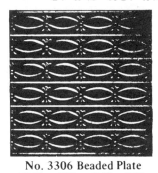

No. 3306 Beaded Plate
24" x 48" or 24" x 96"
This Plate does not have our Standard Dot
and Dash Bead Construction.

No. 3310.   6" Multiple
24" x 48" or 24" x 96"

No. 3303 Flush Back Panel
12" Multiple
24" x 48" or 24" x 96"

No. 3307 Flush Back Panel
24" Multiple
24" x 48"

No. 3311 Flush Back Panel
6" Multiple
24" x 48" or 24" x 96"

STEEL CEILINGS
MOLDINGS

Cornice No. 3314

5" Projection, Length 48"

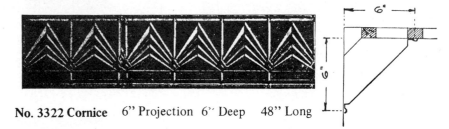

No. 3322 Cornice   6" Projection   6" Deep   48" Long

Cornice No. 3313   Depth, 4 inches. Projection, 4 inches.
Length, 48 inches.

No. 3316 Cornice   3" Projection   4" Deep   48" Long

No. 3317 Cornice   2½" Projection   2½" Deep   48" Long

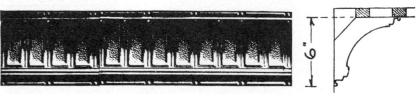

No. 3320 Cornice   6" Projection   6" Deep   48" Long

No. 3315 Nosing   2 3/4" x 48"

No. 3319 Cornice   6" Projection   6" Deep   48" Long

No. 3318 Cornice   1 3/4" Projection 1¼" Deep   48" Long

© 1974.
Kenneth Lynch & Sons
Wilton, Conn. 06897

LYNCH ORNAMENTAL STEEL CURBING
MADE TO ANY SIZE AND SHAPE

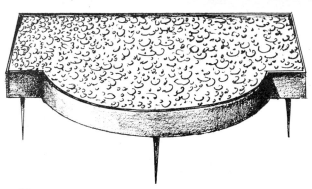

No. 4355. English bow front garden shown with stone mulch held neatly in place.

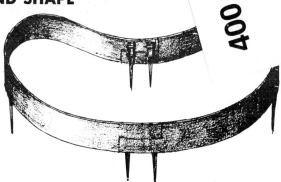

No. 4359. Kidney-shaped design; any size.

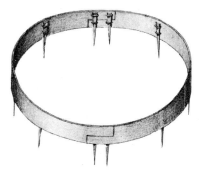

No. 4348. Simple garden ring made to any diameter.

No. 4364. Square Parterre, made in any size.

No. 4358. Triangular design with scroll corners.

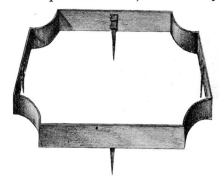

No. 4341. Typical Parterre showing breakback corners; any size.

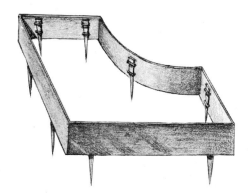

No. 4342. Inside Breakback, generally used in units of four as shown on the accompanying plan.

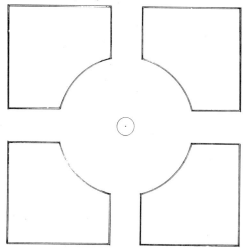

No. 4342. This illustration shows a typical garden lay-out for a sundial in the center and walks coming from four sides. Furnished in any size.

© 1974.
Kenneth Lynch & Sons
Wilton, Conn. 06897

399

LYNCH ORNAMENTAL STEEL CURBING

MADE TO ANY SIZE AND SHAPE

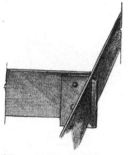

No. 4340. Drop-in-place T connection.

No. 4337. Typical cross connection.

No. 4336. Typical right angle connection.

No. 4338. Typical T connection.

No. 4346. Breakback corners made to any radius.

No. 4347. Scroll-like terminals with socket to receive lanterns, sign posts, etc.; made to any size.

No. 4345. Curbing shown with sockets added for stanchions and sign. Specify what spacing you desire.

No. 4353. Typical terminal; any size.

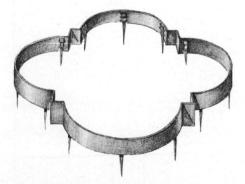

No. 4356. Typical garden design made to any size.

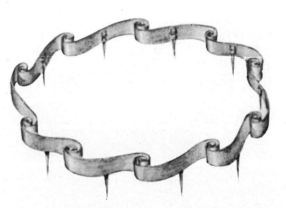

No. 4357. Very nice serpentine design formed into a circle. Scrolls must be made large enough to count in the design.

400

© 1974.
Kenneth Lynch & Sons
Wilton, Conn. 06897

WALL FOUNTAIN

No. 4549. Wall fountain of beautiful detail. The Dolphin itself is a lovely thing to behold. It is 60 in. high and 56 in. wide. Lead. It is possible this could also be furnished in Armorstone.

© 1974.
Kenneth Lynch & Sons
Wilton, Conn. 06897

ALL CORRESPONDENCE TO: BOX 488, WILTON, CONNECTICUT 06897-0488.
(203) 762-8363   FAX (203) 762-2999

AVAILABLE LITERATURE

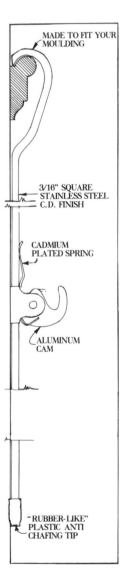